Praise for

JACK'S NOTEBOOK

"Both innovative and inspirational, *Jack's Notebook* swings open a long-neglected door to the creative process. All of us are creative, but many of us do not know how to access our creativity. Like James Redfield's *Celestine Prophecy*, Gregg Fraley uses story to convey principles that deserve a wide audience."

—Julia Cameron
The Artist's Way

"Gregg Fraley's idea of teaching creativity principles using a novel is fascinating; the story he tells is engaging. It's unique and exciting. *Jack's Notebook* will bring creative thinking and creative problem solving skills to a much broader audience."

—Sidney Parnes, Ph.D.
Developer with Alex Osborn of the
Creative Problem Solving (CPS) process

"Rather than relying on divine intervention to solve your challenges, read *Jack's Notebook*. This book cleverly teaches you how to build the skill of deliberate creative problem solving. This is crucial for thriving in today's volatile age of change."

—Stephen Shapiro
Author, *24/7 Innovation* and *Goal-Free Living*

"Story and metaphor can make the imponderable ponderable, the impossible possible, and the improbable probable. Using the framework of creative problem solving, *Jack's Notebook* does exactly that. It is the quintessential, user-friendly guidebook to living a life of creative possibilities that transform into realities. In simpler words,

I know this guy. I work with him. He uses this stuff. His dreams happen. It works. Buy this book."

—Doug Stevenson
Partner in The Innovise Guys podcast
AllCreation.net

"The processes of making ideas a reality have made creativity and innovation hot topics in the prevailing world economies. However, few people have the gift of making creative process accessible and readily applicable to all. Gregg Fraley's deep knowledge of creative problem solving, his gift of storytelling, and his wonderful humor come together in this compelling novel. And *Jack's Notebook* gives fresh breath to a topic that otherwise could be very dry and academic. It leaves you feeling good about your own creativity and wanting to practice what you have learned from Jack's trials and tribulations well before you read the last word."

—David Magellan Horth
Center for Creative Leadership
Coauthor of *The Leader's Edge*

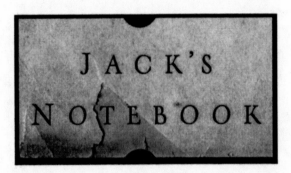

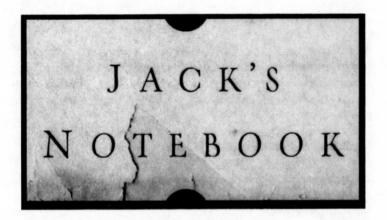

JACK'S NOTEBOOK

**A Business Novel about
Creative Problem Solving**

GREGG FRALEY

Published by
THOMAS NELSON
Since 1798
www.thomasnelson.com

Published in Nashville, Tennessee, by Thomas Nelson, Inc.

Thomas Nelson, Inc. titles may be purchased in bulk for educational, business, fund-raising, or sales promotional use. For information, please e-mail SpecialMarkets@ThomasNelson.com.

Publisher's Note: This novel is a work of fiction. Names, characters, places, and incidents are either products of the author's imagination or used fictitiously. All characters are fictional, and any similarity to people living or dead is purely coincidental.

Library of Congress Cataloging-in-Publication Data

Fraley, Gregg.
  Jack's notebook : a business novel about creative problem solving / Gregg Fraley.
      p. cm.

  ISBN: 978-1-59555-247-1
  1. Problem solving--Miscellanea. 2. Management--Miscellanea. I. Title.
HD30.29.F713 2007
658.4'03--dc22

2006030532

Printed in the United States of America
07 08 09 10 QW 6 5 4 3 2 1

CONTENTS

INTRODUCTION

Creativity is a lot more than artistic expression. It's a myth that to be creative you must be artistic. *Everyone* is creative whether he is artistically inclined or not. Creativity is about problem solving, decision making, *and* self-expression. It's also the foundational thinking skill for innovation. If you use your thinking to create solutions for any challenge in your life, you *are* creative. Very few of us have trained our creative brain. It's a huge opportunity because even a little training in creative problem solving can lead to breakthrough results.

Thomas Edison, Henry Ford, Steven Jobs, and Anita Roddick (founder of The Body Shop) are all creative because they create *novel things that are useful* in their domains. Where is creativity required in your domain? Are you selling a product to a hard-to-reach CEO, reinventing an old product line, or dealing with a teenager? You need creativity! The tougher the challenge, the more you need creative thinking to come up with innovative ideas.

When we meet challenges, our work and lives expand with possibility. When we fail to meet a challenge, it's just the opposite; we're frustrated. We all work hard at our challenges, but we rarely invoke our innate creativity. Instead we try to critique and analyze our way to a solution. Unfortunately, these important thinking skills don't lead us to invent something new. What's needed is a better balance of imagination and analysis. With improved creative-thinking skills we can meet more of our challenges, solve more problems, and take advantage of opportunities by creating *novelty that's useful*. That is what this book is all about, more novelty that's useful by using our creativity.

With good ideas, you can create new products, new services, and possibly a newly energized life. Ideas are the most important asset any person or organization has. It's very straightforward: if you have more ideas, and better ideas, you'll be more successful—however you define success—at whatever your goals are. Of course, you have to take action on those ideas if you want to enjoy the fruits of your labors.

> IT'S A MYTH THAT TO BE CREATIVE YOU MUST BE ARTISTIC. EVERYONE IS CREATIVE WHETHER HE IS ARTISTICALLY INCLINED OR NOT.

So, *Jack's Notebook* is for anyone who wants more ideas. If you are struggling to move ahead in your career, if you're an executive with a thorny corporate challenge, someone trying to solve a messy community issue, a family trying to sort through an emotional conflict, or an entrepreneur looking for ways to make the most of limited resources —this book is for you. If you have a "mess" on your hands, you have found a useful tool.

This business novel contains a simple method, a process really, for creative thinking that is powerfully effective in solving both business and personal challenges. The method is my own extension of something called CPS, which is short for creative problem solving. CPS was developed by advertising maven Alex Osborn, who coined the word *brainstorming* in his book *Applied Imagination*, and the scholar Sidney Parnes, PhD. It is, simply put, a process for becoming deliberately creative—you apply your imagination to challenges in a thoughtful way. In fact, CPS asks you to consider *how you think*. How you think separates those who merely hope for creative ideas from those who actually generate them. When you begin making more deliberate and conscious choices about how you think, you'll leverage your creative thinking in matters that are most important to you. And it's not difficult.

Don't be intimidated by the words *method* and *process*. The basics of CPS are easy. In the simplest of terms, it's about list making and choice making. If you are faced with a challenge, do this: first make a list of options or ideas—and then make a choice. But remember to make your list without judgment. When you stop and critique an idea, you hinder the flow of the imagination. Instead, delay judging your ideas until after you've created a full list. This is the essence of the CPS process.

I'm a creativity and innovation expert. I've spent many years studying, teaching, and doing creative problem solving for individuals and large companies. When I thought about writing a book about creative thinking, I realized that the category needed . . . innovation! Don't get me wrong—there are some incredible books on the subject, and I would encourage anyone interested to jump in and read the works of Sidney Parnes, Michael Kirton, Edward de Bono, Michael Michalko, and Mihaly Csikszentmihalyi, to name just a few. I stand on the shoulders of these talented writers and thinkers. They've done such a good job on the academic and theoretical side of things that I believed something new was required to reach even more people with the message of deliberate creative thinking. I believe that the best way to reach people with this message is through a story.

Stories communicate in ways that academic books and traditional business books simply cannot. I want my readers to learn a concept with some emotion attached because it's easier to digest and easier to remember that way. I want you to feel it. I was inspired by the fables found in Patrick Lencioni's books and Eliyahu Goldratt's seminal book *The Goal*. Stories bring the principles of business leadership, team building, and manufacturing to life.

When I'm not writing business novels like this one, I work with mostly large companies to create new products and services. I conduct "ideation" sessions—the buzzword that means "brainstorming" in the corporate world—where thousands of ideas are generated in just a day or two. I've had the satisfaction of seeing ideas become market-leading brands.

I've been a founding partner in a few companies of my own, and I can tell you from personal experience that this method works for entrepreneurs. You might think that creativity is something that borders on the touchy-feely—and you would be right—but CPS is not about touchy-feely. It's about results.

By reading *Jack's Notebook* you'll learn how to think differently. You'll learn the specific CPS tools and techniques that will take your creative thinking to breakthrough levels. You'll learn how to better understand challenges, how to generate more ideas to meet them, and how to create action plans that get bottom-line business results and deep personal fulfillment. If you're not completely sold yet, it might help you to know that I was as skeptical about a deliberate creative process as anybody in the beginning. I was a very tough sell on the hard Return On Investment (ROI) of creativity. When I first learned and started using CPS, I was an ordinary software salesman, but with CPS, my stalled career skyrocketed. Five years later I was involved as a founding partner in a successful software start-up. Now I'm a successful speaker, writer, illustrator, and consultant.

I learned about CPS in the late '80s while attending the annual Creative Problem Solving Institute (sponsored by the Creative Education Foundation, www.creativeeducationfoundation.org). I took the Springboard course and was amazed to learn a method existed that focused on creative thinking. It wasn't a lot of touchy-feely stuff without results. It was just the opposite. It was serious, exciting, and fun all at once. I was also amazed to learn how quickly you can become very good at brainstorming.

But CPS is not simply brainstorming. It includes that technique, but it's within a structure that helps you use your creativity in all aspects of problem solving, from objective setting through action planning. CPS is not an artificial construct either—it merely formalizes what we often do naturally. Some skilled problem solvers don't use a formal method like CPS, but if you look at what they do, you'll see that they take all the same steps. When faced with a truly scary challenge, even skilled natural problem solvers get lost or overwhelmed. CPS gives us a form to follow when we are lost in the complexity or fear of a difficult challenge.

CPS Process

The diagram shows the six steps of CPS:

1. Identify the Challenge
2. Facts and Feelings Exploration
3. Problem Framing and Reframing
4. Idea Generation
5. Solution Development
6. Action Planning

These six steps occur within three major phases: Problem Exploration, Brainstorming, and Getting into Action. If you're just beginning to use CPS, then it might be easiest to start applying just the three phases. With these, you can practice CPS anywhere—even when driving a car. Later, you can begin working through the six steps more rigorously.

In *Jack's Notebook* the characters will be going through all six steps. Not always in order, and not always every step. As you become more aware of what step you need at a certain time—really what type of thinking you need—you simply can use that one and skip the others. In the back of this book, you'll find a CPS Quick Reference Guide, a chart that summarizes the steps of the process. You'll also find Jack's Notebook with Author Tips, which gives you the lists Jack makes during the story. It also includes a few more CPS tips from me. I encourage you to create your own notebook and start working on a challenge of your own as you read this story.

1 : THE RIDE

Where Jack identifies
the challenge of his life

Jack enters the first major phase of CPS, Problem Exploration. He meets Manny Gibran, a professional problem solver, who prompts him to begin the first step: Identify the Challenge. In other words, Jack must identify what he hopes for and what possible outcomes he wants in his life. Manny encourages Jack to use the words "I wish" to create a list. Manny also urges Jack to defer judgment of those wishes because criticizing too soon will hinder the creative process.

Deferral of judgment is a good idea even when you aren't in the middle of making a list. It's a good practice for everyday life. Things are often not what they seem. If we take more time to understand a situation, then ideas and opportunities often arise. If we move quickly—too quickly—to critical judgment, we close doors.

1

The hot coffee soaking into his jeans jolted Jack awake. Cursing under his breath, he grabbed a handful of paper napkins from a stack on the counter and blotted the spill. The muted sounds of the tennis club, the repetitive thwacking of the tennis balls from the courts, had lulled him to sleep. He noticed spilled coffee inching toward a frayed lamp cord. He rushed to blot it up before it reached the wire and just made it. Under the wrong circumstances he might have been electrocuted. He could see the headline: "Arlington Heights Tennis Club Employee Aced by Coffee Spill." The headline would be accompanied by a gangland, murder-style black-and-white photograph of him lying dead on the floor—visible coffee stains on his jeans. At least he'd go out with a bang.

He glanced at his watch—still forty minutes until closing time.

Jack was tired, and it hadn't helped that he'd skipped lunch and dinner. Being both a night manager at a tennis club and a bartender at a local pub paid the rent but were not jobs conducive to regular meals and sleep. Since his car was not working, he spent hours on the train getting to and from the tennis club job. He walked the few blocks from his apartment to his bartending gig. It was work just getting to work. Worse than all of this, Jack was as bored as a human being could be. As he threw away the wet napkins, he noticed that his hands were trembling; he really needed to get some sleep.

Jack poured himself more coffee and ate some stale pretzels.

At twenty minutes to midnight Jack got into the closing routine. Just after twelve he locked the front door behind him, and a gust of cold wind sent a chill up his spine. He thought with regret that he should have known to wear his raincoat. It was a long walk to the train station, so he zipped up his jacket and broke into a jog. He was so tired he couldn't keep jogging for long, and he slowed to a walk.

The smell of rain filled the air. In the distance rumblings and flashes indicated an approaching electrical storm, and it was still about thirty miles to his apartment. To get there meant a four-mile walk to the Metra's Northwest Line, a long ride downtown, a transfer to the CTA Blue Line, and then another short walk.

Such is life for the young, bored, and desperate, he thought, *filled with trains and walks*. He'd given up on what he really wanted to do, photography. He'd studied photography in college before he dropped out after his junior year. Despite a few successful shoots over the past few years, including weddings and freelance photojournalism, jobs were few and far between, especially for someone who was under-equipped and underfinanced. He had no idea how to take it to the next level. Nothing he'd tried had worked, and it was frustrating.

It started to rain. A drizzle at first, then it quickly built up, and Jack found himself in a downpour. In a minute the ice-cold water soaked through his sneakers and socks, and he still had at least two miles to go.

His body started shaking involuntarily, and he was angry with himself. Sighing, he said softly, "I'm not going anywhere." He wanted to take control of his life. *What gives a person control?* he wondered.

He asked himself, *What do I need?* An answer floated into his head—ideas. *I need more ideas. Is that too simple? Too easy? I need more ideas, and better ideas, about how I can help myself,* he thought. *But how to get them? And how to get off my rear end and do something?*

The rain was getting worse; lightning flashed nearby. He started jogging again, flapping his arms to stay warm, with his back to the infrequent cars passing by. Walking by a public park, he noticed an open-air pavilion with an extended roof. He ducked under the overhang and listened to the rain pelt the tin roof. The center of the electrical storm was right on top of him. Suddenly, the lightning flashed and thunder clapped—so close, so loud and surprising, it knocked him to the ground.

Jack came to a moment later. The air smelled strange, and his body was shaking uncontrollably. His mind was foggy at first, but then he remembered he was going home. He slowly started moving again. Everything was working, so he must have dodged the lightning bolt, or at least the worst effects of it. He was suddenly very happy to be alive.

As he stepped out from the shelter and began walking, a car horn beeped behind him. He jumped and turned around. A fire-engine red Jeep Cherokee pulled over, its emergency lights flashing. For a moment, Jack thought it was a cop. It wasn't. The window on the passenger side slid down, and the man inside said, "Sorry to startle you there, do you need a lift?"

Jack hesitated for only a moment, making a quick judgment that he definitely could use the help. "Yeah!" He hopped in the car and was glad to see that the seats were vinyl since he was going to get them all wet.

As if reading his mind, the guy said, "Don't worry about the seats; they'll wipe right off." The man reached behind to the backseat, and then a hand towel appeared as an offering to Jack.

"Wow, a towel," said Jack. He gratefully accepted it, wiping off his face and neck and blotting his hair.

"Where you going?" The man's voice was deep and resonant, like an announcer. There was the slightest hint of an ethnic accent, which Jack couldn't place. His friendly tone put Jack at ease.

"I'm going home—actually walking to the Metra station, then I make some transfers. I live close to downtown, in Wicker Park."

"Well, I'm heading into the city; you want a ride in?"

"Absolutely!"

Jack tried to get a better look at the driver. It was dark in the car, but the streetlights gave Jack some help now and again. The man wore old-fashioned horn-rimmed glasses, and his long black hair was combed back and gathered behind his neck in a ponytail. His strong chin sported a thick, well-trimmed goatee. He looked intellectual, like a professor. Jack also noticed that the guy had a real beak on him. Jack, on the other hand, looked younger than his twenty-six years, with his boyish face, blue eyes, fair skin, and trim physique.

Jack glanced into the backseat and noticed a fancy red western-style shirt in a plastic dry-cleaning bag. He wondered why anyone would wear something like that.

"It's for a square dancing class," the man said, noticing where Jack was looking. "It's like something out of *Urban Cowboy*, eh?"

Embarrassed to be caught snooping, Jack asked, "So what's in the city?"

The man looked over and smiled. "Going to work."

"This hour?"

"Yeah. Weird deal. I'm looking at an office building—I'm trying to solve a wiring problem, and the only time we can go in and really poke around the building is after hours. I have to get into spaces that might cause some dust or make some noise, so the powers-that-be thought it best I do my investigating after hours. I had a previous dinner date this evening, and this is the earliest I could get down there."

Jack now noticed the man's hands. They were big hands with a few scars, hands that had seen some heavy work, though maybe not so recently. "You're an electrician?" Jack asked.

"No, not really. I'm just helping a client of mine out with a problem."

Jack shook involuntarily, and the man said, "You're cold. Let me turn on the heat."

"Thanks. And listen, thanks for the ride too."

"*De nada.* You're welcome," the driver said.

"So, what's it all about—looking at this building, consulting or whatever. You said it was a wiring problem?"

"It's an interesting problem to me, but you might find it rather boring," the man said, glancing over at Jack.

"No, go ahead. Do you work for a consulting company?" asked Jack, just wanting to continue the conversation.

"I work for myself. I'm a professional problem solver."

"Never knew there was such a thing as a professional problem solver," said Jack.

"Sure, there are a few of us out there. To be more specific, I facilitate a method, a problem-solving process, called CPS, which stands for creative problem solving. Actually, a lot of people—maybe even most of us—are in some way professional problem solvers," the man observed.

"We all have problems, that's for sure," said Jack. "You mentioned a process. What was that again?"

"CPS," the man said.

"CPS, that sounds interesting. I never thought of creativity as a process," Jack said. "How are you using it with what you're doing downtown?"

"There's this old building I'm looking at. It wasn't constructed to handle digital-era wiring, so there's no good place to put the data lines and all. It's a problem. They could probably handle this without me, but they're busy, and they're panicked, and the easy way to handle the problem is very expensive. What they really need is a cheaper way to get it done. So I got the call. Really my job is to do three things: explore the problem or challenge, brainstorm some problem or ideas, and get into action."

"That sounds simple enough. How'd you get into this thing you do?"

"It just evolved," the man said.

"I've tried that evolving. It's not working so well."

"Give it a chance. You're a young guy." The man smiled.

"Well, as you can see, I'm walking around in the rain—I'm not exactly the sharpest knife in the drawer."

"Raw intelligence and good sense are two different things. One's the engine; the other is driving skill. And circumstances can put people, even very bright, sensible people, into some tough situations. Like you, walking around in the rain. Of course I don't know why you are out walking around in the rain. Could be that walking around in the rain tonight was your choice. And even if it wasn't your choice, it could still be the best thing that ever happened to you. Every problem is an opportunity." The man paused for a moment and smiled again. "Sorry, people get annoyed at me sometimes when I say that. Anyway, you sound bright enough to me. What are you up to?"

"Right now, I'm just a slob trying to make his way home," said Jack.

"Like the song Joan Osborne did, right? I liked that song. Funny, the reaction to it. You'd have thought it was a sin to think of Jesus in humble circumstances. But really, if you don't mind, tell me, what are your circumstances? I'm not here to judge, I'm just curious."

"What do you want to know?" asked Jack.

"Hmm, well, to start with, what do you wish for?"

"What do I wish for?"

"Yeah, what's your dream? What's on the list?" The man was persistent. "I'll tell you why I ask for your list of wishes," said the man. "It's the first step in solving a problem. The first step in CPS is identifying the challenge; it's where you think of an objective. You have to know what result you want, in other words, what you wish for."

"So you make a list of wishes about things you want?"

"That's right."

"I don't have a list of wishes," Jack said.

"Okay, so it's not formally written down or anything. Just from the top of your mind—what's the first thing you think of when I ask the question, what do you wish for? I wish . . . "

"I wish I were a photographer," Jack said, without blinking an eye. "I was just thinking about that as I was walking home."

"Okay, photography. What else do you wish for?"

"That's pretty much it," said Jack. "I mean I hadn't thought much about it."

THE FIRST STEP IN CPS IS IDENTIFYING THE CHALLENGE; IT'S WHERE YOU THINK OF AN OBJECTIVE. YOU HAVE TO KNOW WHAT RESULT YOU WANT, IN OTHER WORDS, WHAT YOU WISH FOR.

"We have some time to explore this—unless you want to listen to the radio instead?"

"No, no, that's okay. It's an interesting question. Nobody's ever asked me that before," Jack reflected.

"It's a question you can ask yourself anytime you want—it puts your brain in motion. In order to get what you want, you have to know what it is. That's the first step. Doesn't matter if it's a business problem or a personal one."

Jack thought about this for a minute. *Why is this such a tough question?* he wondered.

"Hey, anything's allowed. I mean, do you wish you had a car?" asked the man.

"Yeah," said Jack.

"Okay, that's two wishes on the list. What else?"

"I wish I had a girlfriend." Jack thought, *That'll never happen.*

"Three."

"And I wish I had a better job. But, oh, I said photography already . . ."

"That's okay, we're just making the list right now; keep flowing, don't judge it. When you defer judgment you open the door to your own imagination. I mean, there could be other cool jobs for you, right?" said the man.

"Right," said Jack, still thinking about the not-judging-it remark. Not judging it. Making a list and not judging it. Jack judged everything. "Tough not to judge," Jack finally said.

"We're all great judgers, aren't we? Critical thoughts come up all the time, but I try not to let it get in the way of my imagination," said the man.

"So, okay, I wish I had my raincoat with me," Jack said. "I wish that I could find a way to have more fun in my life." At this point, Jack remembered the insight he'd had after dodging the lightning bolt. It prompted him to say, "And I wish that I had more ideas, I wish that I had better ideas, I wish I were the idea guy."

"Now you're rolling," said the stranger.

He was rolling. When you really started just saying what you wished for—and didn't stop to analyze—it just flowed. Jack was surprised he had said out loud the wish for ideas. It had just come out in the stream of other wishes.

"Funny how when you get going with that listing, things just sort of pop out," said Jack.

"It happens when you stop judging your own ideas. You've got an interesting list going. So, keep going. What else do you wish for?"

"It gets tougher to think of things once you stop," said Jack.

"Yeah, but push through it. You have more to say. I bet you have more wishes buried—just under the surface."

"Okay." It didn't matter what he said, did it? He'd never see this guy again. Plus he was so exhausted from the rain and cold, he didn't have the mental strength to resist, so he said what was really there for him, right at that moment. "I wish I had finished college," Jack said, "I wish I could confront my demons. It would be nice if I knew what was going to happen to me. It would be nice if I had all sorts of skills to complement what I already know . . ." He paused, thinking, then continued, "I wish I knew more about computers, e-mail, and the Web. I wish I had a family, kids someday . . ."

"Okay!" The stranger laughed. He had a big, easy laugh. "That's some list."

Jack wondered about this guy. "So, what's your name?" asked Jack.

"Manny Gibran," the man replied.

"Sounds like a Hispanic name."

"Not exactly, the name is more Middle Eastern. But I am Hispanic—my mother was Mexican. Manny is short for Emmanuel, which is not all that common of a name in Hispanic culture, but it was the only name my mom and dad could agree on. My father was Lebanese."

"Lebanese—are you Muslim?" Jack was immediately sorry he'd said that out loud. Since 9/11 and the other terrorist bombings, he'd become more suspicious of people who were, or looked like they were, from that part of the world. Jack had never really known a Muslim, not even one—never went to school with one, never had a beer with one. He knew his mild prejudice wasn't rational, and he made a mental note to try harder to be fair.

Jack quickly said, "Listen, it's none of my business what you are. You're just a nice guy to give me a ride."

"Actually, no, it's not a problem; I like talking about my background. I think it's sort of interesting. To me, anyhow. So to answer your question—no, I'm not Muslim although many Lebanese are. A lot of people don't know that many Lebanese are Christians. My father was what they call a Maronite Christian. My mother, God rest her soul, like most Mexicans was Roman Catholic. She was a mestizo, a mix of Spanish and Indian blood."

"How'd a Lebanese guy end up marrying a Mexican woman?"

"They met in Mexico City. My father fled Lebanon during their civil war. He immigrated to Mexico. There's a Lebanese ex-pat community there."

"I've read something about that war. It was pretty brutal from what I hear."

"It was. It destroyed my family, scattered us to the winds. War is so senseless. It's always senseless—no matter what the politics are or what the story is. There is always a better way."

Jack had the feeling that the guy was sincere. His quiet demeanor and voice radiated authenticity. There was no need to worry about him.

"How'd you get here to Chicago?" asked Jack.

"That's a long story. The short version is that after my mother died, my father came up here to find work. We lived near Mom's relatives. The mestizo part of the family ended up helping to raise me. I spent some time down in Texas along the way."

"Sounds like you had a tough childhood," said Jack.

"Not so tough. It was kind of nuts, but our family stuck together," said Manny.

They were making good progress toward the city and were now in the denser urban neighborhoods that ring around the center of Chicago. Jack loved Chicago—its combination of grit, polish, and charm meant *home* to him. The street lamps had haloes in the cold mist. He looked down the long straight avenues disappearing into the fog. The heater was still on full blast, and it was making the car stuffy. He was still thinking about the wish list, how it would be a good idea to have that list to read through and think about. He felt an urge to write it down before he forgot it.

"I have this urge to write down that list I just made," said Jack.

"It's a good instinct, actually. Here, I'll give you something."

Manny fished around in a leather bag under his seat and produced a blank notebook. He gave it to Jack.

"Here, start tracking your thinking in this," said Manny.

"Thanks," said Jack amazed. "Do you keep spare blank notebooks in your bag to give away?"

"Well, I had that one because I'm about to begin a new project, and I haven't even touched it yet. I've got a dozen more at home on the shelf—so you take this one, it's on me," he said.

Jack had a ballpoint pen in his jacket. He opened the notebook, which was a simple spiral sketchbook with blank pages, no lines. He took a minute and jotted down the wishes he'd come up with earlier. It felt good to do it. Why? He thought about it until the answer came to him: it was, very simply, a start.

Jack was thinking ahead. In about five minutes they would be in his neighborhood. The ride was almost over, but Jack wanted to get to know this guy, wanted to stay in touch. And maybe Manny would be a good contact—he seemed like he knew things.

"Listen, I was just thinking . . ." began Jack.

"Yeah?"

"Well, do you, like, ever need a photographer?"

"Matter of fact, I do now and then," Manny said, fishing around in his shirt pocket with one hand. "Here, take my card. Send me an e-mail with your rates and such."

"Okay, thanks," said Jack.

Not what he had hoped for, but he did have the card. E-mail was a problem. Jack didn't have a computer and didn't have an active e-mail account. He'd have to go to one of those Web cafés and get that together.

"Where do you live?" asked Manny.

Jack wasn't sure he wanted Manny to see where he lived. Not because he was afraid of him anymore—he seemed like an okay guy. But because he was embarrassed. His apartment wasn't a total dump, but it was nothing to be proud of.

"Why not just drop me off at the corner of Noble and Milwaukee?" suggested Jack.

"You sure?"

"Yeah, yeah, I need to pick up some stuff at the convenience store," he lied.

"Okay, Noble and Milwaukee—that's right off the exit, isn't it?"

"Yeah, you can hop right back on," said Jack.

They rode in silence, but then Manny said, "I forgot to ask your name."

"Jack Huber."

"Nice to meet you, Jack." He extended his hand. "You a Jack that's short for John?"

"Yeah, but everybody calls me Jack, always have." Jack took Manny's hand to shake it. He'd been right, this guy had hands that were able, had seen some hard work. They were strong. Handshakes for Jack were usually a cursory thing, something you had to do, but Jack sensed something different about Manny's handshake. There was something more sincere about it. Jack's hand was warm as it dropped away. *What a nice piece of luck to run into this guy*, he thought. Jack noticed he wasn't cold any longer. His frazzled fatigue had changed to a calm, relaxed state.

Manny glanced over and smiled. It was a knowing smile, and Jack got his first look at Manny's eyes. Through the glasses, they were large, deep, dark, and liquid brown. They radiated kindness.

"Jack, I hope you send me that e-mail—maybe we could do some work together. If you're interested—maybe I can help you work through that wish list you made."

"I'm interested. Why would you do that? Why would a big-time consultant spend time helping me?" said Jack.

"I have my reasons," said Manny. "Do you want to work through the CPS process?"

"Sure," said Jack.

"All right then," said Manny. "We'll be in touch . . . Oh, one last thing before you go. Review that list and pick one wish that really grabs you, one that really gives you energy, okay? Then, go out and find out as much as you can about it—turn over every stone."

"Turn over every stone . . . okay, will do, and thanks for the ride," said Jack.

"*De nada*," said Manny.

Manny stopped the car in front of the White Hen convenience store. Jack said thanks again and hopped out. He watched the car pull back into traffic and move toward the highway. Jack stood on the corner. It had stopped raining. The new notebook was in his hands. As he walked the few blocks home, he scanned the list. Reading it gave him a glimmer of hope—and that was something.

2: TURN OVER EVERY STONE

Where Jack begins to explore his challenge

Jack chooses photography from his list of wishes and thus identifies his challenge, completing step one of CPS. When he makes his list of wishes, he uses divergent or imaginative thinking. When he chooses from those wishes, he uses convergent or critical-analytical thinking. In CPS, these two types of thinking are separated, even though they usually are not separate in real life. Separating them is a fundamental aspect of better problem solving.

In this chapter Jack begins step two of CPS, Facts and Feelings Exploration. He thoroughly researches his challenge, and he faces the challenge in spite of his fears. In deliberate creativity, you take the time to develop a deep understanding of the facts and feelings that surround a challenge before generating ideas. He also begins an invaluable file folder of research data.

Getting out of bed was usually a problem for Jack, but today was different. His head buzzed with the memory of the previous evening as he swung his legs to the floor.

He felt "lit up." *I should get zapped more often*, he thought, remembering the lightning storm.

Jack looked at the wish list he had jotted down in Manny's sketchbook. Some wishes seemed like things that could actually happen. Some were just curious, odd that he had said them aloud, odd that he had written them down. The wish that stood out for him was the wish about wanting to be a photographer. It was a dream he'd pursued for some time but one that seemed impossible. He'd pretty much given up. Manny had said to pick one and then "turn over every stone." Jack picked up a pen and circled the wish about being a photographer.

Okay, so I'll try again, he thought. *Now what? Turn over every stone—How does one go about doing that?*

The business card Manny had given him was on the table next to the bed. Jack picked it up. *Nice card*, Jack thought, *made of expensive linen paper.*

Here's what I'll do today, thought Jack. *I'll get an e-mail account and send this guy a message, a thank-you note.*

Jack took a quick shower, shaved, and got dressed. He thought he'd go down to that coffee shop on Milwaukee Avenue—what was it called? A weird name—Geek's, that was it, Geek's Web Café. Given the name, he knew they must have a Web connection. Jack hadn't used a computer much since he'd quit college five years ago. Buying a computer was just not in the budget, and honestly, he didn't want one.

So he'd go down to Geek's and send Manny an e-mail with his hourly rate and his day rate, get some coffee and a bite to eat, and start looking into being a photographer. Jack looked around his apartment for his raincoat. The apartment was small: a tiny kitchen, a Spartan bedroom, a cluttered living room, and a bathroom. He'd put up some poster-sized prints of his black-and-white photographs; he had some books, an extensive vinyl record collection that had been his late father's, a few CDs, and an old nonworking jukebox. What might you call this style of decorating? Eclectic ghetto? He found his raincoat on the floor by the door, right where he'd forgotten it the previous day, and closed the door behind him.

It was a decent day, sun out, clear blue skies, and a bite of cold in the air. March in Chicago is a heartbreaker. One minute you think spring is here, the next minute you think you're in Manitoba. Jack sauntered along, not in a hurry, enjoying the walk through his neighborhood, Wicker Park. The area was gentrifying, but it was still home to a weird mix of people—artists, professionals, blue-collar workers, students, old folks, and all flavors of ethnic groups. It was a fun place to live—friendly pubs and diners, clubs to hear live music, non-chain record stores, and good used book shops. Jack liked the diversity. He liked the life of it; it felt like home.

A few minutes later he arrived at Geek's with some color in his face, the cold March air having done its work. Jack noticed Geek's logo—a caricature of a nerdy looking guy wearing taped-up glasses and a bow tie having a coffee with a chicken.

Not much was happening inside Geek's—a few people having some coffee and keyboarding. He went over to an empty booth with a sleek black computer screen mounted on an adjustable arm on the wall, a wireless keyboard sitting on the table. He put his raincoat on the seat, tossed his new sketchbook on the table, and walked up to the counter to order a coffee.

A young woman appeared behind the counter. She appeared to be an organic type, wearing no makeup or lipstick. Her long and abundant light-brown hair sprouted dreadlocks, gathered loosely at the top of her head and held with a long paisley scarf that flowed down her back to her waist. She was wearing a too-small black vest over a blue spandex sports bra top, her midriff showing above a pair of drab olive, hip-hugging cargo pants. No tattoos he could see. She was on the slim side.

Jack tried not to be too obvious in checking her out. As he moved closer to the counter, he got a better look at her face. Her almond-shaped green eyes were set into high cheekbones, and she had a mannish chiseled chin, a strong, young, and fresh face. She smiled.

"Welcome to Geek's. What would you like?" She said it sincerely, not sounding like she'd said it a thousand times.

"Your largest Americano, with two inches of room, please." Jack held up his hand with a two-inch gap between his thumb and first finger.

"Okay, lots of room, anything to eat?" She marked his cup two inches down with a grease pencil.

"What's good today?"

"The lemon muffins are fresh out of the oven." She waved her hand at a tray in the display case.

"I'll have one of those."

"You sitting over there?" She pointed toward Jack's booth.

"Yeah, I'll be over there trying to figure out how to set up an e-mail account," Jack said, halfway hoping she'd offer to help but then asked, "I noticed you have some Scotch tape back there—do you think I could snag a couple of pieces?"

The young woman stared at Jack, clearly giving him the once-over. *Turnabout is fair play*, he thought. *I was staring before. Or was it the e-mail thing? Or maybe it was asking a complete stranger for Scotch tape.* Anyway, he felt like an idiot. Now she looked mildly amused. She turned around and pulled off two lengths of Scotch tape. Turning back to him, she held them out to Jack on her index finger. Jack transferred the tape to his own fingers, slowly and carefully in order not to tangle them. It was an oddly intimate moment.

"There's tape—for the man who's obviously needing to piece something together. Or is it for repair? A broken heart perhaps?" She giggled. "Anyway, don't mind me. Just goofing. I'll bring your Americano over. You'll need to pay me for some computer time. It's five bucks minimum, that gets you the first hour."

"I won't be on that long," he replied.

"That's what they all say," she laughed.

Jack sat down. He opened his sketchbook, the gift from Manny. He taped Manny's card to the page after his wish list. He faced the screen. A box in the middle of the screen said "Press Enter." So he did. Another box popped up asking for a user name and a password. *Am I supposed to know this? Or do I just make one up?* He sat pondering this question for a minute. *This is how computers hurt you*, he thought— *they make you feel stupid. Okay, so I'm stupid.*

"What do I do about user and password?" he asked out loud in the general direction of organic dreadlocks girl.

"Oh, sorry, should have said that. Just use Geek13 for user and password. Case doesn't matter."

"Thanks." Then "Geek13, Geek13," he mumbled to himself, entering the codes by hunting and pecking with his two index fingers.

He hit Enter again. The cursor, which had been an arrow, now took the form of an hourglass, and a second later Jack was startled by a crescendo of music—the computer talking back to him. The desktop screen appeared. *Where does one go for e-mail again?* he wondered. He opened up Internet Explorer and then tried to remember how to get a free e-mail account.

Dreadlocks girl came over with his Americano and lemon muffin. She seemed to be moving slowly. "Here's your lemon muffin . . . is something wrong with the workstation?"

Jack motioned with his hand toward the computer, rolling his eyes. "No, but there's something wrong with me. Something very *seriously wrong* with me. I don't know what I'm doing here. I can't remember how to open up a free e-mail account," he admitted.

Dreadlocks girl giggled. Jack felt like crawling under the table, but then she asked, "Do you want some help?"

"I think I'm hopeless."

"Well, you do *look* hopeless," she said, grinning.

"Can't you help keep hope alive?" He said this with a mild hint of a Jesse Jackson in his voice.

He felt another appraising look from her and saw a glimmer of amusement in her eyes. *She thinks I'm funny,* he thought. *Hope is alive.*

"Oh, okay, seeing as how it's part of my job and all. I might have to jump up and serve, but yeah, sure. So you want an e-mail account?"

"Yeah."

"Yahoo offers free e-mail," she said. Together they went through the process of setting up an account. Jack was delighted with dreadlocks girl, whose name turned out to be Molly. She was helpful and patient, and when she left to serve customers, he got out the business card and typed in Manny Gibran's address. Staring out the window,

Jack composed his thoughts, and then he plunged into writing the note. He spent some time with it, finally getting something he felt was to the point and professional. Sitting back, he drank his coffee and reviewed the note.

```
Dear Mr. Gibran,
    Many thanks for the ride into town
last night, I really appreciate it. I
thought our conversation was interesting—
I'd like to know more about that method
you mentioned, CPS?
    I'm writing to thank you, but also to
follow up on the photographic services I
mentioned. My day rate is $400. Film,
developing, and prints are billed as
incurred. My half-day rate is $250.
Please write or call if you have any
photographic needs.
                            Regards,
                            Jack Huber
```

Satisfied, he clicked on the Send button. *Sent and done,* he thought to himself.

An accomplishment. And it wasn't that difficult. Most of his friends had e-mail, so perhaps now he could start communicating with them.

He stared down at Gibran's card, admitting it would be nice to know more about this guy. *Maybe he's on the Web.* He typed in the name and clicked on the Search button. The screen blinked, and a list of links appeared. Jack saw Manny Gibran's name sprinkled many times through the text on the screen. He spent some time reading through the various links. After a few misses, he finally clicked on one that brought up a two-year-old newspaper article from Seattle. It was a story about some consulting work that Gibran had done to prevent accidental explosions in a munitions factory. This was definitely him;

there was a picture of him talking to people on the shop floor of the munitions plant. The article speculated that his work had probably saved lives. There were pages of links describing various projects he'd worked on and CPS training he'd given. A third link was a magazine article that briefly traced his life story.

The article said his father had been a sort of handyman who had succeeded in Chicago doing small construction contracts. Manny Gibran had apparently helped his father, working beside him. Later, Manny had made a fortune trading options using a software product he'd written himself on an early Apple computer. Then came the problem-solving consulting. There was a list of companies he'd worked for—all over the globe.

Jack was amazed. He couldn't imagine why Gibran would want to bother with him. What relevance would his meager photography skills have to a guy like this? Why would he want to help me? Jack slumped in his seat. He figured this information would be good to keep in a research file.

"Hey, Molly," he called, feigning a south side Chicago accent.

"Hey, what?" she answered, picking up on the accent and feigning right back.

"How do I print?"

"Just a minute." She finished up something behind the counter and came over. This time, she took the mouse, and in a second, she opened the Print box and chose the right printer. She pressed Print and retrieved the page from the printer across the room, and brought it back to him. "That one's free of charge," she said. "My kindness to strangers does have limits though." She grinned. "What are you researching?"

"Well, I was looking into a potential client, a man I met last night who might hire me to do some photography."

"Photography? Are you a photographer?"

"A novice one, yeah. I'm hoping to expand my business."

"Do you have a Web page?"

"No, why?"

"Anybody in photography needs a Web site so potential clients can see their work. Or find you to do some work. If somebody was looking for a . . . I don't know, say a photographer based in Wicker Park, you would want them to find you, right?"

"Of course."

"Okay, so do you know how to use FrontPage?"

"I can read the front page of a newspaper," Jack quipped.

"Funny. Want me to show you? It's not such a difficult program to use," she said.

Molly introduced him to FrontPage, and after a bit of tinkering, he had created the beginnings of a Web site. Just the very basics: a background, font, and more. So far, it was simple and straightforward—a clean design. But he wasn't sure what he'd sell on the Web site.

He got another coffee and started to research photography. Even though he rarely got to do it, he loved Web surfing. It felt a bit like being a kid in a candy store. You could find out almost anything. What a great way to explore a challenge.

Jack made more notes in his notebook. He listed the various classifications of photographers, and he made a note that he needed to learn more about digital media. His current experience was limited to a basic digital camera he'd bought a couple of years ago. *Yeah, I'll get that done by Friday,* he thought cynically. The Web was at once exhilarating and overwhelming. He pushed himself away from the table.

That's when he looked at the clock on the wall. He'd been in Geek's for over three hours. The muffin was a distant memory, and he was hungry again.

Molly was still behind the counter. She looked up and caught his eye. "Would you like another coffee?" she asked.

"I was thinking more about lunch."

"Is that an invitation?" She was openly flirting. "All we have here is breakfast food."

"Sure," he said, wondering if she was serious.

She came out from behind the counter and walked over to his table, slipping the strap of a canvas bag over her shoulder. She was ready to go.

"How much do I owe you for the computer?" asked Jack.

"I should charge you for another two hours, but I'm going to give you the first-timer's discount—on one condition."

"Okay, what's the catch?"

"Catch is we really *do* go to lunch."

"Did you think I was kidding?" he asked.

"No, so let's go."

Happy to go with the flow, Jack put on his raincoat and picked up his sketchbook. They walked out of Geek's and headed up Milwaukee Avenue.

"What did you have in mind?" he asked.

"I just want to get some soup and half a sandwich. There's a health food store with a lunch counter about two blocks from here. Is that okay with you?"

Jack agreed, and they walked along in the midday bustle and chaos of Milwaukee Avenue. Jack noticed her confident stride and great posture. She'd put on a pair of huge Jackie O–style sunglasses. She was carrying a black-and-white notebook. *Were those her initials, MD, in the bottom right corner? Or did she aspire to be a doctor?* Once they arrived at the health food store, Molly went to the counter and ordered the soup of the day. Jack asked for a vegan sandwich, not that he was a vegan—he just thought it would look good. They sat together at the end of the counter.

"So how did you end up at Geek's?" Jack asked.

"I saw a sign in the window, I went in, and I got the job."

"You grow up in Chicago?"

Molly paused for a moment before answering, "No, I just moved here a few months ago. I grew up in Milwaukee. I don't know many people here in Chicago."

"You a reggae fan?"

"I am, but I guess you're asking because of the hair."

"That would be a yes," he said.

"The hair is more of a fashion thing—I just like it this way. I'm not a Rastafarian or anything. I made a decision a few months ago that I was going to look exactly how I wanted to look, with no holding back. I may be overreacting to years of . . . restrictions . . . but mostly I just wanted to look different than I used to and have different hair," she explained.

"I get that," Jack said, nodding approval. "So, why'd you want to have lunch with a perfect stranger?" Jack regretted asking as soon as the question left his mouth.

"You're not really a stranger—we were around each other all morning, weren't we? Anyway, do I need a reason beyond curiosity?" she asked, looking him in the eye.

"No, no—curiosity is good, glad you asked. And I appreciate your getting me started today. I had to get that e-mail out. Might be an opportunity for me to work with this guy I met last night."

"The business card you had?"

"Right. Name is Manny Gibran. Turns out he's some kind of esoteric problem-solving consultant. I'm hoping he'll hire me to do some photography for him. He also offered to guide me through some business challenges."

"Do you do a lot of photography?"

He thought she looked interested. "Unfortunately, no. I don't get much work. I bartend at a place called SMASH, and I have another job out in the burbs at a tennis club." Jack sighed.

"The jobs we do so that we might do other jobs." Molly smiled grimly.

"Yeah, exactly. I feel like I'm on a treadmill. I hate the tennis club. It's out in Arlington Heights, and it takes forever to get out there now that my car is toasted. I really wish I were doing more photography." Jack recalled his wish list of the night before. "What do you wish for?"

Molly leaned back in her chair. "What do I wish for? That's a good question. I don't know. Peace . . . friends."

"Peace and friends?" Jack was surprised with this answer.

"Yeah, just the freedom to live my life the way I want to, and a few good friends to talk to."

"That seems possible."

"It does, doesn't it?" She said it as if she were convincing herself. But then she changed the subject. "You were thinking jobs, right? Well, I wish for interesting work, I want to get a job doing Web site design. I don't know quite enough to get work doing it. I'm good with the writing and the graphics, but I don't have any experience with the more technical aspects of it. And I haven't found entry-level work yet."

"You seem to know your way around a computer."

"To a degree. More important than that, I think I know how to learn a technology."

"What do you mean exactly?"

"I mean, I've mastered some technical skills, but I don't want to stand still. In my mind the key to dealing with technology is simply to continue learning it, to keep after it. You focus on it. You do research. You read books, take classes, practice. Practice in a safe place where you can make mistakes." She smiled. "I really feel like if you want to learn about anything, you just have to turn over every stone."

"Turn over every stone?" repeated Jack. He thought to himself how odd it was that he'd just heard that same thing the night before. "I usually think of research as something scientists do."

"Well, I'm the scientist of my own life."

"Where did you learn all this?"

"I have . . . had . . . a good friend back home. She's my mother's age, and I worked for her two years after I graduated college. She owns a market-research firm. At her company, I was able to develop my computer skills because she let me experiment and explore. In college, I'd taken several classes, but there's nothing like real-world experience."

"A market-research firm? Like those mall surveys?"

"No, not exactly. We did deeper-level research into consumer behavior. Have you heard of focus groups?" Molly asked.

"Didn't they say Clinton ran his government around them?"

"They said that, yeah. And I'm sure his administration actually did lots of focus-group research. But I don't see that as a bad thing. It's really a technique for listening to people and learning about how they think. It's not a panacea, but it can be useful—and I'm sure Republicans do focus groups as well."

"I need a focus group for my life," Jack joked.

"I don't think it would help you. I think you just need a better understanding of what you're trying to do. After all, you're hopeless." Molly jabbed him in the ribs and laughed.

Jack laughed and said, "There's sure a lot to know. It's overwhelming."

"It is overwhelming. Sometimes I feel like I'm drowning—in technological change."

"I hear that. Throw the woman a life raft."

"You don't throw a life raft, you throw one of those . . . what are they called? Round thingies," she said.

"Okay, so throw that woman a round thingy," Jack said dramatically. "Hurry up. No, no, not the square thingy, not the triangle thingy, the round thingy! Quit fooling around . . ." Jack was waving his hands around as if he were directing the other men on deck.

"Stop." But she was smiling, amused.

Jack felt instinctively that he could always work with someone who possessed a sense of humor like this, especially somebody who could be amused when it was really not all that funny. "I have an idea," he said.

"Uh-oh."

"No, don't worry, it's just, maybe we really should be throwing each other a round thingy. Actually, now that I think about it, I think the word is *lifeline*. In fact, what we need is, like, a life raft. More than a lifeline or a round thingy—something that buys us time. That's what a life raft does, it keeps you floating until help comes along. It seems to me that's where we both are, in the water waiting for a ship to come by and pick us up."

"What are you getting at?" she asked, looking at him curiously.

"Look, I know we just met, but so what? I know we can be friends. And we can help each other, you know, be really supportive of each other. We'll do the life-raft thingy together."

"Okay. But I want to be clear here. We're friends, right?" Molly asked.

"Yes, friends," said Jack, looking at her curiously.

"We have to have an agreement about that," she stated gravely. "I . . . I can't get involved with a guy right now. I mean, you seem like a nice guy and all, but romance is the last thing I need in my life. What I really need right now is just a friend." She looked down into her glass of iced tea.

Jack's heart sank. He felt very tired all of a sudden. "So we met each other about four hours ago, and you're worried about romance? Why?"

"It's a long story. And I don't know you well enough to tell it."

She was looking out the window. *Well, there's no need for drama,* Jack thought. *She's nice. We can be friends, and if that's all there is—so be it.*

He took a deep breath. "Just friends on the life raft then. I need a friend. We can be just people who help each other out, like you did for me this morning. And I'd like to do something for you—I'm not sure what at this point. Could we start there?"

She looked away from him, and he wondered if she was tearing up. Then she turned her head quickly back toward him, and now he thought he caught a flash of anger, but then just as quickly, her eyes softened. He noticed her eyes were definitely filled with tears though. She dabbed at her eyes with a napkin, then looked at him and openly appraised him.

"I'm sorry. I just met you, and you'll be thinking I'm Miss High Maintenance. The truth is I am sort of high maintenance, but hey, I'm working on it. My life has been limited by . . . well, by how I grew up. I guess that's true for all of us. Anyway, I do think I can trust you. I really do." She paused and lifted her glass of iced tea. "So we're just going to be friends and help each other, right?"

"Right," said Jack.

"Okay, then when do we start on this life-raft style mutual cooperation society?" She was smiling again.

"I think we already have." Jack smiled back.

"Let's talk more about it," she said.

"Okay, hit me," he said.

She punched him lightly on the shoulder and then said, "Well, I like the mutual support idea and that we'll be friends. The other thing I'm thinking of is, I don't know quite how to say this, but the word is *challenge.*" Molly looked at Jack straight on. "Challenge," she repeated.

"Sounds like an argument," he said.

"No, not like that. I mean, I was watching you this morning. You stepped into something unfamiliar and sort of new today, didn't you?"

"Yeah, a couple of things," he said.

"Right. That got me interested in you. Tell me—how does it feel to do something new?" Molly adjusted her body posture and angled toward Jack. Her face came forward toward him.

Jack thought the closeness was sort of intimidating, but on the other hand, those eyes, still a little wet from the tears, were good to look at up close. "Too busy doing it to think about it just yet," he said.

"That's fair, but talk to me about it. What are you thinking or feeling?"

Jack paused before answering. "Well, it's fresh, it's involving, it's interesting to learn a new thing, meet somebody new. It's not boring. It's the opposite. It's a bright moment. I feel like I'm doing something worthwhile, like it might go somewhere or lead to something."

"And if it didn't lead to something?"

"It would still be worth it, you know. Just the doing of it was something that made me feel more . . . alive."

"See, that's what I was getting at with the *challenge* word."

"So you mean more like 'challenge yourself'—keep moving forward doing things?" he asked.

"Yes, more like that. So, I challenge you."

"Okay . . . And I challenge you back."

"To keep moving forward . . ." she said.

". . . and learn new things," he said.

"And . . . to have more interesting days," she continued.

"And have fun," he said.

"All the time!" she said.

They laughed.

"By the way, what's your name, your last name, I mean?" asked Molly.

"Huber. And yours?"

"Dunne," she said.

Jack noticed that she had had to think a split second about her name, like she was somewhat reluctant to say it.

"So we're friends, Jack, and on the life raft together," she said.

"Yes, friends," he said.

3: As the Stone Turns

Where Jack does a deep dive into his challenge and learns how to observe

Jack continues Facts and Feelings Exploration, and he learns observational research, a simple and profoundly effective technique for getting a better understanding of something. You simply watch—very carefully—a customer, a process, even a malfunctioning piece of equipment. By watching with an open mind (by deferring judgment), he uncovers hidden information. He and Molly also conduct some informal qualitative research; they use interviews to uncover a deeper knowledge of consumer behavior, wants, needs, likes, and dislikes, which increases the odds of having ideas that will gain market acceptance.

Jack also begins another brainstorm and exercises his divergent thinking. By practicing this technique, he becomes a better idea generator. He also formulates challenge statements. He looks for the Who, What, When, Where, Why, and How. A list of Jack's Facts and Feelings Exploration can be found in Jack's Notebook in the back of this book.

Busy days passed, and Jack continued his part-time jobs. He spent long nights bartending at SMASH, and he made the endless and boring train rides back and forth to the tennis club. But things seemed different. Molly, for one thing, but that was just part of it. Between working at the bar and the tennis club, he'd done something he'd never done before—in-depth research. Thorough research. Jack started looking at all things photographic, and he assumed he knew nothing. There was a certain freedom in admitting to yourself that you were ignorant.

He turned over every stone he could find. There were so many stones to turn over. Jack spent time at Geek's doing Web searches and making notes in his sketchbook. He paid a visit to Columbia College and checked out their photography and media courses. He'd even stopped into a couple of commercial photo studios on the off chance they might need some extra help. Unfortunately, they didn't. He'd learned something, though—that it didn't hurt to ask. He asked a lot of questions, to the point that he seemed to exasperate some folks. Still, once he was finished, they seemed to regard him differently. He had his sketchbook with him all the time, and he made a lot of notes.

After all this fact finding, Jack still wasn't sure he knew exactly what kind of photography might best suit him. He was interested in doing studio work, but that wasn't something you could get into overnight—lots of space needed, lots of expensive equipment. Jack wouldn't even know where to start to find customers who'd buy that kind of service. A studio business could take years to build up.

There was portraiture: head shots for actors, models, and speakers. Or photojournalism and fine art photography. There were a lot of choices to make.

Now and then Jack would look over the facts and notes he was gathering in his sketchbook. And while going back through, he added new thoughts and new facts if he had learned more. Sometimes he'd take a highlighter and mark things he thought were especially important to remember, think, or learn more about. Usually he did this just before he went to bed. He found that it helped him sort out what he needed to do tomorrow.

One thing seemed clear: there was no quick path to success in photography. You had to build a career one photo at a time. It was a bit frustrating because all his research seemed to do was raise more questions. He'd started a list of questions on one page of his sketchbook, things that he wanted to learn more about. He was hungrier than ever for some actual freelance work.

He'd sent the e-mail to Manny and had checked back at Geek's for a reply, but nothing appeared in his lonely in-box except for a few cheerful messages from Molly, and spam. *So life goes on*, he thought. *Manny Gibran's an interesting guy, obviously a busy guy—and a guy with no real need for me. So much for the alluded-to freelance work, and so much for the hoped-for guidance from this so-called problem-solving guru.*

Then there was Molly. She continued to be guarded about any thought that they might be getting involved romantically. They'd talked about it again—it was something she was making sure he was "clear" about. It puzzled Jack because he could feel it was more, even for her, but for once in his life he wasn't going to push it. She clearly needed the personal space.

She was mysterious without trying to be. It was what she didn't say, didn't talk about. Jack noticed that she was in the mode of always looking over her shoulder, literally, when she was walking the streets. And the sunglasses, even on a dark day, it was like she was hiding.

He suspected she had secrets. She would share anything he asked about when it came to learning, she would spend time teaching him, and she was very patient. The off-limit questions had to do with her family and most of her past. She dodged those questions, and so Jack learned not to press the matter.

They met at Geek's when she wasn't working, and they would get the corner booth. It became an ongoing seminar. She showed him a slew of different Web sites, pointing out aspects of what she thought was good about one and unattractive in another. Molly got him hip to a lot of cool design ideas and concepts in no time flat. She also taught him the basics of Adobe Photoshop, and they worked on Jack's Web site a little more. Jack knew it would have taken him years to figure this stuff out on his own.

Molly mentioned some of her work at the research company, and Jack was interested in how they learned—sometimes they just watched people. To demonstrate, Molly asked Jack to meet her downtown in front of the Old Water Tower before her shift started at Geek's. Jack took a train into the Loop and walked north up Michigan Avenue. He found Molly sitting on a bench in spring-like weather. She looked beautiful just sitting there alone, with her face turned toward the sun, her long dreads hanging over the back of the bench, her eyes closed. He stepped in front of the sun and cast a shadow across her face.

She opened her eyes. "*Guten Tag*," she said.

"*Guten Morgen*," he replied.

"Follow me," she said.

She walked across the street and entered a Barnes and Noble bookstore. It was midday, and there were lots of people about. She walked over to where the picture books were kept, then opened the cover of one and began thumbing through it.

"What we are here to do is watch," she instructed.

"Watch?"

"Mostly, yeah, just observe, watch. I may ask a few questions of folks here and there, but we can't be obvious about it."

So they watched. Molly grabbed a book and positioned herself about ten feet away. Jack did the same, one aisle down. What they watched was the table of photographic picture books. Several people stopped by and browsed through the books. Some of them just looked at covers. But others would pick up a book and really look through it. One thing Jack noticed was that most of the shoppers were women. *It might be the time of day*, he thought. *What were they looking for?* As if she had heard his question, Molly wandered casually over to the table and browsed next to a woman who was looking closely at the books. Molly said something, and they started chatting casually. Jack listened.

"I really like Ansel Adams—his prints are so beautiful. There's something about black and white," the woman said.

"Do you have any of his other books at home?"

"No, but I have a nice poster. It's in a thin, black frame. We put it in our guest room."

"Do you have any original photos?"

"Of Ansel Adams? Dear me, no. That would be nice, though, wouldn't it?"

"I mean of any photographs."

"Well, do you mean art photographs?"

"Yes."

"Just one. I bought it at the Hyde Park Art Show five years ago. It's a hand-colored black and white. Picture of an old art deco movie theater. I'd have more, but they are so expensive at the galleries."

"Which galleries do you go to?"

"Haven't been in a while, but used to go to Toppel's on West Chicago Avenue, and I do enjoy the summer art shows—I see a lot of art photography there."

And so it went. Molly and he spent the better part of two hours watching and occasionally talking to people. They left and took a bus west to Wicker Park then walked over to Geek's. As they sat having a coffee, Molly explained her technique.

"Okay, so it's not so scientific what we were doing. You can't draw definitive conclusions based on two hours of observing people. But you do learn things. You hear other perspectives. So what did you hear?"

"Hmm . . . well, I heard that photographic books are often gifts."

"Okay. What else?"

"And black and white is very popular, at least for those folks who liked the more artistic books. And people buy books that match their interests, like all the people buying those Chicago-theme picture books or dogs or babies or birds or flowers. Is that what you mean?"

"Yeah, I mean, you notice what you notice," Molly said. "For instance, I noticed that most of the folks buying books were women. I noticed that they were mostly upper-middle or upper-class types, people with money to spend on a fifty dollar coffee-table book. And I noticed they were somewhat conservative in dress, but maybe that's because they were there on a work break. It could also be we're just here on Michigan Avenue, which is pretty upscale."

"Okay. I know I was supposed to be just watching, but the whole time I'm watching, I'm thinking, *Hey, don't pick that one up, that's terrible,* or *Yeah, that's a classy book of photography; you'll like that.* I'm also thinking, *Okay, if you like that book of Chicago photos, I can go it one better.*"

"It's natural to think of ideas. They flow through your brain all the time if you listen to yourself. Everybody has ideas."

Jack glanced at his notebook. "Maybe it's just that nobody writes them down," he said.

"Writing them down would be a start, wouldn't it?" she said.

. Molly started her shift then, leaving Jack at the booth with his coffee and notebook. He opened up to a fresh page and started making a list of ideas about what kind of photography books he might create. He'd had a bunch of ideas when they were watching people in the bookstore. He jotted down a couple of them: Chicago at night, Illinois landscapes.

But as he thought about those two ideas, he had the feeling that they wouldn't work—the ideas were too obvious, unoriginal. It made him feel hopeless again, and he got depressed. A voice inside him was saying, *No, you can't do that kind of book. You've never shot pictures of that quality in your life, so what makes you think you could do it now?* This was true. Sure, he'd done some good work as a student, and he had the occasional outstanding shot from his meager freelance work, but could he ever be as good as one of those guys who did the books? He didn't even have a camera that was truly high quality. And where would he get one? He didn't have the money to buy one.

How could making a simple list of ideas be so discouraging? Jack wondered if it was normal to get as depressed as this when he was just trying to brainstorm a simple list of ideas for coffee-table books. Then he remembered that conversation with Manny. How they had made the list of wishes without judging it. That night the wish list had come pouring out when he had stopped criticizing himself.

Okay, so today I'm judging, he thought. *Stop judging,* he told himself. *Get into a flow.* He looked at his list of coffee-table books—his list of two—then tried again. It was easier now, now that it didn't matter whether he could do it or not. The list grew quickly:

Chicago at night
Illinois landscapes
Best local rock bands
Street scenes in Wicker Park
People drinking coffee
Outside cafés; Chicago-style
Famous Chicago hot-dog stands
Chicago tourist traps

He looked out the window and noticed a flag in the window of a home. *There are lots of those displays right now. Like shrines.* And with this, he had a couple more ideas.

Chicago-style patriotism
Deep-dish patriotism—Chicago war heroes
*Chicago murals and graffiti**

The last few excited him. He was on to something. He was good at street photography. That's why he put the asterisk on the last item. Funny, he never would have gotten to that idea if he hadn't plowed through all the others. *Magic seems to happen when you stop judging your lists,* he thought. *You first make the list, then judge.*

Molly stopped by his table with a top-off for his coffee. "You look like the cat that just ate the canary."

"I was just thinking about the coffee-table books, just jotting down some ideas on what I might do."

"Can I see?"

Jack hesitated, but then thought, *This is Molly, your friend.*

She reviewed the list silently. Then, "You may have something here, the one you starred. There are these incredible murals all up and down Ashland Avenue. I mean maybe you could do a book that is just a documentation of Ashland. When you drive down, you see all kinds of murals and art—posh, funky, all kinds of stuff."

"I like that . . . Ashland Avenue . . . it goes through about ten different neighborhoods." Jack thought about this.

"Did you ever hear back from that guy?" she asked.

"No, I sent him that e-mail and then, nothing. It gets depressing only getting e-mail from you."

"Hey!"

Jack backpedaled fast. "Truth is, I love getting e-mail from you, and I mean I really love it. It's made my day . . . several times, in fact."

"See if I send you another." Molly smiled and went back behind the counter. Jack decided to log in, and there it was—a reply from Manny:

```
Jack,
    Got your note. Thanks for following up
with me. I apologize for not getting back to
you sooner, but I had a bit of an emergency
to deal with overseas and have just gotten
back into Chicago.
    So how's the wish list? Did you pick
one and start in on doing research and fact
finding? Hope so—you'll get insights if you
do—guaranteed!
    The project I mentioned when we met is
moving forward. I was thinking it would be
great to have some good quality "before and
after" pictures. Any chance you could get
down to the site in the next couple of days
to do the "before" set? I'll walk around
the site with you and point out what needs
documenting.
    Give me a call on my cell phone.
    Hope to hear from you.
                            Manny Gibran
```

Jack was exhilarated. Work! Photographic work! He borrowed Geek's phone from Molly and dialed up Manny's cell phone number. Manny picked up on the first ring and invited Jack down to the office building that evening at eleven o'clock. Molly was smiling, watching him. When the call ended, Jack turned the phone around on the counter and looked at her proudly. "I've got a bit of work documenting a work site."

"That's great."

"Yeah, it is, but now I've got to get ready—I need to borrow a flash unit from a friend of mine. Need to go buy some film. And I need to get down there."

"How are you going to get down there?"

"I'll figure something out. I'll see you tomorrow morning, okay? I'm going back home to start getting ready."

"Good luck."

Jack hustled out of Geek's. He was thinking about how to cover the assignment. He had a decent 35mm camera, which would be good enough for this kind of work. He'd want to use slow film so that if Manny did larger blow-ups, he'd still have fine-grain, good quality. He'd also need to borrow Rob's flash unit. His own unit had some electrical short, and he hadn't gotten it fixed yet. Jack stopped at a phone booth on Milwaukee Avenue and called Rob, his good friend from college—they'd done some film-class projects together. Rob had a lot of photography equipment that he didn't use much anymore, and Rob said he didn't mind if Jack borrowed it.

Jack walked over to Rob's. It was about two miles, but he covered the ground quickly, excited about the assignment and eager to talk to Manny again.

4: A Fresh Perspective

Where Jack learns the concept of problem framing and reframing

Manny introduces Jack to step three of CPS, Problem—or challenge—Framing and Reframing. Through reframing, Manny looks at a problem from multiple perspectives and restates it in different ways. Reframing is something people rarely do deliberately, but it is a key tool in creative problem solving. How we state a challenge puts our minds in motion in a specific direction. If we state our challenge in a limiting or faulty way, we could end up taking the wrong road. Reframing leads to breakthroughs because a problem properly framed is much easier to solve. Manny then assigns Jack the task of reframing his original wish of being a photographer.

In this chapter, Manny and Jack actually undertake all three steps of phase one of CPS, Problem Exploration, more or less at the same time. With CPS, you can move back and forth between steps dynamically to meet your needs. The ability to do this comes with practice.

Jack found the address of the old office building without much trouble. Rob had given him a ride downtown, so he'd arrived at 10:30 p.m., early. The building was locked, so Jack rang the bell. A security guard appeared, consulted a list, found Jack's name, had Jack sign in, admitted him, and then sent him up to the eighth floor. Getting off the elevator, Jack found a small group of workers pulling up carpets and demolishing walls.

Manny was back in a corner, talking to a man in a suit and tie, when he spotted Jack. "Jack, you're early—good. Give me a few minutes to finish up here and then we'll get started. There's some coffee second door down. Help yourself."

Jack put down his equipment and headed for the coffee. Looking around the empty office suite, he thought to himself how depressing and ugly an office looks after it's been abandoned. Stray desks, the odd broken filing cabinet, litter, dust, papers everywhere. Not very appealing.

The coffee was appealing, however—fresh and strong. It had a mild pleasant flavoring. Vanilla. From the window he could see a little corner of the lake and the Field Museum. It was a clear night, and Chicago looked bright, full of promise. Two weeks ago he might have looked at this same view and only gotten depressed. What was the difference? On the surface his life was still the same. Still two lousy jobs, still not a bona fide professional photographer, still no girlfriend. Yet things had changed. He was learning things; he was working in his field—at least tonight. And there was Molly.

Molly. He couldn't remember the last time a woman had been so friendly, had treated him so nicely. He couldn't stop thinking about her—her dreads, the nape of her neck.

"So, Jack, how are you?" It was Manny.

"I've been good," came the automatic reply.

Manny stood there looking at him. He looked different than he had in the car, more professional, even though he was wearing jeans and a work shirt. Maybe it was the clipboard. Then Manny poured himself a cup of coffee and Jack noticed the big workman's hands. It was hard to imagine him as some high-priced consultant.

"So let's talk about you," said Manny. "Last we spoke you were going to pick one of your wishes from the list and turn over every stone. Did you actually do that?"

"I did," said Jack.

"Okay, so give me a summary of how that went for you," said Manny.

"Well, the wish I picked was about being a photographer."

"I thought that might be it," said Manny. "What did you learn?"

"Basically how much I don't know," said Jack. "I never realized how many directions you can go and how much I need to learn technically. I found some classes that I might take at Columbia College. I had some ideas about a coffee-table book; I've got a better sense of the kind of art books people like. And I'm starting to learn some computer tools to advertise my business and add value to the pictures I take."

"That's great," said Manny. "Two questions . . . first, what are you leaving out of your exploration, and two, what's next?"

"I'm not sure what I'm leaving out, and as for next steps, well, I'm guessing it's getting into action in some way," said Jack.

"What I think you are leaving out is where you are in your head and your heart about your challenge. I know you want to move forward, but look deeper inside yourself and get a better sense of why—what's your motivation? I know we don't usually think of feelings as 'facts,' but it might be a fact, for example, that you have a deep fear of success, or you might feel that you don't have the talent. You need to know about these things in order to remove them as barriers. I'm going to make that part of your next assignment—add to your hard facts list a list of feelings about the challenge, okay? We'll talk later about what happens after all this research you're doing."

> WHAT I THINK YOU ARE LEAVING OUT IS WHERE YOU ARE IN YOUR HEAD AND YOUR HEART ABOUT YOUR CHALLENGE. I KNOW YOU WANT TO MOVE FORWARD, BUT LOOK DEEPER INSIDE YOURSELF AND GET A BETTER SENSE OF WHY—WHAT'S YOUR MOTIVATION?

"Okay," said Jack.

"All right." Manny smiled then looked around. "Let's talk about my challenge now. Let me give you some background. This building is a typical old-style office building where they run the utilities and phone cables up next to the elevator shaft, near the center of the building. It's an old building—Class C they call it here in Chicago. Basically, there's no room in the shaft by the elevator for any more power or data lines. It wasn't made for it. There's a new software firm coming in here that wants all kinds of high-speed communication lines and power back-up lines to come up to their floor. Eight floors up. So that's the problem: not enough room in the existing stack to do everything they want, not even close. It's not as simple as finding an empty pipe somewhere. They want to bring in a lot of power, telephony, data, fiber-optic cables, plus some room for growth. If it were just a couple of little wires, we wouldn't have a problem. But they need a channel up to their floor that's big enough to get a person into—for maintenance—a space at least four by four feet. We might get away with something as small as three by three, but that would be the absolute minimum."

"So you want pictures of the existing stack?"

"Yes, we'll do that, but really I want to go around the whole building and shoot pictures of a lot of areas where there might be a possibility for bringing up the new lines. We have to avoid the old stack altogether, but we'll look at it anyway. You never know—there might be something there. Basically, the reason for the pictures is, well, I think they might help me get a fresh perspective on this challenge, this problem."

"But you know what the problem is, right? You need to find another way to bring up the lines."

"Well, that's one way to look at it, but not the only way. What I'm really seeking to do right now is change the way I look at the problem. The contractors have thought about this a bit, but all the thinking, so far, has been geared toward squeezing more stuff into that existing stack. That might be the answer, but I suspect if there were a way, they would have figured it out by now. I have somewhat limited access to this space—the other floors are still operating here—so I was hoping that having pictures might help me think about this, help me study it."

So they traipsed all over the building. They took pictures outside the building, in the basement, in the musty subbasement, which had flooded a few years back during the Chicago River fiasco. They photographed all of the floors they had access to and finally the roof of the building, which was dark. As they walked around taking pictures, Jack was a bit scared because now and then the roof was uneven and seemed soft under his feet. But Manny walked all around, looking high and low, making notes on his clipboard pad about the location of various vents and pipes.

Wherever they looked, they shot pictures from every angle—high, low, up, over, under, around, and through. They peeled back carpet; they even removed sections of false ceilings—getting showered with dust in the process. Jack shot nineteen rolls of film.

"You sure know how to peel back the onion," said Jack. "So do you think you have an answer for the wiring yet?"

"Actually, no, I really haven't found what I'm looking for. I feel closer than I was three hours ago though. You see, what we've been asking, the group of us upstairs, was 'In what ways might we widen the stack?' When I was outside I was thinking, okay, maybe it's 'In what ways can we create an alternative stack outside the building?' That seemed to have more possibility, but it's not an elegant solution, at least not at this point because it would detract from the lines of the building. It might also be a problem to get a change like that approved. See, all the buildings in this area are subject to review by something called the Lakefront Group. It's a design-review board. They probably won't allow the building owners to graft anything onto the side of the building although you never know; they might let 'em on the alley side. It would look tacky."

Manny paused and walked to the window. "Anyway, then I was thinking, 'In what ways might we create an alternative stack within the building?' The issue with that is there are not many vertical shafts in this construction, and drilling a new shaft that goes through seven floors would be costly as well as disruptive to the other businesses in the building—impractical really. Although, that's an assumption to challenge—you never know; there might be a clever way to manage it. Maybe the problem is, 'In what ways might we drill a new shaft economically?' Or, 'In what ways might we drill a new shaft without disruption?'" With that, Manny shook his head in frustration. "I don't know."

Jack hesitated, then said, "I guess I sort of had the idea you were some sort of magician when it came to solving problems like this."

"What gave you that idea?"

"I read up on some of your old projects on the Web."

"No kidding." Manny smiled. "Rumors of my miracles are sometimes exaggerated. I'm not a magician at all—you don't see the failures and fiascos on the Web. I fell on my face many times along the way. Making magic—solving tough problems—is hard work. What we're doing tonight might lead to a breakthrough, or then again, it might not. If I don't figure this out, it's not likely these guys will hire me again. If I do, the folks with that software company going in on eight have a better chance at making it. That means thirty new jobs for developers and marketing people, more later if they keep growing. We're trying to remove a roadblock that would prevent that from happening." He paused before adding, "I love helping new companies grow. It's exciting to see a bunch of people running around, making something happen. New jobs come mostly from small business, so I feel good helping these guys out. If I can help them, well, that really is magic."

"So how do you go about making magic happen?"

> IF YOU REALLY UNDERSTAND A PROBLEM,
> SOLUTIONS COME EASY; SOLUTIONS
> TEND TO SUGGEST THEMSELVES.

"I'm in step three of CPS, and I'm trying to reframe just what the problem is. See, people assume they know. They assume they really understand their problems. Usually, they don't. If you really understand a problem, solutions come easy; solutions tend to suggest themselves. If you're blocked on a problem, chances are you have it framed in such a way that no solutions appear. Like with your photography, a different angle can make all the difference. For instance, how do you shoot a picture of a child?"

"A child?" Jack thought for a moment. "Well, I'd get down low, either even with him or maybe even shooting below him with an up angle."

"And what do most people do when they shoot a snapshot of a child?"

"They shoot it from their own perspective. Adults shoot down."

"What does that snapshot look like? What do you see?"

"Just an uninteresting shot. It looks like every snapshot of a kid you've ever seen. It's an adult view, and it's the same view we see of kids every day. It's boring."

"Okay, and I would suggest to you that understanding problems is just like shooting a picture of a child. You see the challenge better when you shift the angle, when you reframe it."

"Got it—reframing the problem, just like you reframe a picture." Jack was finding this interesting.

"Right. Exactly. By the way, did you notice the language I used when I talked about this?"

"What do you mean? When?"

"Earlier, when I was talking about the external stack and internal stack ways of looking at this."

"Well, wait. Oh, okay, you said something to the effect of, what was it, 'How can we . . . ' No, you said, 'In what ways might we use the existing shaft?' and 'In what ways might we use the outside of the building?'"

"Right. I used just that phrase: 'In what ways might we.' That's a powerful phrase for shifting views on a problem, for reframing. If you look at any problem and restate it using that phrase ten times, it almost has to shift your perspective, and a little magic is likely to occur."

"You've only done five!"

"Ha! Good point! But sometimes even five is enough for magic—we just don't know yet. Maybe the statement for us here is more like 'In what ways might we locate unused space within the building?'"

"That's six," said Jack, smiling.

A bald man approached with a roll of blueprints under his arm. "Here's what you asked for," he said.

Manny opened one up and spread it out on the floor.

"These can't be the originals," said Manny.

"No, they're not, but it's all we have. The originals were stored in the subbasement, and those were destroyed in that flood we had a few years ago."

"Ahh, the famous Chicago flood, where they let the Chicago River into all those tunnels they used to use for mail delivery."

"Yeah, that's the one all right. It was a real mess down there. These blueprints are from the refurbishing this building went through in the early seventies. They were still on file at the architects' firm. See here—they redid the entire building interior, adding the heating and AC units on each floor. They're not as detailed as you'd like them to be," said the bald man.

Manny excused himself and asked Jack to wait. He returned about fifteen minutes later and said, "Thanks for your help."

"Nothing to it, but I'm not sure what we accomplished."

"No, no, this is good. We documented the building as it really is. The blueprints are so incomplete, those pictures will help me study this off-site. Get prints made of each shot, and also get me a CD-ROM of all the images."

"Okay," Jack said, hoisting his equipment over his shoulder.

Manny asked, "How'd you get down here?"

"A friend dropped me off."

"Like a ride home?"

"Okay, yes, thanks."

Jack waited out in front of the building while Manny retrieved the car from a couple of blocks down. Jack put his stuff in the back-seat of the red Jeep Cherokee before getting in front. They rode in silence for a time, both with their own thoughts.

Manny broke the silence. "Cameras are really great tools—the thinking man's gun," he observed.

"Never heard it put quite that way."

"Because I just made it up. Actually, a thinking man doesn't need a gun, or a camera either, for that matter. His greatest tool is structured thinking."

"Structured thinking? I would think that unstructured thinking is what you want—you know, to be more imaginative."

"Why's that?" asked Manny, turning it around on Jack.

"Well, okay, I sort of see unstructured thinking as, like, imaginative thinking. You need the freedom or lack of structure in order to create, right?" Jack looked over to Manny for confirmation.

"The imagination is incredible, essential to creating anything," he said. "The problem is most of us don't use it enough. So that's why I say *structured*. You have to provide a structure for imaginative thought, if only to allow enough of it. You simply need to give it a fair share of your thinking time. When was the last time you really let your mind go into that imaginative space?" Manny looked over at Jack with raised eyebrows.

"Hard to say," said Jack. "I mean, I wonder about stuff all the time."

"So go back to the last time you went into wonderment mode or idea mode, and tell me about it."

"I was at Geek's having a coffee . . ." Jack said slowly.

"Geek's?"

"Yeah, it's my Web and coffee spot," said Jack.

"So . . . you were at this Geek's place . . ." Manny prompted.

"I was just sitting at the table, trying to think of ideas for a coffee-table book—you know, one of my photography. So I was making a list, and as I was making the list I was sort of drifting off, thinking about it."

"And . . ." Manny prodded.

"And I made the list."

"So you never returned to earth?"

"I was thinking about it for about ten minutes, not judging my ideas, which really helped me come up with more ideas."

"I'm glad you didn't judge your ideas. So, then what happened?" asked Manny.

"Well, now that I think about it, what seemed to happen is, I got into analyzing the ideas, like which one would have the best chance, you know, be the most appealing book idea. I guess I've been thinking about it, in the back of my mind, ever since."

"And so you're still churning it around, trying to figure out which one is the magic book idea, right?"

"Right."

"So, ten minutes of imagination, where you generated ideas without judgment, and then days of churning, days of analysis. When was the last time you added more ideas to your list of coffee-table books?" asked Manny.

"Not since then, and that was a couple of days ago," Jack replied.

"Right, so a bit of imagination and two days of random, unconstructive evaluation, critique, and neglect, maybe some more imagination for moments at a time—I'd call that unstructured thinking," stated Manny.

"Hey, give me a break," Jack put in. He wasn't really upset, but the way Manny said that made him feel like an idiot.

"I'm sorry—I don't mean to criticize you. Actually, just making a list of ideas about the book is a bit of structure, so you got off to a good start. And the random thought isn't bad either, because sometimes good ideas pop up. And you like when that happens."

"I guess I didn't leave much time for imaginative thought, did I?" asked Jack.

"You're not alone. It takes a structure to remember to be imaginative."

"I don't think of imaginative thought as work."

"I know what you mean. Most people think that daydreaming is wrong, you know? It's what they got punished in school for doing, for not paying attention."

"Oh, man, you're bringing back some bad memories there," said Jack. They both laughed.

"Schools have a tough time. Not enough resources, kids with different languages, different parental support. I feel sorry for teachers; they have the toughest challenge there is. They are forced to teach for the test, the one right answer, and, well, most problems in life have many right answers, not just one. Training kids to be really great at getting the one perfect answer does them the disservice of training them not to think about all kinds of answers, all kinds of options. Tests aren't wrong, but they create an unbalanced system."

"Why are all kinds of options a good thing?" asked Jack.

"What if the one perfect answer turns out to be wrong?" said Manny, answering a question with a question.

"Then you look for another answer," said Jack.

"One more, right?"

"Right."

"So what it sets up is a pattern of trial and error, which is not necessarily bad. But wouldn't it be better to allow for a lot of imaginative thinking about options up front? And then go back and analyze and evaluate?"

"Well, you'd have more to choose from anyway," admitted Jack.

"Yes, that's the point. You'd have more options to choose from. I don't mean to get too simple about it, but with anything you do, there is a list of options and a selection. All I'm saying is, work the list of options. Make lists—without judgment—then make choices."

"Wouldn't it be great if they taught that kind of list making in school?"

"Precisely! And maybe at least once in a while, the test would be to make as long a list of possible solutions to a problem as you can imagine. You get a great score for generating more options. That would be a beautiful way to train kids to think imaginatively."

Manny looked wistful for a moment, then his smile faded.

"You're talking like a rebel," said Jack.

"A rebel. I guess I am. So are most entrepreneurs. And a lot of the best inventors are people who don't listen to what everybody else is saying. They ignore accepted wisdom. There's a guy in California right now, fascinating guy—name of Woody Norris—who's invented this gizmo that can direct sound like a laser beam. It's amazing. He can like shoot a bubble of Eminem sound across the street at a person. They hear it—but nobody else does. Until he demonstrated it, most scientists thought it was impossible. He calls it HyperSonic Sound."

"Sounds pretty cool," said Jack.

Manny pulled the Cherokee up to the corner he'd let Jack out on the night they met.

"Okay, thanks again for the ride—and all the discussion. I have all this to think about—and I have the film. Prints and the CD-ROM, right?" Jack asked.

"Custom prints of every shot. Get five by sevens," said Manny.

"That's going to add up—be pretty expensive."

"I know. It's okay. Do it. And send me the bill."

"Well, would you mind my putting it on your credit card? The lab needs to be paid when I pick this stuff up."

"Okay, yeah. Have the lab phone me, and I'll phone in my number and all that."

"All right. Thanks for everything," said Jack.

"We'll talk again when you get the pictures back," said Manny. "And if you'd like, we can get back to your challenge and think about your feelings. Then try some of those problem-framing questions; you know, 'In what ways might I . . . ' and just finish the sentence. Make as long a list of those reframes as you can stand, okay?"

"Right. I will. Good night then."

Jack walked toward his apartment, lugging his camera bag and tripod. A car started up somewhere nearby. Jack looked over his shoulder and saw a light-colored van drive down the street. It made him nervous to be out at night with something so expensive and so visible. He twisted the camera bag around to his back, and he carried the tripod at his side. *Nice thing about a tripod*, he thought, *it could work well in a pinch defending myself.*

Inside, Jack first organized the film he would need to drop off at the lab. Then he undressed and took a shower. It felt delicious, the warm water really relaxing him. Getting into bed, he eyed his notebook. He picked it up and paged through his notes.

Then he turned to a fresh page and started a new list. He wrote down his first problem-framing question:

In what ways might I become a photographer?

He thought about this. It was obvious, right? He didn't need to do anything else—he knew this was what he wanted. Still, it wasn't that specific, was it? There were all kinds of photography. He recalled his evening of photographic exploration with Manny. Shot after shot, angle after angle, always searching for another perspective, another view of the problem. *Okay,* he thought to himself, *there has to be another way to look at this.* Tentatively, he wrote another line:

In what ways might I become a photographer?

~~In what ways might I become a successful photographer?~~

In what ways might I become a successful art photographer?

~~In what ways might I become a successful fine-art photographer?~~

In what ways might I become a successful artist?

~~In what ways might I become a successful commercial photographer?~~

~~In what ways might I become a successful commercial artist, specializing in photography now, learning about other related media?~~

~~In what ways might I become a successful commercial artist, specializing in photographic fine-art books, learning about other related media?~~

~~In what ways might I become a commercial artist, specializing in photographic fine-art books, learning about other related media?~~

Jack read back through his list, and even though he was exhausted from the long day and night, he felt energized. He liked the way challenge had evolved, and he thought he had a much better idea of what he wanted to do than simply "be a photographer." He was becoming more specific, more focused.

He arranged his covers and snapped the light off. He started to relax, but then he bolted upright and turned the light back on, taking the time to set his alarm for 7:00 a.m.—he had work to do.

5: A Smashing Night for Ideas

Where Jack and Molly generate a large quantity of ideas

Molly helps Jack reframe his challenge statement one more time. Then together they enter step four of CPS, Idea Generation, also called Brainstorming. Molly facilitates a "force fit," or a "forced association," in which she and Jack create a list of attributes about an object and then apply those to the challenge. As a result, they generate a longer list of ideas about the challenge. The attributes and ideas they create can be found in Jack's Notebook in the back of the book.

Scholars have concluded that the larger the number of ideas you generate, the more likely it is you will have a breakthrough idea. In other words, quantity gets you to quality. You don't have to do it all at once. In fact, if you keep after it for a few days or even weeks, ideas will continue to pop up for you, and it is more likely you will reach the breakthrough stage of ideation. When you think you have hit a wall, try using a tool like forced association.

SMASH rocked with jukebox noise, clinking glasses, and the din of shouted conversations. Fridays were always busy, and this one was no exception. Jack could make all the trendy drinks, but he occasionally got stumped by an old classic. The other night somebody had ordered a Velvet Hammer. He'd seen it in the book, but he couldn't remember the recipe. He hated that. And of course the woman who ordered the drink was upset with him for not knowing it. She sat at the bar and busted his chops until she'd got so drunk Jack had to cut her off, which had provoked a scene.

He had told Molly about the Velvet Hammer incident. At least it was good for a laugh the day after. Molly had said that sometimes the worst events made the best stories later. She had a point.

Eleven o'clock now, and the late-shift hospital workers were just arriving for their first taste of weekend. Many didn't even bother to go home and change, showing up at SMASH in nurse whites or their health-care battle fatigues, those green pullover shirts and the pants with the elastic at the ankles. The nurses tended toward either plain old draft beer or blended drinks like a strawberry margarita. Jack poured beers two at a time and mixed every frou-frou drink known to man.

Jack continued to pour and mix while doing a behind-the-bar ballet with Sandy, doing his best to stay out of his way. Sandy, his bartending partner, was good to work with. He kept up his end of things, and he was up for a bit of fun now and then.

Closer to closing time, Jack's eyes scanned the crowd. He was surprised to see Molly showing her ID to the guy at the front door. He was delighted that she was dropping in, but it was unlike her. She was not a drinker or a partier, as far as he knew, and she was not likely to know any of these hospital workers. *She could only be here to see me,* he thought, *and that's nice.*

Molly came straight over to the bar. *Wow,* he thought. She looked different, not in a granny dress or the army-navy wear she wore at Geek's. Instead, she had on a nice-fitting pair of black jeans with sequins running down each side and a matching jean jacket. A white blouse, really a man's shirt, opened far enough to see a little cleavage. She looked attractive. Her dreads exploded in all directions, not her usual tied-back style. Jack realized that she must have actually arranged them to look that crazy-fun. And she had on makeup. She'd turned heads just walking from the front door to the bar.

"Mr. Jack, I've come to visit you in this den of iniquity."

"Ahh, you haven't seen the half of it, Molly Dunne. A woman in black tonight. You look great! To what do I owe the honor of this late-night visitation? This apparition?"

"Hey, I'm not the Virgin Mary, okay, so enough with the apparition. No special occasion. I haven't been out in weeks, and I just thought it might be fun to see where it is you waste your time and make no money. All the while inhaling the equivalent of two packs of cigarette smoke."

"Welcome to SMASH. Can I buy you a drink?"

"You can. I'll have . . . a Velvet Hammer."

"Oh, you, you are bad . . ."

"Hey, I'm just testing you. I wouldn't know what a Velvet Hammer tasted like if it hit me in the head. How about just a glass of white wine instead? Anything that tastes better than salad dressing will do."

"Coming right up, the just-better-than-salad-dressing special."

Pouring her a glass of chardonnay, Jack smiled to himself. Molly had a sense of humor, busting him on that Velvet Hammer. He'd have to make her one anyway, just for her to taste. But no, he couldn't make one—he needed to have some cream to make it. The recipe called for a tablespoon of cream mixed with one and a half ounces of vodka and a little touch of crème de cacao. There was a White Hen two doors down, though, so he called the doorman over, whispering in his ear and sending him down the street for a pint of cream—no, make that vanilla ice cream. Maybe he could modernize the Velvet Hammer and blend it with ice cream. What would he call it . . . a Velvet SledgeHammer?

"It's really nice to see you here," he told her as he gave her the glass of wine. "You are a sight for sore eyes."

"Now there is a well-worn phrase if I ever heard one," she said.

"I have unfortunately inherited my father's tendency to use clichés. Okay, let me try again. I'm just glad to see you, you are a budding flower in a garden of weeds . . ."

She laughed. "Somebody should take the book of clichés and write new versions."

"There's an idea for your first book," said Jack. "*Clichés Modernized* by Molly Dunne."

"I could write a book, but that wouldn't be the content. Maybe a murder mystery would be more up my alley," she mused.

"A murder mystery. I don't know why, but I think you might be very good at fiction . . . Anyway, listen, I've got to get busy and get this place closed up. I'm going to be busy for about twenty minutes. If you stick around, we can have a nightcap together after we close, and I'll walk you home."

"Okay."

Jack and Sandy hustled about, announcing last call, taking a wave of orders, mixing a frantic round of drinks, cleaning up, and restocking the beer coolers. Jack moved through his chores efficiently and prodded the stragglers out the door.

The last folks to leave weren't the usual suspects, but a table of guys that looked like off-duty cops. When Jack asked them to leave, he said, "Guys, you don't have to go home, but you can't stay here." He expected they would laugh or groan. Instead, they eyed him coolly and left without a word. *Jerks*, Jack thought.

Jack noticed that as Molly came out of the bathroom, she gave the room a quick once-over before she returned to her bar stool.

By 3:30 a.m., SMASH was closed. Sandy had a quick beer and left. Jack locked the door behind him. Molly and he were alone, locked inside SMASH.

Jack pulled his things out from under the bar, including the photos he'd developed for Manny. Then he fixed Molly a Velvet Hammer, using the ice cream, and he poured himself a double Dewar's on the rocks. "So, try my new drink invention—here we have the Velvet SledgeHammer." Jack placed the tall, creamy drink on the bar in front of her.

She used the straw to taste it. "I like it. What'd you do?" she asked.

"I used vanilla ice cream instead of cream. Added a whole scoop to make it thicker than a Velvet Hammer would normally be. Blended it instead of stirring it."

"It's good. Nothing like a new combination, eh? Sometimes the quickest way to make something new is simply to make a new combination of elements. I wouldn't drink it every day, though. These would be great for a Christmas party."

"I'm really surprised to see you here." Jack looked her in the eye.

"I didn't want you to think I was too cool to socialize with you," she replied, meeting his look.

"I never thought that. I know we have an understanding about our relationship just being supportive and all."

"You know, I'm still with that. I'm here as a friend," she said.

Jack took a deep breath. This was not the breakthrough he'd been hoping for, but he simply said, "And that's a good thing . . . you've really been a good friend to me."

"And you to me," she said. "Now, you said you'd be picking up your photos from the other night. Can I see them?"

"Sure." Jack laid out a selection of the shots he'd done for Manny, and they talked about the wiring challenge for a bit.

"What about *your* challenge?" asked Molly.

"My challenge?"

"Yeah, don't go dumb on me—how're you going to move forward with your photography? You know, it's clear to me you have the sensibility, if not all the technical skill and equipment. It's just a matter of picking your spot and going after it."

Jack showed Molly his notebook. She reviewed his "In What Ways" statements, then said, "I like the one you picked here: 'In what ways might I become a commercial artist, specializing in photographic fine-art books, learning about other related media?'"

"Yeah?"

"Yeah, it's pretty precise, *and* I have a suggestion."

"Okay, what?"

"The last part where you say *specializing in* . . . and the rest? You don't need it."

"Why do you think?"

"How to do fine art books isn't the challenge or problem—it's an idea about your challenge. I mean it's a good idea doing fine art books and all, but you don't need it in the basic statement. That is just one idea of how you could be a commercial artist, and right now you don't want to limit yourself to just one way. Same thing with learning about other related media—it's an idea, not a problem. Not a challenge."

"So you want it to say just . . . In what ways might I become a commercial artist?"

"Yes."

"I thought that other stuff was good."

"It is good—those are great ideas, which is what we are getting to now, right? Your timing is perfect. Write them down—as ideas."

Jack noticed that she had said *we*. He was glad she'd said *we*.

"Do you have any paper?" she asked.

"Just my notebook."

"Never mind, we can use these." Molly grabbed a stack of cocktail napkins that were lying next to the cash register. She walked to the end of the bar and came behind it, next to Jack. "Let's just start. We can sort them out later. So, what are some ideas?"

"So what—we're doing ideas now?"

"Yeah, you got anything better to do? You got a hot date lined up for after work?"

Jack chuckled. "No."

"So just write down one idea on each napkin. Just for fun. Let's go, come on."

"Okay."

Jack and Molly picked up their pens and started scribbling ideas. As they came up with one, they read it out loud and laid it down on the bar. They didn't spend any time analyzing as they went.

Molly's last idea in this batch was "Rent the back room at Geek's."

Jack stopped the flow of ideas and asked, "You mean there's a room back behind Geek's?"

"Yeah, it used to be the receiving dock for the warehouse that was there before Geek's."

"High ceilings?"

"Yeah, and skylights."

"No!"

"Yes!"

"Where will I get the money to rent it?"

"Hey, wait a minute, don't get ahead of yourself. Let's keep going here."

"Yeah, but still, that is so cool."

Molly tamed him down. "Listen, don't get too excited. It's an absolute disaster zone, a real mess. It would take months just to clean it up."

"Okay, okay, so where were we?"

"So here are the last couple—having to do with studio stuff."

"Yeah. I'm looking back at my original statement . . . before we trimmed off *and related media.*"

"Right, so what are some related media?"

"Digital photography."

"Then start there," she coached.

They generated a batch of ideas around digital photography. Then Molly said, "Take a drawing class."

"A drawing class? I can't draw!"

"Well, what better thing to do than take a class and learn?"

"But I can't draw!"

"Look, this is a brainstorming session, right? We aren't judging the ideas right now; we're just getting them down."

"All right . . . but drawing?"

"Shut up," she said, laughing. "What are some more ideas on fine art books?"

"I've always wanted to do a series on barns."

"Barns?" She looked at him as if he were crazy.

"Now who's judging?"

"Okay already—barns! I know a barn or two you could get started on." Jack and Molly generated a series of ideas on barns, nature, animals . . . and rock and roll.

There was a long, silent pause.

"I'm fresh out," said Jack.

"Me too." Molly got up from her seat and walked over to the bar. She took a bottle of Southern Comfort down from the shelf and placed it on the bar.

"Uh, I don't think we ought to get started with that," said Jack.

"I don't want to drink it. Just tell me, Jack, what is it about this bottle?"

"What do you mean?"

"Just play along with me on this. Describe this bottle," she directed, holding out her hand like Vanna White.

"Describe it?" Jack wasn't sure where she was going with this.

"Things about it, like, it's clear glass, it's see-through," she said. And she wrote down *see-through* on a napkin.

"Well, it's full."

"So write that down and put it here," she instructed, pointing to a spot under her most recent napkin.

They traded napkins that described the bottle and came up with a list:

See-through

Full

Tall

Brown

Southern

Comfortable

Sweet

Potent

Tea-colored

Old-fashioned

Molly looked at the list. "Okay, so what do those words have you thinking about your challenge?"

"What do you mean? They have nothing to do with my challenge—they describe the bottle."

"I know, we're doing a *force fit*."

"It is a force fit. I don't see it," Jack said.

"So, let's just try one. Bear with me here." Molly looked at the list. "So, let's take the word *potent*."

"Okay, what do we do with it?"

"Well, we're going to use it. *Potent* means *powerful*. What does power have to do with your challenge?"

"Power . . . well, I certainly want my images to be powerful."

"Yes, *and* . . ." she prompted.

"Powerful images . . . maybe I do a series of portraits of the most powerful people in the city."

"So there's an idea. What else?"

"Going the other way, maybe I do a series of portraits of the homeless, the not-so-powerful."

"There's another. What else?"

"I do a photo essay on those folks who are giving power to the homeless—social workers and community volunteers."

"So, Jack, that's why you do a force fit."

"Cool. Three more ideas just like that got us going again. Where did you learn this?"

"My old boss used to use that technique at my old job in Milwaukee. I have a book full of techniques like that for brainstorming."

"You'll have to loan me the book," he said.

"I will. So, let's take another word. How about *comfortable?*"

"Comfortable—fine art. What's the connection there? Okay, so comfortable is easy, it's big chairs, it's a hammock in the backyard under a tree, and it's a warm bed. Okay, I could do a book of sensual figure studies—those posters always sell like mad."

"I'm working hard at not judging here. What else?"

HE LOOKED DOWN AT ALL THE NAPKINS
LYING ON THE BAR. THERE WERE ABOUT
FIFTY IDEAS, ALL KINDS OF IDEAS.

"Comfortable . . . like my mother's living room. Reminds me of landscapes that match the sofa and the rug. You know—most people don't understand fine art. They buy art to match their furniture."

"Okay, so use it, go with it."

"So, I'd do a series of landscapes with different dominant colors?"

"Sure—you could sell those colored-themed landscapes to the stock photo agencies," said Molly.

"And also sell them to the stock image Web sites. Man, these force fits really help get you going, just when you think you're all out of gas."

He looked down at all the napkins lying on the bar. There were about fifty ideas, all kinds of ideas. It was impressive. And it had taken only about fifteen minutes. What was he going to do with all this? He knew there were some good ideas in the batch, but now what?

Molly was looking at the ideas reflectively. She picked up one idea and slowly placed it next to another napkin. She started moving more around, pulling an idea about a poster and putting it with another idea about a different kind of poster, taking an idea for training and putting it with the others. She was grouping the napkin ideas, clustering them. Jack started helping.

> SHE PICKED UP ONE IDEA AND SLOWLY PLACED IT
> NEXT TO ANOTHER NAPKIN . . . SHE WAS GROUPING
> THE NAPKIN IDEAS, CLUSTERING THEM.

As they grouped the ideas, Molly created labels for each group. The groups of ideas included: Fine Art Books, Specific Art Books, General Photographic Ideas, the Studio, and Learning.

Molly looked at Jack quizzically. "So what do you think?"

"I think there are a lot of ideas here, more than I could ever use."

She agreed. They both reviewed the grouped list silently.

"You know, I have the sense that we've missed something," said Molly.

"Really, what?"

"Well, you say you want to be a commercial artist, right?"

"Right."

"What really strikes me about these ideas is that they are, mostly, all photography."

"That makes sense—that's what I know, that's what I'm good at," said Jack defensively.

"It is what you know . . . now. But it's not beyond your possibilities that you could do something differently. I mean, we sort of got 'out of the photography box' a couple of times when we had the learning ideas and the idea about getting into a class on Flash Animation," she said.

"What are you getting at?"

"I'm getting at what is commercial art—in this day and age?"

"Hmm . . . good question."

Molly and Jack discussed this for a few minutes and generated a few more ideas.

Jack looked at the bar again. "These ideas are amazing." He paused. "You know, you've really opened up a whole new world for me." Jack paused again, feeling in his heart that it was more than that, and more should be said, so he continued, "You know, Molly, I don't know anybody who cares enough about me to . . . spend time helping me sort it out. Thanks for helping. I mean, I don't want to get all sappy here . . ." he trailed off, embarrassed, and afraid of what he might hear next.

Molly went quiet. She just looked at him for a good long while. Finally she broke the gaze and walked over to the bottle of Southern Comfort. She fished around in one of her jeans' pockets, pulled out a five-dollar bill, and held it out over the bar. Then she let it drop. After pouring two shot glasses full of liquor and raising her glass, she motioned to Jack to pick up the other. He did.

"I propose a toast," she said in mock ceremonial tone. "We've become good friends; we've helped each other. In the spirit of this fine cordial, Southern Comfort, I toast our friendship, one I hope will bring us . . . not just southern comfort, but a lot of . . . northern comfort as well . . . anyway, that was odd . . . but I mean it—I only want us to have the best of times. So here—to us."

"To us," he returned. Their shot glasses clinked, and Jack and Molly downed their drinks.

"Jack, I've had a ball working with you, hanging out with you at Geek's and all. The thing is, it's not 'work' anymore. I'm saying it out loud. It's been very difficult to keep a distance when I don't want there to be a distance. I know you now, and I think I can trust you. Still, to be honest, it scares me to get involved with someone, but you and I . . . well, it's an idea whose time has come, I think."

Molly reached out her hand. Jack took it and pulled her easily into an embrace. They kissed, and it was a long, soft, sweet kiss. Their bodies pressed together lightly. Molly broke off the kiss first and buried her head in Jack's chest. Jack touched her dreadlocks and felt the strange texture. They felt spongier and softer than he imagined they would be. He stopped playing with her hair and gently cupped the back of her head in both his hands.

"Let's collect all these ideas and get out of here," Molly said.

"I second that emotion," said Jack.

And then they picked up Jack's future off the bar.

6: 100 IDEAS INSIDE JEANNIE'S BOTTLE

Where Jack is interviewed and is left alone to organize his ideas

Still in Idea Generation, Jack forms additional ideas and then clusters them into groups by using sticky notes. Combining ideas allows him to create a new and useful idea. He then participates in choice making, or choice selecting, by creating a subset of ideas and a short list of actionable items. He also takes action on one idea by calling a friend. The lists that Jack makes can be found in Jack's Notebook at the back of this book.

Molly's apartment was a full-frontal assault on Jack's senses. There was a faint smell of incense in the air and a kaleidoscope of color. The place was draped in paisley fabric—everywhere—walls, ceiling, and furniture. The floor was covered by a rag rug that was in turn layered with smaller Orientals. On a small coffee table was a brass Buddha, the fat one with the happy face. The living room had two futons stacked on top of each other, no frame, smothered with paisley pillows. Like Jack, Molly had a small place. The difference was it wasn't just a crash pad like his; it was deliberately created.

"I love your place, it's . . . an environment."

"Exactly. Creativity happens when you are self-expressed in all aspects of your life."

She showed him the kitchen. Small, functional, and not draped in paisley. It doubled as an office. A small table had enough room for one person to eat; the rest of it was taken by a computer, an oversized monitor, and a small color printer. No phone in sight. Artistic, efficient, and private. Very Molly.

Molly took him by the hand and led him into her bedroom. Like the living room, it had an *Arabian Nights* sort of theme. It was darker, even with a small lamp on. Her bed was an old-fashioned brass four-poster, which somehow worked with all the paisley fabric. Jack wondered how she could afford such a nice piece of furniture, the computer, and the Oriental rugs on her salary from Geek's. Another Molly mystery.

They kissed and embraced.

She pulled her head back and spoke slowly and in a low voice. "So, the deal's off. It's a new deal. I want to be intimate with you. But you're going to be upset with me, I think."

"Why would I be upset?"

"Because I want us to be intimate in some ways, but not physically —not yet. Is that possible? I want us to know each other intimately— I want to know your heart."

Jack took this all in. He was disappointed. He looked down at her without speaking for a long while. He searched his heart for what he felt, and it was clear to him that he wanted a future with this woman. "Okay, I do want to be intimate in some ways too. So how do we do this?"

She led him back into the living room by the hand. Molly sat down on the floor on a large pillow, and he sat down opposite her.

"I have an idea. Let's take this time to hear each other's story from start to finish, no judgments. The only rule is to tell the truth," she said. "I want to know everything about you."

"Let's take turns on this, or else one person might go to sleep."

"Okay, we can break or switch anytime we want," she said. "Will you go first?"

Jack started talking about himself. It was strange because he was so used to being interrupted and saying things quickly in conversations that he at times would have to stop and realize how he'd really given his story short shrift by not elaborating. She just listened. Every so often she would move her face closer to his, and they would kiss. And every so often she would ask a question, like "Why?" Or, "What else?" Or she would simply say, "Tell me more." Jack had never felt so listened to before in his life, and as crazy as it was to think this, he'd never had a more intimate moment with anyone. Jack realized how long he'd been talking and asked Molly to share about herself. She hesitated and said, "Are you sure you want to hear all this?"

"After you just listened to every last detail of my life? I think it's my turn to listen now. And hey, I want to know everything about you."

"Okay, well, hold on to your hat; here goes." She took a deep breath and started to speak slowly. "My mother died when I was quite young, and I've always had the sense that she was a victim. She died in a mental institution, and I've always felt like . . . maybe she wasn't so sick. I don't know exactly how to say this, but let me just say it. I've not gotten into my background much with you because I didn't want you to know how weird it is." She paused.

"It's okay, please, your family doesn't have an exclusive on weird. Tell me what happened," Jack said gently.

"Well, the reason I'm here in Chicago is I've basically run away from my family. I'm dodging my father. See, Dad is kind of a nut case, and he's got a lot of money, and he's just a sneaky old dude. He doesn't know where I am right now, and I don't want him to know."

"Is it that bad? How sneaky can he be?" asked Jack.

"Real sneaky—in a class by himself. It's weird, but I'm just now getting used to the fact—after months of living alone here in Chicago—that every move I make isn't being watched. I was brought up like a cloistered nun. Couldn't go places, couldn't date, wasn't allowed to have friends outside school. I even had a 'bodyguard' that followed me around when I was in college. He doubled as my full-time chauffeur. There was no bucking the system either. It was a bad scene."

"What else? I have a feeling you're just scratching the surface," said Jack.

"It's a long story. See, Dad is a successful businessman, a powerful man. I should probably say *was* because he really hasn't done much business since Mom died, but it didn't matter much because he was incredibly wealthy before I was even born. Anyway, he cut way back on work after Mom died.

"Actually, after Mom died, Dad became more and more strict with Bridgette—that's my younger sister—and me. For a little while, Bridgette and I at least could go to movies and restaurants and school events, things like that. But with each passing year, it became more like living in prison. He went through our clothes and books—we had no privacy at all. No friends were allowed to visit our house; we couldn't be on any sports teams—we went to private school and came home. That was our life.

"The worst part was that he severely disciplined us if we stepped out of line—we were denied meals, made to kneel and pray for hours on end, locked in our rooms for as long as two days. Thank God for the help of the housekeeping staff and the cooks, and sometimes the sisters would visit."

"Sisters?" asked Jack.

"Nuns. Dad was a big contributor to their order, and after Mom died they were always coming by to check on us. It was kind of weird, but they were nice to us. For some reason Dad gave them a lot of respect, and if they asked him for something, he'd almost always come through."

In spite of the late hour, they continued to talk, each taking turns until the sun started lighting up the blinds on her windows. Jack started nodding off, and she gently pushed him down on the pillows and covered him with a blanket.

When the CD alarm went off two hours later in Molly's room, blasting songs from the *Romeo and Juliet* soundtrack, it was jarring and dreadful. Molly pulled herself up and went to take a shower. Jack found her stereo and switched the sounds to a local radio station, the jazz campus station from the College of DuPage. Slowly, he pulled himself together. He drifted into the kitchen and looked around for coffee. He found some and began preparing a pot.

Molly came out of the shower in a huge paisley towel, which made Jack smile. She ran around the apartment, getting dressed quickly. Then she came out to the kitchen.

"Ahh, coffee. One of the advantages of partnership—somebody to make the coffee while you shower. Wanna take a shower?"

"Yeah."

"So go, run in there. I'll fix us something to eat."

Jack came back into the kitchen ten minutes later, showered and dressed. Molly had him sit in the chair at the table. She had toasted some bagels and had set out light cream cheese, peanut butter, and jelly. Jack started fixing up a bagel, and she sat on his lap. His hands full with butter knife and bagel, the best he could do was kiss her and nuzzle her neck.

"I love you," he said.

"I love you," she answered.

Jack dropped the bagel and knife on his plate and looked into her eyes. Her eyes, those sparkling pools of green, they seemed to have grown larger overnight. They sat silent in the chair, embracing.

"Last night was wonderful," she said. "I've never felt so close to anybody—and now I know all about you. I almost wish we could just stay here for about . . . oh . . . the next month and just keep talking like that."

"I was just thinking that I'm basically your slave. I mean, if you asked me to rob a bank right now, I'd do it."

"So, go rob a bank. Heck, there's an ATM a block down—that would be good enough."

They laughed.

"It's weird to feel this powerless. I would go rob a bank, or an ATM, if I thought you were serious, Molly. I mean, I would find a way to make it work even though it would be crazy."

"I know what you mean."

Jack hugged her tightly and said, "So tell me more about Bridgette."

"I feel bad because I've left her alone up there. Bridge is in school.

Well, she's trying to go to school anyway, at Marquette in Milwaukee. I'm really afraid for her. We talk on the phone occasionally, but I can't even tell her where I am. She's a mess. See, for me, everything that happened just made me angry and more determined to get away. Bridgette, I'm afraid, has lost hope; she's kind of beaten. I think she's clinically depressed. She needs help, really needs help, but Dad will only let her go see a priest. And the priest she's allowed to see is in Dad's pocket."

"Your father is paying off a priest?" Jack was incredulous.

"He pays off a lot of people," Molly said. "It's not *the* Mob, it's more like *his* mob."

"How do you know all this, I mean the mob part?" asked Jack.

"Because I'm a very good observer, and that's one of the ways I kept myself from going nuts. I made a study of it—it gave me a sense of control when I really didn't have much," she explained. "It's also how I've been able to get away and stay unfound. These dreadlocks and a pair of sunglasses go a long way. But I'm crazy with guilt about leaving her up there alone with Dad," said Molly quietly.

"Amazing. I'm still trying to get a grip on all this, okay? Why do you think your father is so . . . controlling?"

"Boy, that's a question I've spent half my life thinking about. I've no doubt at this point he's mentally ill. And part of his illness is that he's an over-the-top Puritan, actually old-school Catholic, especially when it comes to his family. With everyone else he doesn't have such standards, and, I don't know, he's a type of high-class gangster. What caused it all, way back when, is the real mystery, although I have my suspicions. My grandfather was a hard man—Dad was abused as a child, I'm sure. But the really creepy person was my grandmother. I only met her a couple of times. My father hated her, and he wouldn't let her anywhere near us. Dad told me once that when he was very young, if he did anything wrong, she would lock him in a closet. Sometimes for more than a couple of days. He wouldn't be let out until his mother said he was 'purified.' I think he's buried all this and never really come to terms with it. It's warped him. My mother saw the good in him—the ambition, the charm—and she thought she could help him deal with all the trauma. But she couldn't do it; he needed professional help. When my mom died, I was just a little girl, but even when she was home there was always this tension in the air. Dad was always after her and yelling about something. He was so much older than her, it was almost like he was her father and not her husband."

"Molly, this sounds like a movie . . . but, well, you're here now, and you're living your own life," said Jack. "Are you okay?"

Molly smiled. "I'm fine; today is a great day. I'm glad I could finally tell you some of this stuff. You're the only one in Chicago that has a clue about who I really am. And now I feel great. Love is like a B12 shot, isn't it?"

"It is," he said.

"Listen, I've got to leave and get to work. I'm due down at the Geek's in twenty minutes. What I'm thinking is, why don't you stay here for a while if you want? Take some quiet time and sort through all those crazy ideas we put on napkins last night. Maybe create a few more. Here," she said, going to the living room and bringing back the napkins. "Put them up on the wall, see if you can think of a few more, and start getting a sense of which ideas really seem like winners to you. And, Jack, don't automatically reject the really wild ones. Let them live a while. Keep hope alive."

Molly was now back in action, back in "do" mode. She could switch pretty fast from one to the other. *I could be more like that*, he thought.

"I'll do that, thank you," he said. "I love your apartment. It's fun to be here. I feel like I'm inside Jeannie's bottle."

"Hey, I loved *I Dream of Jeannie*. That was such a goofy show. So you can stay here in the bottle working, and when you want, you can smoke yourself out and come over to Geek's. Or whatever."

"I'm off to the tennis club this afternoon," lamented Jack.

"Right—we've got to rescue you from that, don't we? We'll think of something."

With that, Molly gathered up her things and was out the door, stopping for one more kiss on the way out. Jack sat at the kitchen table, eating his bagel, relaxed, tired, and elated. Okay, so Molly had a wacky family. He wanted to know more. And how had Molly stayed so well-adjusted?

It must have taken incredible courage for her to leave her home. But then he wondered if she was being paranoid. *I mean, what could her father do to her down here? And what was he afraid of?* For all the bohemian trappings and goofy fashion, she was pretty grounded, at least as far as he knew. No evidence of drugs. She had her head on straight; she worked hard. She knew what she wanted to do, and she was going after it.

Jack hoped he was a part of it.

Jack looked at the stack of idea cocktail napkins on the table. They were intimidating this morning. There were so many ideas it was hard to imagine picking one and running with it. He really ought to be doing about ten of them all at once.

He picked up the stack and started taping them up on her kitchen wall. They were still sorted into the groupings they'd come up with the night before. He paused as he put up the idea having to do with renting the space in the warehouse behind Geek's. The idea was exciting and so impractical. It was crazy—and yet . . .

My own studio, he thought. *Not just a photo studio but a commercial art studio. We could do art for the Web and for corporate brochures and for ads and stuff like that.* Molly could work with him. The two of them were almost competent enough to pull it off. Of course, there were all kinds of problems with the idea. According to Molly, the place was a mess. And then they had no money; they had no clients—not even potential ones. *Maybe I'm not ready for a step that big,* he thought.

He started looking at all the ideas, and he had some fresh thoughts. Some new ideas came to him in a rush. He picked out a black Flair pen from a coffee mug filled with pens and colored pencils and found a pack of sticky notes. He looked at them, thinking they would have come in handy last night. He added an idea to the Studio cluster, and another nearby:

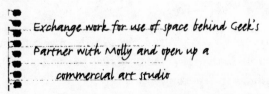

Exchange work for use of space behind Geek's

Partner with Molly and open up a
    commercial art studio

In the back of his mind, he'd been thinking about the long train ride and how he might get out of it. Maybe he could get a job at Geek's and trade his time for use of the space. It wouldn't hurt to ask.

He spent the next hour processing through the ideas. He added more to the Learning, Studio, Marketing, Brochure, Documentation, and More New Business idea groups. He had a fresh head this morning, and the ideas just kept coming, piggybacking off the session Molly and he had done the night before. What he liked about today's ideas was that they were more specific and practical—like getting a yellow pages listing. Obvious now, but he hadn't thought of it before. The ideas from the night before were a stepping-stone to today's.

Funny, he thought, *how your own view of yourself*—in his case, as young, underequipped, and underskilled—*can stop you from doing some simple things that might help you grow.* For some purposes, his skills as a photographer were more than adequate. He knew the basics, he knew composition, he could take good shots. He could even do weddings respectably, recalling those misty fog shots he'd done of that young couple by the lake. Heck, his skills were a good match for covering any "event." It was just the crazy nature of weddings and the fear of blowing an important shot that had him in risk-reduction mode. Events. Jack started writing another note: "Promote yourself as an events photographer."

> *FUNNY,* HE THOUGHT, *HOW YOUR OWN VIEW OF YOURSELF*—IN HIS CASE, AS YOUNG, UNDEREQUIPPED, AND UNDERSKILLED—*CAN STOP YOU FROM DOING SOME SIMPLE THINGS THAT MIGHT HELP YOU GROW.*

Okay, so what kind of events? Chicago had a huge convention business. Jack wrote down a slew of ideas of how he could tap into the convention business and sporting events.

Jack paused there for a moment, looking around the kitchen. He saw that Molly had a copy of *The Reader*, a free newspaper with local music happenings and such. He picked it up and was glancing through it when he came to a page of people dressed in black tie. The pictures were all snapshots—nothing fancy, just simple pictures of people at parties. Parties? Well yes, they were having a good time, but actually these were charity events. Charity events. This had him thinking about fashion shows next.

And hairdressers.

He remembered that Rob's wife, Cheryl, was a hairdresser and that she was always going out to do hairstyles for fashion shows. Every salon he'd ever been through had some kind of glamour shot on the wall. He imagined that some of those were done by beauty product manufacturers, but he'd bet the shop stylists wouldn't mind having some shots of their own best work.

Jack looked up at this whole new batch of ideas. Then he counted them: ninety-nine ideas. It was interesting to him that just fifteen minutes earlier, he had thought he was fresh out—all out—of ideas. That's when he thought of the events thing, and he thought of about twenty more in the blink of an eye.

Why hadn't he done this type of thinking before? He had the sense that some of these ideas were things he could have been doing all along. *If I'd been working on this all along, I would be doing photography full-time now,* he thought. *I'd be successful.*

The future is paisley, he thought as he looked around the room. And he smiled remembering the incredible conversations of last night and this morning. He never realized how romantic just talking could be! He settled back in his chair, enjoying his coffee and finishing his bagel. *This is good stuff,* he thought, *lots of good ideas here. Amazing—I have one short of one hundred ideas for making a better life for myself— and maybe not just myself.* Ninety-nine ideas. The sticky notes on the walls screamed for one more idea to make it a full one hundred. There was something wonderfully perfect about one hundred ideas. Just one more. One more. He looked at the peanut butter jar. What did that suggest? Food, restaurants, menus.

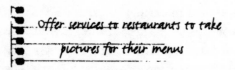

Offer services to restaurants to take pictures for their menus

Okay, one hundred, even! It was exciting. All kinds of ideas, new business ideas, educational ideas, money-making ideas, unrealistic ideas, long-term ideas, short-term ideas. The question now was what to do with all of them. Some of them could take years. But some of them he could do today. Like calling Cheryl—he could do that right now. On an impulse, he picked up the phone and dialed.

"Rob—it's Jack. Yeah, good, I'm good. Right, I'm not calling from home—you must have caller ID. Yeah, it went okay. Thanks for the ride downtown. Say listen, Rob, would you mind if I called Cheryl? I want to ask her something about what hairdressers do to get their best do's documented. What? Okay, okay, *coiffures*—what they do to get their best coiffures photographed. I mean, they must want that sometimes, right? She's at work? Do you think I could call her there? Okay, thanks."

Jack wrote down the phone number on Molly's newspaper. Then he dialed the number.

"Yes, may I speak to Cheryl, please? Thank you. Cheryl? Hi, it's Jack, Jack Huber—right, Rob's friend. Listen, sorry to bother you at work, but you know I'm a photographer, right? Right. Right. Well, I have a question for you. I was just wondering how hairdressers get photographs of their best work—their best coiffures?"

And Jack listened to Cheryl. It turned out that stylists often lamented not having photographs. They got some at educational seminars, events put on by the hair products companies, but not all the hairdressers participated in them, and they weren't every day. They also got some photographs from fashion shows, but again, shows didn't happen every day, and getting a good shot of their work was more luck than planning. He had more questions, but he didn't want to keep her on the phone too long when she was at work, so he asked if he could call her again at home. Then he thanked her and hung up.

How many good salons were there just in Lincoln Park? A dozen?

Maybe he could give them a day rate and just shoot pictures all day at one salon. If they had enough notice, they could have some of their best customers lined up. No, that wouldn't work, they couldn't possibly get them all on the same day. Then again, maybe each hairdresser could have one or two show up on a specific day, which might be enough to make it worthwhile. He'd have to ask Cheryl. This could be a good way to generate some cash. It would be like school pictures day, except for hairdressers. He'd put together a brochure with a day rate, maybe a half-day rate and an hourly rate just in case they would prefer that. And prices for both black-and-white and color prints. They would probably want color.

Jack looked at the one hundred ideas on the wall. So many ideas, what to do?

Jack picked up a red pencil from Molly's desk. He started reviewing the ideas. *Maybe the thing to do is just pick, say, five of these ideas, and then* work *them.* He knew intuitively that ideas weren't always perfect. Those cocktail napkins and sticky notes were not all little plans up there on the wall. Each one of these ideas, particularly the bigger ones, would require more thinking, more research, more sweat to make them into something really workable. *More sweat,* he thought.

> HE KNEW INTUITIVELY THAT IDEAS WEREN'T ALWAYS PERFECT. THOSE COCKTAIL NAPKINS AND STICKY NOTES WERE NOT ALL LITTLE PLANS UP THERE ON THE WALL.

Jack spent the next hour choosing his five best ideas:

- Do a brochure offering photographic documentation services for businesses
- Partner with Molly and open up a commercial art studio

- Promote yourself as an events photographer
- Exchange work for use of space behind Geek's
- Read a book on starting a new business

This is so interesting, he thought. *All five of the best ideas, at least what I'm thinking right now are the five best, were done in the second phase of Idea Generation. The idea of working in exchange for using the space at Geek's was a build on the earlier idea of renting the space. The seed of the exchange idea had come early, but the better idea, the more practical one, came this morning when I was doing more imaginative thinking. Manny was right when he said people didn't allow enough time for it.* Jack was just beginning to see that even a little more imaginative thinking could be incredibly productive.

He was also surprised by what the five ideas, as a group, seemed to be telling him. They were telling him to start a business. He didn't think of what he wanted to do as "a business," yet the ideas seemed to scream it. The five top ideas, now stuck in their own area on the wall, were almost like little people demanding a giant to hear them. Maybe he wasn't doing this right.

Jack picked up the pen again and went back to the wall with all the ideas. He circled the ideas that he thought he could do right away or that he should come back and revisit:

- Get a yellow pages listing as a photographer
- Check with the city of Chicago on permits for
    soliciting at public events
- Find out who hires photographers for the city
- Check the newspaper every sunday for
    upcoming events
- Call Cheryl and ask about who does fashion shows

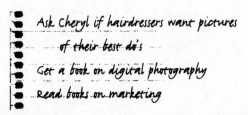

Ask Cheryl if hairdressers want pictures
of their best do's
Get a book on digital photography
Read books on marketing

Looking at the ideas, he realized that he had done all this thinking, with Molly's help, in the last twelve hours. *A half a day of imaginative thinking that might determine the course of the rest of my life.* Of course, maybe not—maybe none of this would work out. He'd had big ideas before that hadn't worked out.

So, Jack thought, *it's time to take some risks and try some of these ideas out. I really don't even have pride to lose. Matter of fact, I have pride to gain.*

Jack spent another whole hour writing down the ideas into his notebook. Then he pulled the napkins and sticky notes off the wall and stuffed them into an envelope he took from Molly's desk. He looked at his watch—almost noon. He had to get home, change clothes, and spend two hours getting out to the stupid tennis club. He had a feeling he wouldn't be doing it much longer.

7: RAZOR'S EDGE

Where Jack develops his ideas into a solution and gets into action

Molly leaves town, and Manny shares why he has decided to help Jack. Already, Jack is Getting into Action, the third phase of CPS. Together, he and Manny begin the fifth step of the third phase, Solution Development. They look at an idea and make it better—more workable, more doable, less risky, more exciting, and more acceptable to others. Manny first asks Jack to make a list of criteria that can be used to evaluate his ideas. Criteria are important to keep in mind as ideas are evaluated and improved. For a more extensive use of criteria in Solution Development, see Jack's Notebook in the back for an Evaluation Matrix.

Manny also walks Jack through the PPCO Technique or Positives, Potentials, Concerns, and Overcoming Concerns. Listing Positives and Potentials forces Jack to see the big picture. When listing concerns, Manny asks Jack to use the words "In What Ways Might We," which positions the concerns as solvable problems. Then, they take each concern individually—generating some ideas to manage or overcome it. Manny calls this the Development part of R&D, of Research and Development.

Jack woke up on Friday morning and thought about everything that had happened in just the last few days—what a crazy and interesting week it had been.

He'd shared with Molly the ideas that had seemed to scream out for action, his narrowed-down lists. They'd had some long talks over pasta and a bottle of wine about just what to do. It was a process of refining ideas, paring them down, building them up, evaluating them, and then doing it all over again. In this process it occurred to them that they should be business partners. But where to start?

They shook hands on their partnership. Jack had a good feeling about working with Molly. They were romantic, sure, but they were more than that; he felt they were also equals, partners in a broader sense than just business. It was interesting to him that a romantic relationship could have a work dimension.

Molly told Jack more about her family. It was troubling to hear; the last desperate days of her dead mother in particular. Molly also mentioned a secretive group of "security" guys who worked for her father. Her biggest concern was her younger sister, Bridgette. She was afraid her sister would attempt suicide, and one of the few regrets she'd had about starting a new life in Chicago was leaving her behind. She'd talked to her recently, and things were getting worse for her in Milwaukee.

His growing sense of her strange history made him all the more uneasy about the last conversation he'd had with her.

Molly had phoned him at the tennis club last night and said she was going home to Milwaukee for the weekend and would be back on Monday. No explanation—just that she "had to go home for a while, to see my sister." Molly hadn't been any more specific than that, which was pretty weird given all they'd talked about. He thought he detected a sort of breathlessness in the tone of her voice. She didn't usually speak like that. The call didn't last long, and Jack didn't have time to react or ask questions. She didn't leave a number in Milwaukee.

The call was a real letdown. Jack wanted to spend every waking—and sleeping—hour with her. Of course, he still had work to do, so maybe this was a blessing in disguise.

But still Jack wondered, the sudden exit to Milwaukee, was it about them? Given her fears of her father, why was she going back now? What was happening? Maybe it was just an explosion of self-expression now that she finally had a choice.

Now he had to get back to today. Jack called Manny, got his voice mail, and left a message saying the prints and CD-ROM were ready and that he could drop them by, just to let him know where.

He hung up the phone and stared at the ceiling. Now what? Picking up his notebook, he looked at the list of short-term things to do. He wrote on top of the page "The Short List." *Okay,* he thought, *no time like the present.*

He picked up the phone again, called directory assistance, and figured out who to call for yellow pages listings.

Next, he called the city and was bounced around from office to office in his attempt to figure out whether it was legal to solicit for photographs at city events. With no resolution on that, he gave up.

He made more calls. He talked. He asked questions. He made notes in his sketchbook and kept plugging away on the short list. He called Cheryl at home, and they had a discussion about the idea of an instant picture service for salons—where they would use electronic cameras and do prints at the shop. She didn't like the idea. She was high on normal photographic prints because they were more permanent and had better quality. She did think there was business at the salons, though, and she encouraged Jack to call the owner of her shop, Tony Cooper. She said he was a real nice guy and that she'd talk to him later today, so Jack should call him tomorrow.

Mañana. Always tomorrow, Jack thought.

He reviewed the short list again: *Check the newspaper every Sunday for upcoming events.* He didn't have Sunday's paper, or any other paper for that matter, at his apartment. He could go down to Geek's and see if they'd kept a copy, and if they hadn't, he'd use the Web. For the first time in his life he wished he had a computer at home. If he had one, he could have found out then what he wanted to know. He sighed.

"What's a poor boy to do . . . give it away on Seventh Avenue?" Jack recited the old Rolling Stones song from the *Some Girls* album. That had been one of his father's favorites. Jack had listened to those songs so many times; the lyrics were easy to recall, always floating around in his head. That and all the other music his father used to play at home. His father, his face, was a distant memory to Jack now. And yet his music, the stuff he was always playing around the house, was as fresh and ever present as if it were yesterday.

Jack remembered his father's sudden death with renewed sadness and disbelief, reliving that time for a moment. His father had died of a heart attack when Jack was about to start his senior year in college. The bottom had fallen out of Jack's life, and he'd dropped out of school. They had been close. They shared a love of music, and his father was a good advisor. When he died, it left Jack feeling like he was all on his own. His mother wanted to help him, but Jack resisted her advice because, well, it didn't seem right to him. She wanted him to go back to school and get an accounting degree! School wasn't such a bad idea—but accounting?

Jack got off the bed—his office at home—and went over to the stereo. It was the only thing of earthly value he'd received when his dad died: the old turntable, beat-up speakers, the glowing tube amplifier, and his record collection. The stereo had been state-of-the-art years ago, and it still sounded pretty good. He flipped the switches and started looking through the stack of albums, roughly still in his father's alphabetical order by artist. He found the *Some Girls* album and put it on the platter.

As the music played, Jack thought his father would probably like what was going on for him right now. He was in the process of reviving a dream he'd almost given up on, and he was in love with a beautiful woman. Yeah, he'd approve.

The phone rang. He turned down the volume on the Stones and answered.

"Jack, it's Manny. Got your message, and yes, I'd love to get those prints. Where can we meet?"

"Umm, how about if we meet at Geek's, down on the corner of Milwaukee and Noble Street?"

"Right, you mentioned that place."

"Yeah, and they have good coffee."

"That's fine, so, how about I meet you there at 11:30?"

"Great."

"See you there, then."

They hung up, and Jack hustled down to Geek's. It was strange to see somebody behind the counter besides Molly. The man making espresso this morning was in his midthirties—Jack had seen him before. He was clean-shaven, head and all, giving him a rather severe sort of look.

"A regular coffee of the day, please," Jack ordered.

"Sure enough. You're Molly's friend, aren't you?" asked the clean-head-look guy.

"I am. It's funny not seeing her here."

"Funny for you. She sort of left me flat here."

"She did leave town in a big hurry," admitted Jack.

"I mean, I know things happen and all, but I was hoping to get somebody to take her shift until she comes back, and I can't find anyone. So, you know, I've got to do it myself. I guess I'm not used to real work anymore," he said with a bemused grin.

Jack felt a friendly vibe from this guy. He was a bit worried at first that he was going to hear a raft of complaints about Molly, but it was obvious there wasn't too much of a problem.

"We all do our best to avoid real work, don't we? By the way, I'm Jack."

"Jack, yes. Mine's Layne. Here's your coffee."

"Thanks."

Layne kept busy behind the counter, serving a small rush of customers. Jack recognized his name because Molly had mentioned him a couple of times—Layne was the owner of Geek's. Poor Layne was having a bit of trouble keeping up with things, and Jack recalled how efficient Molly was behind the counter, so smooth that you really didn't notice. You took it for granted—until you saw someone like Layne doing the same work.

He sipped his coffee while considering where to sit down. His eyes scanned the shop, but it dawned on him that Layne was someone he actually wanted to talk to. He waited until the mini-rush was over, and he eased up to the counter again.

"Layne, Molly tells me you have some unused space in the back."

"Back there?" he asked, gesturing behind him. "Yeah, it's a huge space, but not much I can do with it. Can't afford to heat it, and I really don't need any more space for the coffee shop. Plus it's a huge mess. Why'd you ask?"

"Molly was telling me about it. Thing is, I'm a photographer, and I'm looking for some studio space, but really, it's kind of a pipe dream 'cause I'm just getting started."

"Hey, man, don't lose that dream. I never thought I'd get Geek's open either. It took me two years to figure out how to finance this. I kept working the plan, and I finally figured out a financial model people were willing to give me loans for, and now I'm open for business. You want to look in the back?"

"Yeah."

"Here, follow me. Brace yourself." Layne locked the register and put the key in his pocket.

"I may have to run out front if I hear the doorbell ring," he said.

Layne walked to the rear of the shop and opened a door. It led to a dark, narrow hallway and another door. He opened that door and they both walked through.

Molly was right—it was a huge space with a warehouse receiving-and-shipping feel to it. The ceiling arced over the space—about twenty-five feet high in the center, with wooden rafters exposed. And there was still hardware up there for moving large things around—pulleys, hooks, tracks, and the like. In the center of the ceiling was a skylight, letting in some sunshine in spite of a thick film of dirt. The soft, natural light illuminated an amazing array of junk: piles of construction refuse, insulation, old desks, broken chairs, ancient light fixtures, piles of wooden pallets. He saw what looked like old computers, maybe thirty or forty in a haphazard pile. Building materials, cinder blocks—some broken, some whole. Also, stacks of drywall, 2-by-4s, half-used cans of paint, an old bicycle, a doll with its head broken off, and several jukeboxes. And this was only the first layer. Behind the junk was more junk—of what composition was anybody's guess.

It was a colossal mess covered in dust.

Jack broke the silence.

"Didn't they use this set in *Blade Runner*?"

Layne laughed. "Hey, yeah, they did. Rutger Hauer is buried under that pile over there, and Harrison Ford is out front having coffee with a replicant. Yeah, told you it was bad. A real disaster zone. But I got the whole building with the lease for the coffee shop. It was an all-or-nothing sort of deal. This space is a complete waste really. I haven't had the time or the energy to even think about sorting it out. I had a woman come in here to see it a couple of weeks ago. She was looking for a place to give dance lessons. She took one look and laughed herself all the way back to Lincoln Park."

"It's big enough for a dance club."

"It is. I looked into it. Thing is, I couldn't get a liquor license here to save my life. It would take years to finagle and more money than I can throw at it. Nothing but trouble, a night club."

"So who does all this crap belong to?"

"Me, I inherited it. Company went out of business left most of it. The rest of it was abandoned here. I guess the former owners let people use the space for storage."

"Well, if it was cleaned up it would be a great space for photography, but like I said before, I'm just getting started," said Jack.

"How do you feel about hard work?" Layne was grinning.

Jack looked at him. He had an idea where this was going. "Hard work? That's my freakin' middle name," he said, trying to contain the excitement he was feeling.

"Here's the thing—I could pay somebody to clean this mess up, but that would be cash out of my pocket. And I don't have a plan for this space anyway, you know? I don't really *need* to do anything with it. On the other hand, if I could get some rent back here, I'd be happy. It would help me make the lease payments. So are you serious about a studio? Do you think you can really get one going? Do you think you can make it pay?"

"I don't know, but I'm sure going to try. I mean, I have no equipment, no resources. All I've got is a ton of ideas."

"That's where it all begins," said Layne, pausing to look around the room and then back at Jack. "Okay, so here's my offer. You clean this mess up, and I'll give it to you rent-free for a year. When I say *clean*, I mean all this crap out of here and the place painted. I'll supply the paint. After a year, then we'll talk about a new arrangement."

"Layne, that's an amazing offer. Thing is, if I clean this mess up, it may take a year, and I won't have the time to make it pay off."

"Okay, so rent-free for a year and a half, and I'll agree to $1,000 a month rent for a year after that. That gives you a space, free or darn cheap, for two and a half years."

"And free coffee?"

"Don't push it." Layne laughed. "No free coffee—I'd go broke. But you can jump onto my high-speed data line for a nominal fee. Does this make sense to you?"

"It makes sense," said Jack.

"I'll draw up some paperwork then, to make it official. It'll take me a few days. Meantime, have at it back here," Layne said, grinning. "Your middle name is going to be 'Freakin' Dusty Hard Work' for quite a while, I'm thinking."

Jack was in shock. This was a dream come true. He had no idea if he could make it work. He had no idea how much trouble it would be to clean up that room. But right now he didn't care—he had a studio, a real working space.

Layne extended his hand. Jack shook it. They looked each other in the eye for the briefest of moments, and then Layne excused himself and walked back through the door, leaving Jack alone. In his studio.

Looking around more closely, he found the power panel and opened it up. Not bad—enough capacity for heavy-duty lighting equipment. Then he opened up the back door, which was actually a small step-through door and part of a much larger hangar-style door. Out back were an alley and a dock raised about four feet off the ground, so you could back a truck right up to the hangar-style door. If he could get a truck, it wouldn't be hard to get stuff out.

He started poking through the various mounds of trash. There was lots of scrap lumber—if he wanted to build anything, he was covered. The computers had an AT&T logo and looked ancient. One was cracked open with the circuit board exposed and the wiring gleamed gold. Under a canvas tarp was a huge pile of shrink-wrapped stationery, very old and a funky light green color. Jack picked up a ream and cracked the plastic seal. Inside, the paper was dry—*still usable*, Jack thought.

Then he heard the door open. It was Manny.

"Manny, I'm sorry! Have you been here long?"

"No, I just walked in. I asked the guy behind the counter if he knew you, and he sent me right back here to find you," Manny said, looking around the room. "And this would be your average industrial space gone to seed. What a glorious mess."

"Yeah. No doubt. I just cut a deal to rent this space for two and a half years."

"No kidding?"

"No kidding. We're standing in the new headquarters of Jack Huber Enterprises."

"Wow, congratulations. I'd uncork the champagne, but I'm not prepared. Maybe we'll save that for your grand opening. Given the state of things in here, I'm guessing that will be in about, what, two months?"

"I was thinking more like six! I have no idea what I'm going to do with all this stuff."

Manny was already poking through the piles. "Actually, while it's a mess, a lot of this stuff is reusable. If you sort it out, there are people who would love to take this stuff off your hands. You could list it on e-Bay maybe. Look at this paper over here—nothing wrong with it. Could be used by teachers. These are art supplies. And these computers—there are people who take these things apart and salvage the gold off the circuit boards. What I would do is sort through all this stuff and make a list of what's here. Then, just make lots of phone calls until you find out what people will come and take off your hands." Then Manny peeked out the back window. "The good news is this dock'll make it pretty easy to load up trucks. What people don't want, you can rent a big Dumpster and just push it all right out the door."

"You make it sound easy."

"No, not easy. It'll take weeks to sort out and find new owners for all this wacky stuff. And you'll have to minimize what you just pitch because it's sort of expensive to get rid of."

"Okay, I've got my work cut out. But hey, let's go get a coffee, and I'll show you those prints."

Jack and Manny closed up behind them and returned to Geek's Café. Jack looked at the café space with new eyes. Layne must have carved this space out of the front offices of the old warehouse. You'd never know it, though. Geek's looked like it had been an old-fashioned coffee house for fifty years, except for the computers.

They sat down at a booth, and Manny looked through the five-by-seven custom prints. He studied them intently, and then he started sorting them into piles. After some time, he stacked them all up and put them back into the envelope.

"Find what you're looking for?" asked Jack.

"Not really. I was hoping it would be like on the cop shows, that something would just jump out at me from these pictures, but nothing really does." Manny smiled. "It's good to have these anyway—as documentation. And thanks for the CD-ROM too." He reached into his pocket and pulled out an envelope with Jack's name on the front. "Here's a check for your fee.

"Tell me, what's been going on with you? I mean, besides the new studio."

"Yeah, the new studio—I'm a little freaked out right this second. I think maybe I bit off more than I can chew," Jack said.

"That's a natural feeling, but you can handle it," Manny assured him.

"I think you're right. I tell you, what's been going on for me is, well, everything. I've really been thinking imaginatively about what I'm going to do with myself. I've had a lot of help from Molly."

"Molly?"

"Molly is . . . well, she's a good friend, and we've been working together to learn some things and do research and think up lots of ideas on how I—we—might tackle things. She works here at Geek's. I mean, she normally works here, but she had to leave town to visit her family in Milwaukee."

"Tell me more about her."

Jack hesitated but then looked at Manny and smiled. "I think I'm falling in love with her. We've been friends for a little while—we just help each other out, and we're now business partners."

Manny smiled in return. "How does she help you out?"

"Well, we talk a lot. And she teaches me computer stuff, and I'm going to teach her photography," said Jack.

"She's into technology?"

"Yeah, she's a Web designer."

"So she could do a Web page for somebody?"

"It would depend on how extensive it was, but yeah, that's her area."

"Interesting. So—you love her?" asked Manny. "Have you been hit by the thunderbolt?"

"Uh, yeah, I do love her, and 'the thunderbolt' is a good way to describe it. She's only been gone a day, and I already miss her. In fact, I can't get her off of my mind. Maybe because she left in such a hurry."

"So what's next for you?"

"I'm not sure, other than two months of cleaning! And I have a short list of ideas to implement. I'm working on a lot of things."

"So you've moved into Action Planning already? What have you decided to do?" asked Manny.

"I guess what it boils down to is I'm starting a business, with Molly, to do photography and commercial art, including her Web design stuff. Generally that's the idea, but we're still figuring out how to go about it. I have a couple of ideas on areas we could focus on, like events photography and—how do I put this—photography for hair-stylists. I mean, I don't know how to start a business, I don't know everything I need to know about commercial art, I have no customers, and I have no cash."

"But you have a location!"

"I got that going for me," said Jack, doing a Bill Murray. "Heck, I don't even know the actual address."

"Small problems," said Manny.

"To you. I'm scared to death. I mean, I don't know where to start," said Jack.

"Make a list," advised Manny.

"You're big on lists, aren't you?"

"Yeah, I am."

"I have a list of things I want to do—of ideas, I mean. Thing is, they are just ideas. I don't really have a plan. So really I don't know what my next step is."

"Okay, so here's what I tell my clients when they are in this spot . . ."

"Wait a minute. How many of your clients are in the position of not knowing what to do? I mean, your clients are all big shots, big companies with lots of money and lots of experts," said Jack.

"That's true, but whenever they start something new, they are in exactly the same place you are. They have some ideas. They have the sense they are good ideas. But they don't know exactly what to do. There's always ambiguity around starting something new. You have to embrace that. With my corporate customers, it's just happening on a grander scale, but it's the same thing. You've heard of the term *R&D*, right?" asked Manny.

"Right, Research and Development."

"This is Development. Idea development and business development," said Manny.

"So, how does one go about idea development?"

"You look for ways to make the idea more workable, more doable, less risky, more exciting, and more acceptable to others. You need to have some idea of the criteria you'll use to evaluate the idea. You want to take the idea and build it into something more than just an idea. You want to build—and I hesitate to use this word because it's so over-used—you want to build a *solution*."

"And you do this by . . . ?"

"Like I said, you start by making a list."

"A list of what?"

"I'm getting to that. So tell me, what are your ideas?"

Jack got his notebook and read some of the items from his list:

> *Do a brochure offering photographic documentation services for businesses*

Partner with Molly and open up a commercial
   art studio
Promote yourself as an events photographer
Exchange work for use of space behind Geek's
Read a book on starting a new business

Manny took the notebook from Jack and looked over the list for a few minutes.

"This is good. And look, you've already taken some action on one of them. Now you have more problems you need ideas for!" He laughed. "All kidding aside, you've taken care of the space; you just cut a deal. Congratulations. It proves that the best ideas are the ones you actually take action on. Until you act, you have nothing except words on a page."

> UNTIL YOU ACT, YOU HAVE NOTHING
> EXCEPT WORDS ON A PAGE.

Manny stopped a moment and seemed a bit distracted. Then he continued. "The rest of these ideas are all related to the new business idea, so it's really not so much about evaluating one versus the others. You can do them all, maybe. Between the idea for documentation services and the events photographer—there is some choice to make there. The choice might be made for you based on what comes through your door. Do you have a sense of which might work better for you?"

"I've done both," said Jack.

"Okay, then what is more exciting for you?"

"Probably events."

"Define *events*."

"To me it's like meetings, conventions, sports, and . . . oh, yeah." Jack laughed. "Hairdressers."

"Interesting. Let's make a short list of something," said Manny. "Thinking about your idea of an events-photography business . . . what criteria would you use to evaluate that idea? For instance, if it takes you three years to get this business off the ground, would that work?"

"No, it really has to start doing well in a few months at the most."

"So, one criteria for evaluating your idea would be 'generating cash in three months.' What else?" said Manny.

"Well, it has to be work I can actually do," said Jack.

"Okay, we'll add that to the list as 'in my skill set,'" said Manny. "Do you want to also say, 'or Molly's skill set' since you are in this business together?"

"Yes, right, can either of us do it," said Jack.

Manny said, "Anything else?"

Jack thought for a bit and then said, "Well, it occurs to me that if it generates cash and I can actually do it, the only thing left is simply getting the work . . . so how about 'can find the work.'"

Manny nodded. "You might also say and 'can I sell the work?'— yeah, that's a feasibility criterion. We'll add that on." He paused for a moment. "So you have financial and skill-set criteria and, finally, what amounts to marketing or sales criteria. One thing you could do is look at each idea you have and run it up against these criteria—give it a score. That's called an *Evaluation Matrix*. It's one way to further develop your list because if you see a hole or a weakness, you can then address it and improve the idea. There's another way to do it as well . . . we'll try that in a minute . . . but before I go there, what was it you mentioned about hairdressers?" Manny asked, smiling.

"I have this idea that maybe hairdressers want to get shots of their latest stuff—the do's, you know? I have a friend that works at a salon, and she says it actually makes some sense—wants me to talk to the salon owner, a guy named . . . what was it?" Jack asked, looking at his notes a few pages back. "Yeah, Tony Cooper."

"There you are. So you need to make that call and ask about fifty questions. Better yet, go see him and bring the donuts." Manny paused and reflected for a moment. "I'm thinking you can't decide right now. Commercial art, events photography, and photographic documentation are pretty closely related. Seems it's not so crazy to think you could do all three, at least to start with. You really don't know yet where the business is most likely to come from. As a new business, you have to be really flexible. I can't tell you how many times a business's original intention had to change in order to make a go of it. By the way, do you know the three most important things with regard to a new business?" Manny asked.

Jack looked blank. "No, what?"

"Well, first there's cash flow."

"Yeah."

"Then there's cash flow." Manny started grinning. "And finally . . . there's cash flow."

"I'm getting the idea that cash flow is sort of important," said Jack, grinning himself. "So how do we build this solution you were talking about?"

"Let's try this. Let's work through a tool called PPCO, which stands for Positives, Potentials, Concerns, and Overcoming Concerns. To start, let's bundle all these ideas into one. We'll call it, just for the sake of a label, JackNewCo."

"Okay."

"JackNewCo will be a commercial art studio specializing in photo documentation and events photography."

"Sounds like a TV ad already," said Jack.

"Let's go with that. This is a TV ad where all you can say is what's positive . . . so tell the audience what's positive, for you, about this idea? I'll write down what you come up with."

"Positives about JackNewCo?"

"Right."

"Okay, so like, how about, it would focus my efforts?"

"Good, yes. Another positive?"

"Molly and I might make a decent living."

"That's actually more of a potential, but I'm going to write it down, we need those too."

"There are always events happening," said Jack.

"Okay, right." Manny jotted that one down.

"Molly will be a great partner."

"Uh-huh."

"The studio is big enough for almost anything."

"It is. Keep going," Manny coached.

"We could do photography and all kinds of commercial art. There's space for a lot of people."

"Yes, true."

"Documentation is something businesses need for insurance."

"They do," said Manny.

"There must be a ton of books out there on how to start a business."

"Okay, good. Now stop. It's time to list the potentials."

"I might make a decent living."

"We got that one."

"Actually, I started out with *we* might make a decent living."

"Right."

"We might be able to build up this business into something really big."

"Got it."

"It will be fun work, fulfilling work."

"For sure."

"I will learn a lot."

"Check."

"It might enable me—us—to have a more interesting lifestyle."

"Yes."

"We might do something very valuable for our customers."

"Okay, great. Now what are your concerns? And for this part, when you answer, put everything into a phrase that starts with, 'In what ways might we.' For example, 'In what ways might we reduce the risk?'"

Jack fell into it and came up with seven more concerns:

> In what ways might we avoid the most
> common mistakes of new businesses?
> In what ways might we avoid an
> embarrassing failure?

> In what ways might we speed up the cleanup
>   of the studio?
> In what ways might we get some cash to fund
>   equipment and general start-up costs of
>   this JackNewCo?
> In what ways might we generate cash?
> In what ways might we find customers?
> In what ways might we get Molly back to Chicago?

Manny was writing furiously, keeping up with the concerns. When he had caught up, he reviewed the list.

"So, the drill now is to think of answers to these concerns," said Manny.

"But I don't know the answers to these concerns."

"But you might have some ideas, right?" encouraged Manny. "I think you have some ideas, Jack. You always have some ideas." Manny looked at the list. "'Avoid the most common mistakes of new businesses'—try that one."

"Doesn't the government have some sort of thing? I saw a commercial on TV once."

"You might be thinking of SCORE. SCORE is a nonprofit business advice group. They have counselors. They work with the SBA—Small Business Administration—but they are not actually a government agency. They're a good resource. If you sign on to the Web here in Geek's, I'll bet you can find out all you want to know about SCORE here in Chicago."

Jack spun a monitor around and did just that. He found the SCORE Web site and saw that there were three offices in the Chicago area, one on West Madison in the Loop that he could walk to in about fifteen minutes. Jack printed out the address.

"Feeling better about avoiding common mistakes?" asked Manny.

"A bit."

"Good. Now, let's look at this 'embarrassing failure' thing."

"We can skip that one—we've already addressed it," said Jack.

"True, we've reduced risk and found you a resource for advice, but this gets to the emotional side of it, doesn't it?"

"Yes."

"So let me ask you a question. Do you plan to give this everything you've got?"

"I do plan just that."

"Think about it again. What might hold you back from trying as hard as you can to make this work?"

"What might hold me back . . . fear, I suppose."

"So fear of failure, causing you to hold back, which might actually contribute to . . ."

"Failure."

"And if you were able to face that fear and then go after this with all you've got, then what might happen?"

"I might succeed."

"You might. And you might not. What if you try as hard as you can and still fail?"

"I guess I would just fail."

"And you wouldn't walk around saying to yourself, 'If only I'd tried harder.'"

"Right, I wouldn't. Actually, though, I might. I don't know."

"Does failure with your head held high make you any less of a person? Is that something to be embarrassed about?"

"No."

"Is a learning experience—given you're not in jail or physically harmed—ever a total failure?"

"I guess not."

"Have we addressed this concern then?"

"Yes. For now anyway."

"Jack, I know this sounds like Norman Vincent Peale stuff, but a positive attitude about this is key. I'm not saying you won't have doubts or worries. An entrepreneur lives in a constant state of worry—that's reality. But you have to learn to work with it and just keep going. You wouldn't be human if you didn't have worry and fear. I hope when the going gets tough, you'll have this 'way of thinking' to fall back onto. It will help you keep going when things seem impossible or out of control. Problem solving, creativity, decision making—whatever you want to call it—is done better when you have a resolute motive. Let me ask you a question. Do you really care about this idea, this new business idea?"

> AN ENTREPRENEUR LIVES IN A CONSTANT STATE OF WORRY—THAT'S REALITY. BUT YOU HAVE TO LEARN TO WORK WITH IT AND JUST KEEP GOING.

"I do—for certain."

"The more you care, the more passion you have in your heart for it, the better your chances are."

"Okay, I hear you."

"So have we addressed your fears?"

"My biggest fear is I'll accumulate a lot of debt and the business will fail."

"So . . ." Manny prompted.

"So maybe I make a rule that I don't incur debt until I know I have income to cover it."

"That would reduce risk—good. Let's take another. We've already talked about cleaning up the studio . . . Uh-oh, here's a big one—'funding.'"

"It's a big one all right," said Jack, suddenly down again.

"Do you have any ideas on raising money?"

"I really don't."

"Well, you might raise some cash selling off all that trash in the back."

"That's a firm *maybe*."

"Can you raise any seed money from your family?" asked Manny.

"No, nobody in my family really has any money."

"I can relate. Okay, let's talk about this. Thing is, right this minute, you don't need cash. I mean, it would be helpful to set up shop and make stationery and buy lunches and stuff like that, but you're not planning to set up a computer network, a photo lab on-site, and a studio with eight-by-ten format cameras—I mean, not day one, right?"

"Right. It will take some time before we're even ready to do that sort of thing."

"I'll tell you right now you'll never get a loan without showing somebody you are already in business and already generating revenues."

"As usual, only those who really don't need a loan can get one."

"Ironic, isn't it? But it's understandable—would you loan money to somebody who doesn't look like they are in a position to make any? How would you ever get your loan back? What you need to do, Jack, is generate some cash by selling services."

"How do you mean?"

"You need to find work that will bring in enough cash to start funding the company. In the first phase of your business, you are the bank. A loan becomes possible when a banker, or an angel investor, can look at your business idea, your model, and your cash flow and see that with a little more cash you could make even more. If it looks like what you need money for is growing an existing business, the money's much easier to get. Betting on a brand-new venture is a lot tougher of a sell to an investor. Unless you have some heavy credentials, like an MBA from Harvard, or an incredible reputation, you really have to prove your worth," explained Manny.

"I see all that. I mean, it makes sense. What's tough, though, to be honest, is I'm just scraping by. I can't stop work at all the part-time jobs until I can make enough at JackNewCo," said Jack. "That's my dilemma."

"Do you have any assets at all?" asked Manny.

"I have a few cameras, but I need to keep those."

"Anything else?"

"I have a broken-down car."

"Really? What kind? What's wrong with it?"

"It's an '82 Honda Civic."

"What model?"

"A hatchback with a four-speed standard shift. The transmission is shot. And it's got some kind of problem with the gas pump. And the electrical system is skitzy."

"Where is it?"

"Back behind my apartment."

"How about if I buy it from you for five hundred dollars?"

"Really? Why would you do that?"

"I'd buy it because I have a cousin, Angel, on the west side that turns over cars. He buys clunkers like yours and gets them working; then he sells them. I should probably look at Blue Book value, but I'm going to guess it's just a little less than five hundred dollars."

Jack thought about the offer for a minute. He hadn't used the car in months. Even if he had the dough to fix it himself, he had the sense his old car was in need of constant repair. Once fixed, it would be fine for a bit but would break down again. Then there was the insurance, which he had allowed to lapse. *The car is a rolling time bomb for me*, he thought. Five hundred dollars was a decent offer.

"So I'll sell you the car," he agreed.

"Great, I'll tell Angel, and we'll arrange to pick it up. So, let me pay you." Manny whipped out a checkbook and wrote out a check for $500. He tore it off and handed it to Jack. "Things happening too fast for you?"

"Yes!" Jack said, taking the check. And he did what he normally did with money or a check—he folded it up as small as he could and put it in the little key pocket of his jeans. He wrote down a note that he'd need to get all the stuff out of the car and find the deed and such to sign the car over to Manny.

"That should hold the wolves from the door and get you started with that mess back there. The thing you need to focus on now, with regard to money, is getting some paying work." Manny looked down at the list. "'In what ways might we find customers?' That's such a big topic that it should be a separate discussion. Obviously, you'll need to come up with a marketing approach. Your call with Tony Cooper is a beginning. Once you're through that meeting, let's talk again about what you should do in marketing."

"Why are you doing this?" Jack suddenly asked. As much as he didn't want to look this gift horse in the mouth, he had to know. After all, Manny barely knew him, he wasn't family, and he had no reason to be so nice.

Manny didn't seem surprised by the question; in fact, he seemed to be expecting it. "It's a long story."

"So, give me a synopsis."

Manny sat back in his seat and looked at Jack for a moment. "So, what I'm going to tell you is just between us, right?"

"Agreed."

"And I'm going to ask you—just for this conversation—to open your mind up to the possibility that very strange things happen sometimes, and that you just have to go with them." Manny looked at Jack for confirmation.

"Okay."

"So, here's the story. I was in Texas about twenty-five years ago. It was late summer. I'd done some farm work for my great-uncle, he'd paid me, and I was hitchhiking my way back to Chicago—this was back when you could still do that. I was walking up the highway late at night, and a bunch of rednecks pulled up and started harassing me. I ran into the fields, but they came after me in the truck, caught me, and gave me a beating. I came to a few hours later and managed to crawl back to the road. I was hurting pretty bad, bleeding from my head and nose. My insides hurt so bad I was thinking I might die right there."

"Whoa, how'd you get out of that mess?"

"Well, here's where the story starts sounding like a fairy tale. I was out there at the crossroads, passing in and out of consciousness. I was praying for help. Then I was dreaming, and my mother showed up in the dream. And you know, I barely remember my mother, but when she popped into this dream, I remembered her face, and it was so great to see her again. You probably think this is crazy . . ."

"No, not so crazy," said Jack quietly.

"Well, she talked to me. I could see the two of us sitting at a café—we were having coffee together. She told me I was going to live—and that I was going to be very successful in the future. She had something to ask me. It's hard to put into words, because it was all without words, but she asked me to use my success to help people. And not everybody-all-the-time like a priest or something, but more like an artist who would ignite the spark in people. And it was all that vague and all that specific. I knew what she was asking—and I swear it was asking; it wasn't telling. And I agreed to do this thing."

"That's incredible," said Jack.

"Yes. You probably think I'm really full of it," said Manny, "but because of this, ever since, I look for people . . . like you, for situations where I can make a difference."

"So what happened?"

"Well, I woke up in a hospital with IVs coming out of my arm. I'd had surgery. I'd had internal bleeding, and the doctor said it was a miracle I'd lasted so long out on the road. Some old cowboy saw me—he picked me up and brought me in. Turned out he was a real good guy, a simple guy."

"When I got let out, he took me into his home. He lived alone and ran a small horse ranch and boarded horses for rich folks and such. All over his ranch you saw how everything he did, he put a bit of himself into it. I mean, every little thing—fence posts he made, barbed wire, water tanks he made from old train cars, special straps and harnesses he used when training his horses. He was always looking for ways to do every little thing a bit better or different. He was always exploring, tinkering. He never got frustrated when something didn't work; he just kept on trying. He wasn't a big talker, but what I learned from his actions was how great life could be if you have a curious mind. And his curiosity was made more powerful by this simple quality of kindness and this incredible patience with things—allowing things to grow, evolve."

"What an experience," said Jack. "How long were you there?"

"A couple of months. Oh, and I forgot to mention, he taught me how to ride horses. I'd rode horses at my uncle's, but the cowboy, his name was Ed, really taught me a lot about technique, and he put me on the road to becoming a real horseman," said Manny.

"So do you think God gave you that vision of your mother and put that old cowboy—Ed—onto a rescue mission?" asked Jack.

"Yes, I do. Do you think I'm crazy?"

"No, no, I'm sort of struck by how you are to me right now what that old cowboy was to you."

The table went quiet for a minute. Then Manny said, "Maybe so, and what you'll figure out is that you're going to be that way for somebody else down the road."

"Hard to imagine me being in a position to really help somebody."

"Believe it. And so now that we've gone completely woo here, let's get back to the task at hand," said Manny, looking at the list. "What's our last concern?"

"How might we get Molly back to town."

Manny squinted his eyes and looked at Jack for a moment. Manny sat back in the booth.

"So where is Molly?"

"She's up in Milwaukee."

"Has she called?"

"No, I talked to her just before she left. I don't have her number up there, but she said she'd be back on Monday."

"Man, you really are love struck, aren't you? The thunderbolt!" Manny paused and said, "She'll be back soon. In the meantime, go find some business. I'm gonna go now, Jack—I've got to sit down with these pictures again and see if anything pops out at me. How about if I swing by your place, say Tuesday morning, and pick up the car?"

"That'd be fine. Come by at nine. Thanks, Manny—really. Thanks for the checks."

"Hey, thank you. These are great pictures, and Angel's going to make money on your old clunker, so it's just business."

"Not just business, no."

"Well, no, not just business, but it's true—Angel is looking for jalopies, and if I can help you with that and him with that, then no harm, no foul."

"Just thanks again."

"Don't mention it. Now, a parting shot for you. Write down a plan for your business. Start off by listing these three things: Assistors, Resistors, and Resources. ARR is going to inform your planning. People often forget that a good plan not only leverages the people and things that can help you but also addresses resistance. As always, you'll make a list, and as usual, don't judge as you make the list; just list as many ARRs as you can. When you get done with that, use those lists and our PPCO stuff to create an action plan with specific steps to get your business going. It will be a different plan if you do ARR first, so don't skip it, okay?"

Jack agreed; then he and Manny talked a few more minutes before Manny got up to go. Jack gave him an awkward hug.

Watching him walk out, Jack thought, *This guy is like a guardian angel in the flesh.*

8: TONY, TONY, TONY

Where Jack makes a very specific plan

Jack enters step six of CPS, Action Planning. He proceeds with his new business idea by creating a plan and taking action on his to-do list. He also reviews his Assistors, Resistors, and Resources. Assistors are people who can help make your idea a reality or a success, Resistors are those people or things who can hinder your progress, and Resources are any means that can move you forward.

Meanwhile, Jack's intuition is telling him something might be wrong with Molly. Intuition is a calculation done in your brain that takes into account everything you know. When a thought continues to nag at us, it's usually a problem or challenge we should consider putting into the CPS process.

Tony Cooper—the quintessential driven man. He'd worked unceasingly building his hair salon business for fifteen years, and it was an unqualified success. A busy salon on North Clark Street, T. Cooper's Hair Designs was frequented by a Who's Who of Chicago professionals and celebrities. Also a teacher of hairdressers, Tony was much in demand for product demonstrations and fashion shows. His passion was fashion—he loved everything about it.

Friday is a nutty day, Tony was thinking to himself. Wall-to-wall customers. He might cut fifteen heads before the day was over. Still, it was fun—he wouldn't have it any other way. He had tried to cut back, but his customers wouldn't be pushed off onto another cutter, even though he had excellent people working for him.

It was only about 2:30 p.m., but the day was wearing him down already. And now here was Jenna telling him he had a call. He had about three minutes before his next head was out of shampoo, so he took the call.

"Tony Cooper."

"Tony, this is Jack Huber. Cheryl said I should give you a call. I'm a photographer, and I had this idea of doing photo shoots for hairdressers—you know, to document their best work."

"Really? I'm sort of busy right now, but, briefly, tell me more."

"Well, what I had in mind was for me to come into the salon, maybe on your day off. You could arrange for one or more of your customers to come in and get cut, and I'd take some pictures in front of a portable backdrop."

"Hmm. I've always wanted to have a bit more control over photographs. I get some here and there, but it's always sort of unpredictable. So I like the idea. How much it would cost?"

"I'd charge you my day rate and expenses. Prints are extra."

"Okay, what's the day rate?"

Jack took a deep breath. He mentally added a few more dollars to his old day rate.

"Four hundred, twenty-five dollars," said Jack.

"That's all?" Tony asked frankly. Now he was more than curious.

"Well, I'm just getting started with this."

"Do you have any references I can call?"

"I do, but not in fashion photography."

"Ewww, that's sort of a red flag. You've got me worried now. Listen, we're off on Mondays—why don't you come in here and let's talk it over. Thing is, I do need photographs. I'd like to have more of a formal portfolio of the work I've done. I can use them here in the shop, and there are industry publications I could send them to. But if I go to all the trouble to arrange for models and makeup and all that stuff, I want to make sure we get something we can use."

"I can get you some good shots. What time Monday?"

"Come in first thing, 8:00 a.m."

"Okay, I'll see you then."

After Tony hung up, Jack put down the receiver and took a deep breath. He thought he'd had it at first, then he thought he'd lost it, and it ended up about halfway—he had neither got it nor lost it. And getting this job had taken on a greater importance since he was really starting a business. Cash flow and real customers were what he needed to prove he was viable. And to cover expenses. He saw it now as the key to everything. With customers and cash coming in, he could fund things like buying equipment and improving the studio space. The studio would be just a burden unless he could start using the space and make it pay. Well, Tony had sounded encouraging. If he could get Tony to try him out, he was sure he could deliver.

He'd be in business.

Jack wrote in his notebook a reminder to do some research on the proper lighting set-up for headshots. He'd need to borrow some real lighting equipment.

This is a great possibility, he thought. He'd have to call Cheryl over the weekend and thank her. Plus, maybe she'd have some ideas on how best to close the deal with Tony. And he'd have to talk to Rob about borrowing a lighting kit.

Rob—now there was a friend he hadn't spent much time with the last couple of months. Jack called Rob and asked himself over to visit on Sunday. Rob gave him some grief about being a meal-mooching bachelor, but Jack knew it was just friendly banter. He asked Rob if he could run down the phone number of the guy with that lighting kit, and Rob said that he would.

The weekend passed by quickly. Sandy had to go out of town, so Jack got more hours tending bar. Fine, he needed the money, and he needed to stay busy so he wouldn't think about Molly. He worked at SMASH Friday and Saturday night, and then he opened the tennis club and worked till 2:00 p.m. on Sunday. He fell asleep on the train ride coming back into the city, and it was just enough rest to keep him going. But by the time he headed over to Rob and Cheryl's on Sunday night, he was exhausted.

As he approached their apartment, his thoughts turned once again to Molly. The weekend of work had kept his mind elsewhere, and it did feel good to be pocketing more cash than usual. But at the moment, he found himself really missing her, even though it felt a bit obsessive. He wished he'd been alert enough when she called to ask her more questions. Jack didn't think of himself as an intuitive person, but he just had this feeling that something was wrong. She had taken such pains to escape her father's sphere of influence and keep her location a secret, so why go back now? Maybe she was checking in on Bridgette on the "down low."

Rob and Cheryl greeted him at the door. Cheryl was making decent money working for Tony Cooper. She'd just graduated to full-time hairdresser after a rather long apprenticeship, and she was enjoying the first financial and professional success of her life. Jack could see the difference it made for her. She was more confident, less worried, and she even held herself differently when she walked. It's interesting how just holding your head up can make a difference in how people see you. Tonight, Jack could tell that Cheryl felt good about herself. She sparkled.

She made some coffee while Jack and Rob sat in the living room, talking and listening to some music. When Cheryl joined them, Jack gave them both the update on his life. He was a bit amazed himself at what had gone on in the last few weeks. He told them about meeting Manny and the work he'd done for him and then about meeting Molly and all that he'd learned from her. He didn't say that he'd fallen in love with her. He didn't have to.

"When are we going to meet her?" asked Cheryl.

"If it were up to me, you'd be meeting her now," said Jack.

"She's back tomorrow, right?" Rob questioned.

"That's the rumor."

"When she gets back, let's all go out and see a movie. You two can come over here first, we'll have some snacks, and then we'll take the train over to town," said Cheryl.

"Sounds like a plan," said Jack.

"Speaking of plans, what are you thinking of pitching Tony Cooper Monday morning?" Cheryl asked, curious.

"Well, like we talked about on the phone, I'm offering to do shots of his best coiffures."

"First tip, do not use that word *coiffures*. I know you think it's cute, but he'll think you're spoofing him. Rob is the one who uses that word."

"Right, okay—no coifs," Jack said, looking sideways at Rob.

"I spoke to Tony after you got off the phone with him on Friday. He asked about you. He wants to do it, but he's not sure he wants to bet on a rookie," said Cheryl.

"Yeah, I suspected that would be the key issue," said Jack.

"So, how are you going to deal with that?"

"I don't know exactly. I can give him Manny as a reference, but the work I did for him was so unfashiony."

"It won't hurt to give him a reference, but it won't put you over," said Cheryl.

"Tell me more about him then."

"Well, he works like a madman. I don't know how his wife deals with it. He's hyper. Drinks a lot of coffee. And he's impatient when he's frazzled. He won't be on edge when you see him Monday morning, though. He'll be more relaxed because the shop isn't open. And did I say that the guy can cut hair? He's incredible—very skilled—and he's one of the few I've seen at that level who is really good when he's talking about it, teaching it. I've learned so much from him."

"Interesting guy, huh? So what is he interested in besides, you know, hair?"

Cheryl was a font of knowledge about Tony. "Everything. He never has any trouble talking to the customers because whatever they do fascinates him. He's really into the stock market—and car racing. What else? Oh, yeah, he has this idea about a new kind of salon, one that would be more man-oriented. He thinks men, especially older men who grew up getting their hair cut in barber shops, aren't really all that comfortable in a mixed-sex salon. His idea is to do a men's-only thing and really do it up like a kind of super barber shop—have cigars and sports, manly stuff like that."

"Man, that's a great idea. My father would have loved that! Of course, I couldn't afford it," said Jack.

"I keep thinking it'll be like in the *Godfather*, you know, some guy will draw the blinds and you'll get popped just sitting in the chair," said Rob.

"Where did that come from?" asked Jack.

"When you start talking about an old-fashioned barber shop, that's what comes to mind," said Rob.

Cheryl rolled her eyes and shook her head. "Anyway, Tony's been researching it. He just might do it one of these days, knowing him. He's kind of a bold guy—tries things."

"Bold guy, huh?" Jack asked. "I think my approach with Tony is to be flat out honest. If I downplay the risk, he'll think I'm trying to put one over on him."

"That's good. He'll like that, I think."

They had a pleasant evening. After they watched a movie together, Jack bowed out.

Walking home, he decided to pop into an Irish pub. As he sat alone at the bar, he paged through the notes in his sketchbook, turning his attention to the ideas he'd discussed with Manny last Friday. The one that stood out was the new studio and that huge mess to clean up. Reading the notes on the studio got his mind into a certain kind of zone. It wasn't just being excited about the possibilities. It was more than that. What he felt was a conviction that the future was almost a foregone conclusion—all he had to do was execute to make it happen. This was a new feeling for Jack. It was confidence.

Jack's impulse was just to start doing things. But then he remembered the conversation he'd had with Manny about structured thinking. What would Manny do right now? It came to him immediately: make a list.

But a list of what? Reading his notes from the conversation at Geek's with Manny, he recalled Manny's parting shot: Assistors, Resistors, and Resources. He started making that list and really got into it. Ideas occurred to him—people who had offered to help, friends with equipment he could borrow, old employers he might be able to sell some services, the list went on. Now, to do the plan. What is an action plan anyway? It occurred to him that it's really just a better way to make a good old-fashioned to-do list. He made the list at the bar and moved things around into a more logical order. He had a few more ideas on just how to go about some things—breaking down the ideas into more detail. What he noticed is that his plan was a lot more complete than any plan he'd ever done. It wasn't just a list of things to do, which always seemed kind of boring and dreadful when he'd done them in the past. No, this wasn't something he *must* do; it was something he was excited and confident about doing.

> IDEAS OCCURRED TO HIM—PEOPLE WHO HAD OFFERED TO HELP, FRIENDS WITH EQUIPMENT HE COULD BORROW, OLD EMPLOYERS HE MIGHT BE ABLE TO SELL SOME SERVICES, THE LIST WENT ON.

Reviewing his notes, it struck him as funny that he was calling and thinking of the business as JackNewCo. *We need a better name than that,* he thought. *After all, it's not just me. And we need a logo too.*

He sketched a couple of ideas for logos. What would they call the company? Huber-Dunne? That sounded like a law firm! What could you do with the initials "HD"? On the page, they looked like two strong letters. HD could stand for "Hard Driven." What else? He free-associated for a few minutes on what HD could mean: Hard Driven, Heavenly Direction . . . what else?

Maybe High Definition. He liked the sound of that. High Definition Inc. Maybe.

He put his sketchbook aside for a moment, making a mental note to ask Manny what to do when brainstorming just went into utter goofiness. He'd have to think some more about the name. High Definition, Inc.

What would Molly think?

"She'll be back tomorrow," he mumbled out loud. *Have faith*, he thought to himself. *Have faith*.

Pulling himself together, he picked up his notebook again. He stared at his to-do list—maybe not perfect, but a good start, a list he could work with. *They'd need help with finances in general*, he thought. He was really concerned that he and Molly would mess everything up if they didn't get wise really fast to business legalities and taxes. Books? Who would keep the books? Jack knew next to nothing about accounting. So he added a line item in the to-do list for bookkeeping, not sure how he would accomplish that.

All in all, a good plan—and there was nothing he could do right this minute, late Sunday night. Sipping his Guinness, he examined his feeling of excitement about the plan. An image of a roller coaster came to mind. This new business idea was a ride, with ups and downs and surprises. You know ahead of time that a roller-coaster ride will be scary, but you get on anyway for the fun of it. You know there are safety measures built in.

What could he do to improve his chances for success?

He needed safety measures. He needed help. *I'm a novice at business*, he thought. *If I don't get help, I'll fail.* Jack looked again at his plan, and he added these items:

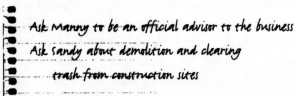

Ask Manny to be an official advisor to the business

Ask Sandy about demolition and clearing trash from construction sites

Manny probably knew how to get started with bookkeeping, and Jack knew he'd be willing to advise. Sandy might be able to advise him on clearing out the studio—given his experience in construction and re-habbing.

Enough of this, Jack thought, *it's Sunday night, and I'm exhausted.*

Walking on Milwaukee Avenue, toward his neighborhood, he thought about the plan in his sketchbook. He thought about who else might help him become successful. Hearing his own footsteps, Jack let his mind wander in a beat with them—Manny, Manny's mother, his own father, Cheryl, Rob, Molly, Tony, the meeting Monday morning. Tomorrow morning!

Lost in the rhythms of his thoughts, he didn't see anything unusual as he rounded the corner near his apartment. Suddenly, he was grabbed from behind, and before he could blink, somebody had a choke hold on him and had twisted his arm behind his back. Jack struggled to breathe.

A man spoke into his ear. "This is a warning, compadre. You're involved with a lady whose family wants no part of you, wants you gone. Molly Dunne's family. Hear this—you and her are over, it's over, bro. She's gone back to her family, and she doesn't want to hear from you any-more. Don't call her. Don't return her calls. And no going to the cops. If you do, you'll wind up dead. We know where you live. I'm supposed to kill you now, but I got a soft heart. I'm only going to hurt you real bad."

Jack's arm was released, and the choke hold quit. He thought for a moment they were letting him go. He was about to turn around when he got hit in the back of the head. He fell to his knees, and someone pushed him down. Then came the kicking. When they had thoroughly worked him over, he was slipping into unconsciousness. He opened his eyes and was blinded by the flash of a camera.

9: FACE DOWN, JUST LIKE ELVIS

Where Jack hits pay dirt and is suddenly faced with an entirely different problem

In spite of being attacked and delayed, Jack keeps his appointment with Tony Cooper. This display of integrity and courage is a part of creative effectiveness. By doing what he said he would do, Jack builds trust with Tony. He also builds something important in himself—a commitment to carrying out his plan and making it work. Keeping your word in spite of difficulties builds a good foundation for creative thinking. Creativity and good ideas happen spontaneously when a person has an open and uncluttered mind.

Jack, in essence, completes the CPS process for the challenge he started in Chapter One. He's into action on his action plan (i.e., his to-do list) for starting his business, and he's already begun to see results as he now has both a studio space and a key customer. He'll need to continue to execute his action plan, though he may even change the plan as circumstances dictate. He has moved through all six steps of CPS; his use of the method is complete. In this chapter, he then begins to use CPS in a more organic way on a whole new challenge.

When he woke up, he was face down in the gutter. He had no idea how long he'd been there, but it was still dark outside. His first reaction was simply to get up, but as he lifted his head and upper body, he felt an excruciating pain from his skull all the way down his spine to the base of his back. His arms buckled, and he crumbled back onto the street.

He remained there, helpless, for some time. Slowly his mind cleared, and the sounds of the street and passersby became more real to him and less like some drug-addled dream. He remembered the mugging now, at least the beginning of it. After the blow to the back of his head, they'd taken turns kicking him all over his body. There must have been two or three of them. Right now it seemed like he could feel those kicks everywhere, especially his ribs. He moved his right arm experimentally—no pain there. Then his left arm. Then his feet. Next, he bent one knee, then the other. Good news—he wasn't paralyzed. He was going to have to try to get up again. He moved his head around on his neck in micro movements, testing to see where the pain would begin. He could move it a little bit without that shooting pain. *If I can just not move my head and neck getting up, I can do it,* he thought. He planned his move carefully, and after taking some deep breaths to get him fortified for the effort, he pushed himself up on his hands, managing to get himself on his feet. His head throbbed as if he were being hit in the head with a sledgehammer.

He backed up slowly to the wall of a building. Once he had the wall to lean on, he felt his pockets. They'd stolen all his cash and his wallet. Then he remembered the threat, and he wondered why they'd stolen anything if the purpose of the beating was to warn him off Molly. He steadied himself against the wall some more, holding still until the throbbing subsided somewhat. *How am I going to walk home like this?* he thought. He'd have to try.

He started walking, slowly, like a drunk, down the street. He'd made it about a half a block—he was almost home—when the cop car pulled over.

"Looks like we tied one on tonight, young fella," said one of the cops.

"No, I'm fine," said Jack, but as he said it, he realized he sounded drunk. So he tried to be more careful with how he spoke. "Somebody hit me coming round the corner back there." Jack was having trouble speaking.

"Right. Well it does look like you're bleeding from the back of your head. You must have hurt yourself when you passed out."

"Didn't pass out, got hit," said Jack.

"Whatever, we're taking you off the street, for your own good, kid."

With that, the two cops grabbed him by his arms and took him toward the police cruiser. They moved too quickly, and Jack cried out, twisting away from them in his pain. The cops interpreted it as resistance.

"Hey, no need to get rough. We can give it back, you know," one warned.

They both took turns giving him a hard shoulder on each side. Jack felt like a tackling dummy. They jerked on his arms. They didn't hit him, but it was clear they were sending him a message not to resist. The pain reached an excruciating pitch. His knees buckled, and he passed out.

This time he came to lying on the backseat of the cruiser, but again, face down. He moaned.

"We better take him by the emergency room to get his head bandaged," one cop was saying.

"Naw, I think we have a good actor here. It's just a scratch—we can dress it at the station."

The ride downtown was a blur to Jack. He passed out again, then woke up once more, but the motion of the car made him sick to his stomach. He vomited onto the floor. The cops cursed. When they got to the station, they literally dragged him in, and the next few minutes were another blur, Jack passing out again somewhere along the way.

He woke up in a holding cell, alone, looking up at the ceiling. Somebody had put a crude dressing on the back of his head—it was held in place by a flimsy strip of gauze wrapped around his head. Jack had completely lost track of time. He rested there, trying to review again what had happened. He'd been mugged, that much he knew. He'd been given a warning. He also realized in a moment of clarity that Molly was probably in trouble. In that instant, his body was shot through with a natural adrenaline rush. He had to do something—and now.

His head still hurt, but he felt good enough to sit up on the steel ledge where he had been lying. *If this wasn't the worst possible luck,* he thought. *I'm busted. I've lost my cash. I'm wounded, might even have a concussion—or worse. I don't even have my ID.*

He looked around for a cop and realized he must be in a row of cells because he could hear, but not see, some activity around him. With some effort, he yelled out, "Hey! I need to talk to somebody!"

This was heralded with a chorus of hoots and jeers: "Hey, so do I," "Somebody stole my shoes," and worse. The effort and the catcalls made Jack's head hurt again. He felt the back of his head and panicked when he saw thick, congealed blood on his fingers.

"I'm hurt! I need to see a doctor," Jack yelled into the hallway.

He tried this again and again for what seemed like an hour. It was exhausting.

Finally, a cop came around and looked in on him. "That you making all the noise back here?"

"Please—I need a doctor. I'm bleeding from the back of my head." Jack was glad he could speak clearly again. "I don't even know why I'm here."

"You got picked up drunk on the street."

"Listen, I was mugged—isn't that obvious? If I fell down drunk, don't you think it would be my face bleeding? I got hit in the back of the head. I was threatened. They stole my cash and my wallet, and I'm the one locked up?"

"What I hear, you're lucky they don't charge you with resisting arrest."

"Resisting arrest? You've got to be kidding. This is a nightmare. I didn't resist, I was just trying to protect myself."

"Save it for the judge."

"I get to make a phone call, don't I?"

"Yeah, you do. You ready to do that now? You were in no shape to do that when you came in."

"Yeah, I'm ready."

"Okay, come with me."

The guard unlocked the cell and led Jack to an area at the end of the row of cells. Jack got a look at his company in the other holding cells. Most of the other cells held several people, and this was not a good-looking group. The place reeked of urine. Jack was grateful, at least, for the fact he hadn't been locked up with the others. The cop put him in front of a phone and a chair, and Jack took a deep breath. Who to call? He had no family in the city. He could call Rob, but Rob wouldn't know what to do. Whoever came would need money to bail him out.

Manny.

Jack dug into the pockets of his jeans, and yes, it was still there. He'd been carrying around Manny's card since the day he'd gotten it. This was embarrassing. Fact was, he didn't have anyone else to call. He dialed the number.

"Manny, sorry to get you up this late."

"Jack?"

"Yeah, it's Jack."

"Why are you calling this time of night?" Manny asked, sounding puzzled—and tired.

"I'm in jail."

"What happened?" Manny's tone changed, concerned now.

"I got mugged over near my place, and the cops picked me up. They thought I was drunk. I've got a cut and a big bump on the back of my head, and I need to see a doctor." Jack's voice broke with the effort to get all this out.

"Where are you?" Manny's voice took on a tone of urgency.

Jack asked the cop, "Hey, where am I?"

"District Two."

"You hear that?" asked Jack.

"District Two," repeated Manny. "Okay, hold tight—I'll be over there in two shakes. And listen, Jack. Don't worry. If you're clean, this is really no problem. Did they give you a breathalyzer?"

"No, they just assumed I was drunk."

"Good, okay. I'll be right over. Just relax."

"Okay," Jack said, clearing the call with his finger on the switch hook.

The cop wasn't paying much attention; he could make another call.

Jack called his own phone number to check messages. This was something he almost never did—nobody called him—but he dialed himself up and entered the security code.

There were two messages on his machine, both from Molly. One was a "just called to see how you're doing" from early Sunday evening. The next one, left around midnight, was pretty freaky.

"Jack, listen—I won't be coming back to Chicago tomorrow. In fact, I won't be coming back at all. It's over with us, and I don't want to see you anymore. I know this is a surprise, but there are things about me you don't know. I guess you'll have to go back to your comfort from the south. Don't try to find me. Bye."

Now he was beside himself. First of all, he didn't believe the message. The tone was all wrong, and it just wasn't the way she talked. In a sense, it wasn't her. It was her voice, just not her style. *Molly wouldn't dump me like this,* he thought. *If she was going to dump me, it would be to my face.* And besides, what had he been warned for if this was all her idea?

So what was going on? He looked at the clock on the wall. It was 4:30 in the morning. He was supposed to meet with Tony Cooper in less than four hours. Jack felt a wave of nausea as his anxieties escalated. He dry heaved. His head throbbed. He felt a trickle of cold sweat running from his armpits down his sides.

"Help me," he said out loud with frustrated intensity.

The cop looked up and met Jack's eyes. "All right, time's up. Let's go back."

Jack was light-headed. The message from Molly put him into a zone of intense fear. His hands were shaking involuntarily. Back in the cell, he lay down and tried to calm himself, but his mind was racing. He closed his eyes, and gradually the fear and adrenaline buzz wore off. He went into a sort of neverland of half sleep, half hallucination. There was a kaleidoscope of images and colors, moving too fast for his liking. He had the sense he was flying, and it was so uncomfortable to be moving that fast in the air that it woke him.

He heard the doors clang at the far end of the hall and then voices approaching, footsteps moving quickly. They stopped at his cell. It was Manny.

"Here he is, Mr. Gibran, safe and sound. We were just holding him until he sobered up—there's no vagrancy charge."

"I should say not. This man has a home address and gainful employment; he's not living on the streets. He's the victim of a crime, and he needs medical care. Why wasn't he taken to the emergency room?" Manny was borderline incensed. He was under control, but it was clear he was angry.

"I can't say, Mr. Gibran. I wasn't the arresting officer."

Manny focused on Jack now. "Jack, are you all right? Can you stand up?"

"Yeah, I still feel a little woozy, but I'm better than I was a few hours ago."

"All right, let's go."

Manny took Jack's arm and supported him as they walked out of District Two. Manny had already taken care of the paperwork. Jack learned later that Manny had woken up one of the top defense attorneys in the city, a guy with connections to the mayor. The way had been quickly cleared for Jack's release.

By a stroke of good luck, the emergency room at Rush Presbyterian wasn't having one of its usual busy mornings, and Jack was in and out of the hospital in about two hours. It helped, of course, that Manny agreed to pay any charges. The doctor cleaned up the wound on the back of Jack's head and speculated that Jack had been pistol-whipped. He used a local anesthetic and sewed up the cut with a half a dozen stitches. He put on a secure dressing and gave Jack a tetanus shot and a mild painkiller. But he insisted that Jack get a full-body X-ray. An orthopedist showed up and looked at this X-ray; it was determined that Jack's neck pain was the result of muscular stiffness—no damage to his spine. He did have a couple of cracked ribs, which the orthopedist bandaged up tightly around his torso. When that was done, they sent him on his way.

It was about 7:00 a.m., and the sun was coming up, its yellowish glow showing low on the horizon between the buildings in Chicago's Loop.

"How do you feel?" asked Manny.

"Now that those painkillers are kicking in, not bad, considering. Tired. And hungry. All of a sudden, I'm ravenously hungry."

"Let's get you home."

"I've got to stay up for another couple of hours," said Jack.

"What are you talking about?"

"I've got an appointment with Tony Cooper at his salon at 8:00."

"Call him and cancel."

"No way. I'm okay now. I just need to get some food in me, and some coffee. And I'll clean up a little before I go in to see him," said Jack.

"You are really, really nuts," said Manny. But he said it in a low tone and with respect.

What Manny respected was the resolve—and the instinct. *There's something very smart about not breaking the meeting,* he thought. Manny knew that a first business meeting is a crucial moment in a customer relationship. Canceling, even with a perfect excuse, puts you in a hole you have to crawl out of. First impressions are, indeed, everything. *If he goes in and makes the meeting—with a bandage on his head—he looks like a man who goes to great lengths to keep his appointments, his commitments. Some people would admire that a lot,* thought Manny. He knew he would.

> MANNY KNEW THAT A FIRST BUSINESS MEETING IS A CRUCIAL MOMENT IN A CUSTOMER RELATIONSHIP. CANCELING, EVEN WITH A PERFECT EXCUSE, PUTS YOU IN A HOLE YOU HAVE TO CRAWL OUT OF.

"Let's see if Lou Mitchell's is open," said Manny. "My treat."

Lou's was open. They went in and were ushered to a back booth, where they had a hearty breakfast. Lou Mitchell's, a Chicago landmark, the ultimate diner, with great skillet omelets and coffee made with purified water. Jack wolfed down his omelet.

Nothing like getting beat up and thrown in jail to whip up an appetite, he thought. With the exception of an achy head, sore ribs, and a sore neck, Jack felt okay. He laughed to himself—the painkillers and coffee had him feeling high. He wanted to tell Manny about the threats the muggers had whispered in his ear, about the messages from Molly, but he wasn't sure if he should. It was just too much to lay something like this on him after all he'd already gone out of his way to do.

"Not to speak of the mundane, now that you've survived a murderous assault, but what's your approach going into this meeting?" Manny asked.

"At this point, just getting through it," said Jack.

"Listen, not that I don't admire the guts here, but if you can't hold a conversation, there's not much point in going in."

"I can manage. What I'm thinking is just to say to him, 'Look, I can do this for you. I've done some decent work.' I can show him some of my prior shots and the newspaper work I did last year—I have reprints of those. And I'm going to offer him a guarantee. If he doesn't like my work, he doesn't have to pay for it." The effort to get all this out made Jack breathless.

"Sounds good. Hold off on the guarantee, though, at least until after you've given him a chance to talk about what he wants, what he needs. In fact, probe on his needs—there's more to know there—and then give him some ideas if anything comes to you."

"Right."

Jack's thoughts drifted away from the meeting. What was it about Molly's message that had seemed so not Molly? He'd have to listen again when he got home. He realized that the emotional deal with himself just to get through to Monday was out the window now. Today was when they were going to get started on the business. He had so much to tell her. Now, he couldn't remember a bleaker morning.

"Jack? You okay?" Manny asked.

"I'm . . . fine. Just thinking about this meeting."

"You sure you're all right to go to this meeting?"

Jack hesitated. Maybe because he was partially delirious, or maybe because he felt a little desperate, Jack decided to tell Manny what had happened to him that night.

"Manny, the mugging wasn't a mugging. It was a beating that came with a warning."

Manny's expression showed confusion then surprise. Before Manny could speak, Jack found himself telling Manny all about the new situation, from the threat he'd received to the phone messages from Molly.

After Jack finished, Manny thought for a few moments and then said, "Molly was supposed to be back yesterday, right?"

"Originally, right. But then the crazy phone message changed it to never, which just isn't like her."

"It is very radical a move to abandon her job, Chicago, you." Manny paused to think. "So, who do you think is behind what happened to you tonight?" asked Manny.

Jack spent some time giving Manny the details of what he knew about Molly's history—particularly her father, Brian Dunne.

"So, you think her father is behind all of this?"

"From what Molly has told me, yes, I think he is."

"That's pretty drastic action for a father to take with an adult child, but then again, he sounds mentally unbalanced," Manny said. Noticing Jack's pained expression, he said, "I'm sorry, Jack, here I am exploring the situation already. Are you all right?"

"I'm just afraid something has happened to her, and I feel helpless." Jack looked up at Manny.

"Well, you're not helpless," said Manny. "Jack, we'll figure this out. It may not be as bad as we're making it out to be. Right now, you're exhausted, physically injured, and have an interview in less than an hour. Let's focus on that. Just get through the meeting, and then you can go home and collapse. We'll talk about this again after you're rested. Let's get you over to your apartment."

With his skimpy portfolio in one hand, Jack held the railing tightly as he walked up the steps to the entrance of the salon. Jack had changed his clothes, shaved, and layered on aftershave. When he entered, Tony emerged from a side room, bouncing out to greet him, smiling. He was younger looking than Jack expected. He was dressed plainly enough—baggy black dress pants and a sparkling white shirt. He had a moustache and wore a pair of thick, oversized black glasses with almost square frames.

"Jack? There you are. Looks like you've had an accident or something."

"It would be the 'or something' category—long story," Jack said as cheerfully as he could.

"Nothing serious, I hope."

"No, I'm fine. My neck is a bit stiff."

"You want some coffee or tea?"

"I could go for a coffee big time, thanks."

"We'll get some right away. Let's talk in the back. Follow me."

Tony led the way past a number of salon workstations. The décor of the shop was art deco to the hilt, nicely done. Art prints from the '20s and original fashion ads for hair products of the same era were hung about the shop. In the front windows hung a series of large color photographs in movie-theater-style frames. The photographs were well done, but they contrasted oddly with the style of the shop. *It would be better*, Jack thought, *to have something that fit the deco thing better, something flapper-like, or maybe thirties Hollywood.* Jack had an image of Bogart and Bacall. Lauren Bacall—now there was a woman with beautiful hair.

"Are you a movie fan, Tony?"

"Oh, I love the movies, all kinds. I don't have as much time to get out and see things as I used to though."

"I was just thinking how nice a movie-style poster would look in your front windows."

"Uh, what do you mean exactly?"

"Well, I was thinking of some shots that would have a more old-fashioned color tone, something warmer than what you have in those frames now. Still featuring the hair, but maybe instead of that white seamless modern look, try something with pastels. And then use deco frames."

"Sounds interesting. Sounds colorful."

"But sorry, let me back up. What exactly are you looking for?" By blurting out a spontaneous idea, he'd gotten a bit ahead of his plan to "probe" Tony's needs first. Thankfully, it had gotten things off to a good start, but if Tony hadn't liked the idea, it might have worked against him.

"Like I said on the phone, I need shots for all kinds of things, including those front window frames. Those are customers, by the way, not models."

"Really? They look great," said Jack.

"I have some really good-looking customers! And for hair photos, unlike say, clothes fashion photography, it really doesn't matter if they're five-feet-two or a willowy five-ten—it's only the hair and the face that matter."

"Those are well done. If you don't mind my asking, what's stopping you from just getting more of those done by the same guy?"

"Same gal—Mernisa. She does a really nice job, but she's expensive. She's also booked pretty solid. And I need a boatload of pictures. I've got a push on to get a lot of industry-level PR, and I need good shots of a whole series of things I do. I've been thinking about it since we talked. I'd like to take a whole Monday and just crank through as many shots as possible, bring in a couple of my better people and just line 'em up."

"We could do that," said Jack.

"Okay, so here's the bottom line. You seem like a good guy, but it's clear you are underexperienced in this area. So you could be a great bargain if you work out, or you might be a colossal waste of time and effort, no matter the price. I'm also afraid that, once you get rolling, I'll never see that day rate you quoted again."

"Tony, here's what I can say. You're 100 percent right about the inexperience. I've done only enough work with this kind of lighting to think that I can do it. But it's no secret how it's done. Take a look at this postcard—I did this with one lighting instrument."

"This is a really nice shot. Not a traditional fashion shot though. I mean, you couldn't do a hair shot with that kind of lighting."

"I'll need to perfect a lighting set-up, and I'm likely to do that better after I shoot a couple of test rolls. Then I'll know just how to do the right kind of lighting on hair. As for the money, well, if you're not happy, you don't have to pay. How's that?"

"Actually, it's more the time than the money, Jack."

"Okay. It's a risk for you. But if I work out, I'll end up saving you time because you'll have what you need in a timely way."

"True, but if you don't work out, I waste a day and get nothing."

"How about if I get my hair done here for the rest of my life? Would that compensate you?"

Tony laughed. "I guess it would."

"Okay, and I'll tell all my friends."

"Okay . . . I'll take the risk. We're on," Tony said. "I need the pictures, so yeah, I'll move forward. And you won't ramp up your day rate? Like, how about I get that rate you quoted for six months?"

"Sure, I can live with that," said Jack.

"Let's plan to do two sessions a month for the six months then," said Tony. "For once I'll have everything I need."

Jack was amazed. This was better than he'd even hoped for. He did some math in his head and realized the income from this job would be a great base for the new business. *Actually,* he thought, *this deal makes my business a reality.*

They talked for a time about logistics and what they would try to accomplish in the first shoot. They discussed the look Tony wanted, how many shots, which clothes, and some other details. Tony was excited by the time they shook hands. And as Jack was leaving the salon, he promised to call Tony back in a couple of days to finalize plans.

When Jack closed the door behind him, a wave of exhaustion and nausea rolled over him. He grabbed the railing and walked down the stairs stiffly, carefully. When he reached the bottom step, he took a deep breath. He was glad it had gone well with Tony. Now his only goal was to get home and lie down. Thoughts of Molly returned, and he wished desperately that he could speak with her. Jack walked over to the Jeep and gingerly got in.

"How did it go?" asked Manny anxiously.

"It's a deal," reported Jack.

"Tell me more . . ."

"Well, looks like we'll be shooting here twice a month for a half a year. So that's seven hundred dollars a month from this work."

"All right. That's great! What were we saying the other day about selling services? You've done it! You're in business, Jack." Manny was grinning ear to ear.

"It's true, isn't it? I mean it won't get me a mansion in Evanston, but it's a good start," said Jack.

"Celebrate the success, Jack. You've taken a huge step today." Manny's grin faded as he looked at Jack. "You look like death warmed over though. Let's get you home, and after you've rested, we'll figure out what to do about Molly."

As Manny drove him back to Wicker Park, what remained of Jack's energy seeped out quickly. It was a short ride, but Jack felt like he could barely hold it together. He desperately needed to lie down.

As they pulled up to Jack's apartment, Manny said, "You know, they don't give any medals for what you did this morning, Jack, but if they did, you would get one. The definition of poise is 'grace under pressure.' You showed a lot of it getting through that meeting under the circumstances. If you have as much business sense as you have heart, well, you're going to be very successful some day."

"From your lips to God's ears. But thanks, Manny. Thanks for everything. And good night, I mean good morning. Anyway—later." Jack laughed, weakly and wearily.

Manny walked him to the door. Jack stepped into his apartment alone, closing the door slowly behind him. His elation over the meeting was tempered by worries about his own health and what was going on with Molly. He had a lot to think about, but he couldn't think, not right now. He undressed, taking great care not to jar his head or neck. And then he got slowly into bed, positioning himself to be as pain free as possible. The pillow below his head had never seemed more delicious. Drifting off to sleep, he saw visions of birds flying—big graceful birds, with wide wingspans, flapping steadily, then floating, floating.

10: SOUTHERN RIDDLES

Where Jack begins to explore a new challenge

Recovering at home, Jack begins step two of CPS, Facts and Feelings Exploration. He has skipped step one, creating a wish list and converging, because it's obvious what his wish is: he wants Molly back.

In step two, Jack's exploration results in a messy confusion, which is typical of many real-life problems. He learns to tolerate ambiguity, a creative thinking skill that allows him to minimize the discomfort and assess a situation calmly. Jack asks himself questions, then waits. A time of incubation is important because it allows his subconscious mind to work.

If you want to take advantage of more of your brainpower, pose questions to yourself, think about them for a bit, and then put them mentally aside. Go for a walk or bike ride, do some stretching, window shop. Often when you return to the question, the answer will be there waiting.

Jack woke up at 4:30 that afternoon, feeling groggy and hungry and, overall, a good deal better physically. His head ached where he'd been hit, sensitive to the touch. However, the bump had gone down, and his neck felt looser, more mobile. His bruised ribs did hurt if he tried to bend over or if he twisted his body even a little.

He fixed himself coffee and a peanut butter and jelly sandwich. He was halfway through the sandwich when he realized he was scheduled to work at the tennis club that evening—in half an hour. His heart sank.

He made a call to the tennis club to tell them, at least, that he would be late—very late. The manager listened to Jack's story about the mugging, and while he was sympathetic, at least on the surface, he said that Jack could have called earlier in the day. The man asked Jack if he was really committed to his job at the club, and Jack had to answer truthfully, no. After a pause, the manager said maybe it would be better for everyone to end the relationship. He said Jack needn't come in—they would mail him his last check.

Jack hung up the phone. Ironic that he'd lost the job just as his new business was taking off.

He lay down on the couch. He was sorry he'd lost the job and that he'd let them down, but he also couldn't help feeling relieved—he wouldn't have to make that crazy train trip anymore. Maybe this wasn't a disaster. He only wished it could have been a clean getaway, giving proper notice and all that.

Now he was down to one job. Bartending. But he also had the Tony Cooper business—if he performed that job well, then he could get by without the tennis job. If he got more business, made more sales, he could quit bartending. *That's another challenge,* he thought, *how to get more business?*

What else is going to change? he wondered, his mind drifting to Molly. It was a scary world right now. His girlfriend was, what? Kidnapped? Jack was afraid for Molly's safety, and he was afraid for his own safety.

On hearing the message last night, his first reaction was that it was coerced. But now he wasn't so sure. If she really wanted him gone, all she had to do was say so. He wouldn't like it, but he'd bow out. But why the threat? Why the beating?

He walked over to his phone and played back the messages on the machine. What was it about that last phrase that rang a bell with him? There was clearly a message within the message because it was not something she would normally say—"I guess you'll have to go back to your comfort from the south." *Comfort from the south. Comfort from the south.* He repeated the phrase over and over in his head. Something there, but what? Comfort from the south is like what? Home cooking? Southern hospitality? An old girlfriend? He couldn't think of anything.

> THERE WAS CLEARLY A MESSAGE WITHIN
> THE MESSAGE BECAUSE IT WAS NOT
> SOMETHING SHE WOULD NORMALLY SAY.

Jack gave up and looked out the window. His mind wandered. He watched a crow pecking away at something on the sidewalk.

Then it hit him. Their toast back at SMASH. Southern Comfort was the drink they'd had the night of the after-hours brainstorm. What had the toast been? "To us," she'd said. So the message was reminding him of their toast. She was saying it wasn't over after all; that it was still "to us."

Jack felt sure he'd puzzled it out. That had been their first true romantic moment, their first unguardedly-in-love moment. He felt a cloud lift. It wasn't rejection of him; she had been coerced. Okay, so maybe he should call the cops? But he had been told not to call the cops.

Her father was warning him off. He was sure the sneaky old dude had worked out a story, and Molly would have to go along because he had her over a barrel. He'd tell her that he'd have me killed, to buy her cooperation. Or he'd find some other way of coercing her. Then he remembered the last moment of the beating—the camera flash. They'd shown her the picture.

He wished he could talk to her and tell her not to worry about him. Was it possible she could pick up the phone? But how would he get her number?

Jack got up with a start and went over to his phone. He had caller ID. There it was, the Milwaukee phone number of Brian Dunne, the number where Molly had called him from and left a message.

He took a deep breath. *Do I call her? And what do I say?* He paced around his apartment. *What if they won't let her speak to me? Am I tipping them to my location? Doesn't matter,* he thought. *They already know my location.*

He dialed the number. It rang four times, and then a man answered the phone, her father.

"Brian Dunne."

"Mr. Dunne, this is Jack Huber, a friend of Molly's from Chicago."

"I've heard about you—you're the bartender. She wants nothing to do with you anymore."

Jack paused. "I'd like to speak with her. I mean, all I got was a phone message."

"You could speak to her if she was here, but she's not. Molly told me she was through with you, so I think the manly thing to do is get drunk and forget about it."

"I'm just a bit concern—"

"I don't care what your concerns are!" shouted Brian Dunne, hanging up.

11: TUESDAY HEARTACHE

Where Jack and Manny start turning over stones

Jack and Manny explore the challenge even further. They research additional facts about Molly, turning over every stone. Jack fully realizes that this problem is too much for him to solve on his own. He knows he needs help, and Manny steps in.

The next morning, Manny and his cousin, Angel, arrived to pick up Jack's car. Then Manny suggested that he and Jack take a ride over to Geek's. They walked in the door just after the morning rush.

"How're you recovering?" Manny asked.

Jack tested his neck by turning it as far as he could to the right and then to the left. It was better than yesterday, but it still hurt. Then he felt the tender areas around his chest. "I'm better. Still pretty sore all over, especially my ribs."

"You'll want to take it easy for a while," Manny replied. "Did you hear anything from Molly?"

"No, but I think I figured out her last message." Jack explained his reasoning.

"So you think 'comfort from the south' was her signal that she was making the call under duress?"

"Yeah," said Jack, "I do."

"It's not something a person would normally say, you're right. I think she was signaling you." Manny paused. "Jack, this is a serious situation."

As they walked up to the counter, Layne greeted them and asked for their order. The three men talked for a few minutes before Jack asked, "Layne, have you heard from Molly?"

"No, still nothing."

"I got a message Sunday on my machine that she might be up there for a while."

"At least you rate a call."

"Layne, I hate to say this, but I think something funny is going on. I mean, have you ever known her to be irresponsible? Like not call if she said she was going to call?"

"Actually, no. She was easily my most reliable employee. I still trust her—I just don't understand why she disappeared."

Manny stepped up. "Layne, I hope you can help us with some information. Jack and I are trying to figure out what's going on. It could be foul play. What can you tell us about her? What do you know about her past employment history and such?"

"I guess so, sure," Layne said. "She had two former employers on her employment application. Just a minute." Layne walked into the back office and returned with a file. He opened it and read the names of the employers out loud. "Legally, I really can't tell you anymore," he said.

"Okay, Jack, let's sit down and talk about this. Layne, give me two double espressos, please."

"Be up in a minute," said Layne.

Manny started in, "We have the names of two former employers here. We don't have much else. Do you happen to know her social security number?"

"No . . . but I know where I could find it," said Jack.

Jack pulled a keyboard over and started typing. As he worked, he explained to Manny that he and Molly had set up a file folder on the Geek's server to hold documents about things they were researching and doing. One of the documents was a FrontPage form—Molly had been showing Jack how to set up data entry fields, and she had used her social security number. In a minute he had the number.

"So what will that get us?" asked Jack.

"We'll soon see," he said.

"Sure," said Jack, glad to be doing anything. He scribbled down the numbers.

Manny pulled a computer keyboard over and adjusted the monitor. Then he went to work. Jack watched as Manny moved quickly through several computer screens. He gathered that Manny was doing background checks on Molly and her father. Manny explained as he went along that credit card companies, the government, and other organizations keep extensive database information on almost everyone. Employers, private detectives, and financial institutions were the typical users of these online services. He also accessed newspaper archives and a slew of other "data aggregators." As he found records, he would print them out. More than once Jack saw Manny enter his own credit card number to pay for information. At one point Manny sighed, and at another point, he gave a low whistle. What the devil was he finding out? He printed a few more things out, and Jack started reading.

An hour and a half later, Manny came up for air. He took off his glasses, rubbed his eyes, and stretched his neck.

"Jack, I'm going back to my place to pick up some stuff. I'll drop you at home. Pack a small bag with a couple days' worth of clothes, and bring your cameras, film, and some sneakers. We're going to Milwaukee."

12: ROAD TRIP

Where Jack and Manny go mobile to explore the missing-person challenge

On the road to Milwaukee, Jack and Manny discuss the background information they gathered about Molly's family. They digest, or analyze, this information to come up with insights, one of which is that they are not dealing with a normal person in Brian Dunne. This is part of phase one, Problem Exploration.

They also realize they need more help, and Manny recruits Linda Hutzel to become part of the resource group. A resource group is made up of people who don't "own" a problem but may be able to contribute facts, ideas, and assistance in finding solutions.

An hour later they were on the road north. It's not a long drive from Chicago to Milwaukee, but getting out of Chicago can be a challenge in the middle of the day. Sure enough, they ran into heavy outbound traffic, and it took them over an hour just to reach the Lincolnshire suburb on the north edge of the city.

Manny filled Jack in along the way with what he had learned doing his background checks on the Web. Most of it rang true to what Molly had told him, but with a great deal more detail.

"We got kind of lucky on this because at one point Dunne was a public figure. There's a lot of historical data about him in the public record," said Manny. He told Jack about what he'd learned.

Brian Dunne was a wealthy businessman who had done it all on his own. His parents were first-generation Irish immigrants, and he'd grown up poor. But he'd been ambitious even as a youth, excelling in school and in high school sports. They'd moved from Boston to the Milwaukee area when Brian was in high school. He went to Notre Dame on a baseball scholarship. He did well in college, and he went into banking after graduation, becoming a bank president by the time he was thirty. He'd moved from banking into construction, and he'd grown a small start-up into a company that did huge public works projects and skyscrapers.

His success, from what Manny could glean, was based on hard work and shrewd—some newspaper accounts had said *ruthless*—dealings. One article looking into his operations compared his business style to Joe Kennedy's. As he acquired more wealth and power, he also accumulated a group of family hangers-on: assistants, lawyers, and security guards. One article speculated that there might be a connection to the Irish Mob in Boston. He had ties to a number of Milwaukee-area businesses and was a major stockholder and even a board member of several midwestern public companies. He kept a low profile but was a major contributor to both political parties and to the Catholic Church.

"What about her mother?" asked Jack. "Did they say anything about her?"

"He'd been too busy with business for any romance when he was young. At some point he must have realized that if he didn't start a family he'd have nobody to leave his wealth to."

Manny continued with his report. Brian Dunne married a much

younger woman, Mary Rhanigan, when he was in his late forties. They'd had two children. Their firstborn was Molly, and two years later came Bridgette. Apparently they were a happy family, at least for a time. Mrs. Dunne and her husband were fixtures in the Milwaukee social scene. Brian had loosened the purse strings and contributed to arts organizations and to the disabled. There was even talk of his running for one of the Wisconsin US Senate seats.

Then it had all gone wrong.

Brian Dunne became more and more of a recluse. He withdrew from the society swirl and the business world, selling many of his assets and resigning board positions. Then, suddenly, Mrs. Dunne was committed to a mental institution, and she died there unexpectedly. The papers had not said much about it, other than it was sad, a tragedy, and so forth.

Jack looked through the printouts in his lap. One had a picture of Molly's parents in better days. They were both very attractive people, and he could see that Molly favored her mother, but he also noted she had her father's strong chin.

"What do you make of all this?" asked Jack.

"Rich families tend to have well-kept secrets, but there's also a lot on the public record, as you can see," said Manny.

"Her father—he's almost larger than life."

"Good way to put it. He's both a success story and a tragic figure, it seems," said Manny. "And if I had to guess, someone who has gone over the edge of eccentricity into insanity."

"Molly came to Chicago to get away from him," said Jack. "I don't have a clue about Milwaukee. Do you?"

"Not really," Manny said. But after a pause, he added, "I do have a friend who lives there. We met at a conference a few years ago, had a nice chat about market projections and predicting consumer behavior. We've been out to dinner a few times when she's in Chicago on business. Let me try to find her."

Manny got on his mobile phone. He got a voice mail and left a friendly message, saying he was on his way to Milwaukee and had a couple of questions for her if she could spare some time to return his call.

Manny looked over and saw Jack's strained expression. "Listen, don't worry. We'll find Molly and straighten this mess out, then you two can live happily ever after," he said with a grin.

"I wish I was that confident," said Jack.

"You know, I just thought of something. She may try to call you again on your home phone."

"I can pick up messages."

"Here, then, call in and check." He handed Jack his cell phone.

Jack dialed his voice mail retrieval number. There was one message: "Jack, I'm sorry for the message I left Sunday. I was at our house in Milwaukee, and my father pressured me to say what I said. He knows about us. He showed me those pictures of you. I hope you're okay. It really scared me. I really never thought he would go that far. Bridgette and I got out last night. She needs help—she's not good, and so I've got to figure out how to help her. We're going into hiding. It's better you don't know where we are for now. So don't do anything. My father plays for keeps. I've gotta go now so they can't trace this call." The message was delivered with a rushed voice and an urgent tone.

"You were right, Manny. That was her."

"And?"

"She says she and Bridgette are hiding, and it's best we don't know where they are."

"Oh great," said Manny.

"And she says she doesn't want me involved in this."

"Why do you think she said that?" asked Manny.

"Because it's bad, and she doesn't want to see me hurt. She must have some idea of how far her father will go, and so she's trying to protect me."

The phone rang. Manny answered. "Linda? Yes, good to hear your voice. Hey, I'm driving into Milwaukee as we speak . . . yes . . . I'm going to be in town for a few days, and I want to pick your brain on something. We're staying at the Pfister . . . no, no, really, that's not necessary . . . have my friend Jack with me . . . no, we can stay at the Pfister . . . okay, okay, we'll stay with you, but I'll be honest, I could use some other help . . . well, it's a long story. What's your address?"

Manny scribbled directions on a dash-mounted note pad. "We'll see you in about a half hour then," Manny said, finishing the call. Then to Jack, "We'll stay with Linda. She knows the city and can help us get around and find things."

"How does one go about locating two young women in a city with more than a million people?" asked Jack. "I mean, we're not the law, and I don't think we have the skills."

"The voice of self-doubt. I'm dealing with that too. I have a feeling we'll work this out in spite of it. This is how you're supposed to feel when you step off into the unknown. I mean, it's just like this thing I'm doing downtown. I have to admit, I'm stumped. I thought it would be slam dunk. I mean, I know there's a way to bring those cables up without spending a million dollars. I can feel it, I can smell it—I just can't find it. It's got me going goofy. Things like that bring me down to earth. I start feeling like a poor kid on the West Side again, the kid who doesn't know squat and doesn't have squat." Manny looked a little disconcerted.

> THE VOICE OF SELF-DOUBT . . . THIS IS
> HOW YOU'RE SUPPOSED TO FEEL WHEN
> YOU STEP OFF INTO THE UNKNOWN.

"I forgot about your wiring thing," Jack admitted.

"I haven't. Matter of fact, if I don't figure it out by this time next week, I'm hosed."

"Hosed?"

"It's a technical term. Actually, I'm not sure where I got that. People started saying that back in the eighties. But in this case it means I'm not going to get paid."

"The eighties—the years of my youth."

"Don't rub it in. And you're still in the years of your youth, in case you don't know it," said Manny.

They were approaching Milwaukee now. Manny navigated the freeway twists and turns, and they ended up in a nice neighborhood on the southeast side of town, near Lake Michigan. They knocked on Linda Hutzel's door and were ushered into a spacious loft-style condo.

"Hola, Manny!" Linda said. "Who's your friend?"

"This is Jack Huber."

Linda shook Jack's hand, saying, "Nice to meet you. You keep good company, you know."

"I do know," said Jack. "Better than I deserve."

"Well, I don't know about that, but hey, come in and sit down."

Jack took a look around. The place was filled with art, sculptures, paintings, even a mobile hanging from the ceiling—and in every style imaginable. Jack wasn't sure if the bicycle hanging from a hook was for transportation or was some kind of art piece. Linda made them coffee, and they all sat down at her kitchen table.

Linda was a slim, taller-than-average, athletic-looking, middle-aged woman with auburn hair. She had an easy smile.

"It's been some time since that conference, Manny. That was good fun, wasn't it?" Linda was staring, her eyes sparkling.

It was soon clear to Jack that Linda was attracted to Manny. Manny, on the other hand, appeared slightly uncomfortable.

"Yes," said Manny. "I haven't sung so much in years."

"That was the best sing-along. So what brings you to Milwaukee so suddenly?" she asked.

"Tell us about you first," Manny requested.

"Well, what's to tell? I'm still a workaholic, but things are a bit slow right now, so I'm sort of jumping out of my skin. I was really busy until about a month ago. Since then I've been doing all those things you put off—you know, sorting my sock drawer, cleaning my closet, deleting old e-mails, stuff like that," she said. "Actually, I'm about to go out of my mind."

"So demand for trend forecasting has slowed down?" asked Manny.

"For me it has. I've been getting started on doing some personal writing and some painting, but I keep waiting for the phone to ring. I don't know—maybe it's time for me to get a new hustle," she said.

"I doubt that," said Manny. "I've been hoping you'd write a book about your forecasting techniques."

"You'd be among the twenty people nationwide that would really get it," she said.

"Well then, how might you broaden its application?" asked Manny. "And maybe it doesn't matter if it isn't a million-seller, huh?"

"Actually, I have thought about how to make it practical at a broader level, but I don't know if the average person really needs to think thirty years out. Anyway, I'm not sure what I'm going to do if things dry up, but I'm not too worried about it. So enough about me. Why are you here?"

Manny looked over at Jack, so Jack explained what he knew about the situation, with Manny filling in the details he'd learned doing his Web background checks.

Linda knew a few things about Brian Dunne, and her story matched what Manny had learned.

"Where could we start looking for Molly?" Jack asked Linda.

"I really don't know, she could be anywhere . . . I wonder how the police find missing people."

"Let's put ourselves in her shoes, then," suggested Manny. "She's avoiding her father, who probably has people looking for her, maybe even the police."

"She's committed no crime," said Jack.

"Doesn't mean they aren't looking for a missing person," said Manny. "Let's try to get into her head and see things from her perspective. She's scared of her father. Her sister is too. And she's visible— she's an attractive young woman with a distinctive look. She wears dreadlocks, Linda."

"That wouldn't stand out much on Walker's Point."

"Walker's Point?" asked Jack.

"Yes, a very diverse neighborhood. Artists, bohemian types, African Americans, Hispanics—all in one big melting pot," said Linda.

"Sounds like a good place to look. But first, I think we need to find out who she would trust. She'd try to get in touch with a friend, someone to help her, don't you think? Probably a girlfriend who could be trusted to keep a secret," said Manny. He looked at Jack. "So let's get out there and start looking. I say we start at Marquette, where Bridgette goes to school. You drive this time."

13: Seeking Perspective Shift

Where a reversal doesn't work and more foul play is discovered

Jack and Manny continue to use CPS to search for Molly and Bridgette. They use an abbreviated version of the CPS process to manage the chaos, to add to what they know, to rule out things, and to seek facts and generate ideas. They decide to use a technique for shifting perspective called a Reversal. They also stop to think about how they're thinking and do "Challenge Triage."

Challenge Triage is really just pausing for a moment and asking yourself what step in CPS you should use. Do you need to know more? Go to step two, Facts and Feelings Exploration. Do you need Ideas? Then begin step four, Idea Generation. Challenge Triage helps direct their next steps in a very fluid situation.

Manny and Jack drove over to the Marquette University campus.

"How are we going to find them? We really don't have a place to start. Maybe find out what dorm Bridgette was in? Talk to her friends?" Jack asked, looking for a parking place.

"Yeah. We could do that. I'm just thinking, though, what if we flip the situation, do a reversal?"

"Reverse what?"

"It's a way to shift perspective. I mean, maybe there is some way for them to see us—to know we're here, as opposed to our knocking on a lot of doors."

"What, like rent a billboard?"

"In a way, yeah. But there's more than one way to get noticed. If they have friends here, we want them to see us and have them report to Bridgette and Molly. What could we do?"

"A billboard . . . I'm still stuck on that," mused Jack.

But then they alternated ideas. Manny went first: "We could picket a coffee shop for having bad coffee."

"We could swim naked in a fountain," said Jack.

"We could start juggling in the center quadrangle."

"Wait a minute—how would they know it was us?" asked Jack.

"Right, her friends don't know who we are, so even if we get on the evening news—darn, it's just unlikely," said Manny.

"Well, let's try the word-of-mouth thing at the dorm first," said Jack. "Then maybe we try the local Web café."

Manny agreed. They spent a little while trying to find someone who knew Bridgette. Nobody seemed to know who she was. Manny finally found out which dorm she was in by looking in a student phone book he found in the student union lounge.

Jack knocked on her dorm room door. No answer. "Well, I guess that's that."

"Not so fast," Manny said, looking both ways before getting to work.

He pulled a tool from inside his jacket that looked something like a very small comb. He quickly picked the lock, opened the door, and walked into the room. Jack was momentarily taken aback, but Manny pulled him into the room.

The place was in disarray—more than the normal disarray of a sloppy college student. Chairs were tipped over, drawers pulled from the bureau.

"We're too late," Jack whispered, getting a sinking feeling.

"What do you think went on here?" Manny asked, trying to keep Jack's mind moving. When Jack didn't answer, Manny did some thinking out loud. "Obviously somebody's gone through this room looking for something. Or maybe it was just a quick exit. There may have been a struggle as well, but it's hard to say. Jack, I want you to check the drawers and get a sense if you think things have been taken out."

> THE PLACE WAS IN DISARRAY—MORE
> THAN THE NORMAL DISARRAY OF A SLOPPY
> COLLEGE STUDENT. CHAIRS WERE TIPPED
> OVER, DRAWERS PULLED FROM THE BUREAU.

Jack looked through the drawers. One drawer had a pair of jeans, but mostly there were nicer clothes than the average college student would wear, more formal. He looked in the base of the closet and saw only dress shoes.

"You'd think a college student would have at least one pair of sneakers," he commented.

"Yeah, you would," said Manny. "If you were in a hurry, you'd take the basics, and that would be part of the kit, I think."

They looked around the rest of the room carefully. Jack ran his hand under the bed and found a stray pill. He showed Manny, and then Manny went into the bathroom.

"Somebody's been sick," Manny called out to Jack a minute or two later. When Jack entered, Manny was pointing to some very small pieces of food stuck to the underside of the toilet bowl rim.

"Gross," said Jack, watching Manny move on to the trash can and pull out an empty quart bottle of orange juice. "You know, that food might mean she's bulimic."

"That's true," said Manny. "That's a possibility."

Then Manny opened the medicine cabinet, rummaged through it, and held up a nearly empty bottle of prescription medication.

"What is it?" asked Jack.

"Ambien—it's for insomnia. I could be wrong about this, but Bridgette may have taken one too many of these. The OJ is something people give to treat somebody who's taken too much of something—it helps dilute the drug in the body. And the vomit—well, puking is what happens sometimes when you take too many pills."

With this in the back of their minds, they looked around the room a bit longer. Jack checked out the books in Bridgette's bookshelf. It was a blend: textbooks, many books about rock music, and some on Zen Buddhism. On the top was a picture of her and Molly. Jack guessed that Molly may have been around twelve in the picture, and since they were all dressed up, he guessed it must have been taken at some kind of a formal event.

After a thorough search, Manny finally said, "Let's bolt."

Next they cruised the Walker's Point neighborhood. But after only a short while it seemed pointless. They needed something more to go on. They stopped and had a coffee at a small corner shop when they couldn't find a Web café. This was a neighborhood full of characters and artists, for sure. *Molly would fit in here,* Jack thought. *This is definitely her kind of area.* He could enjoy this neighborhood himself, but today, it felt mostly cold and uninviting.

"We've hit the wall, and we've only been here half a day," said Jack.

"Keep trying to think of ways to get over the wall, then. Molly would turn to somebody she trusted. She's gone underground, but unless she has resources we don't know about, she would need help. She and her sister need a place to stay, for one thing. They need food. And if her sister is sick, as I suspect she is, they really need a safe haven to rest up. So who is her friend here? I think if we find her best friend, we find Molly and her sister."

"Well, she did say she worked here for a while. Maybe it would be somebody she used to work with," speculated Jack.

"Worth checking out. The other thing is her father."

"He'll be hard to talk to," said Jack.

"Maybe we can . . ."

"What are you thinking, Manny?"

"I'm thinking I walk up to his door and knock on it."

"You're crazy," Jack said, but he said it with admiration.

"I'm not afraid of Brian Dunne. I don't have to be. And Brian Dunne just might be more afraid of this situation than we are. And we really don't know what's going on, do we? We assume that Molly is protecting her sister from Mr. Dunne, but maybe that isn't so. We just don't know," said Manny.

"Why don't I go knock on his door? She's my girlfriend," said Jack.

"Well, you could—but they know who you are, don't they? They might even be expecting a young man to show up. They won't be expecting a middle-aged Hispanic, though. No, let me check out the Dunne house. I'll get a cab over to see Dunne," said Manny. "You take the Cherokee and my cell phone. I'll call you later to come pick me up. Call Linda to see if she can background you on Molly's old employer —you go and talk with someone there."

"Are you sure you want to split up?" Jack asked, not sure how he would do on his own.

"Don't worry about me. I've managed the worst neighborhoods of Chicago and Mexico City—I think I can handle Milwaukee." Manny grinned.

"Okay, call me as soon as you know something. I have a bad feeling about your visit."

"I'll call. Here's the cell phone. Now get to work. Find the facts, Jack."

14: IDEAS ON ICE

Where Jack learns more about the past

Still in step two of CPS, Facts and Feelings Exploration, Jack uses his skills of observation and fact gathering. He also learns by doing when he first meets Harriet Potts; he jumps into a situation in order to learn more about it and to glean the information he needs. Experiential learning is the opposite of analysis-paralysis; you learn by actively doing something.

When Linda Hutzel answered the phone, Jack plunged right in. "I'm going over to this place where Molly used to work. It's called Ideas on Ice. Have you ever heard of it?"

"I have, we're in a related business. Harriet Potts is the principal. I know her. They do market research and ideation."

"Ideation?"

"Yeah, like brainstorming, just a fancier word for it," said Linda. "It sort of sounds psychological, doesn't it?"

"Yeah—anyway, she knew about brainstorming . . . ideation," said Jack.

After Linda gave him directions, he drove over to Ideas on Ice. The offices of IOI Inc. were near downtown Milwaukee in a made-over warehouse. They were up on the fourth floor, and he didn't see an elevator. Jack climbed the stairs slowly, not sure how to approach the task, not sure how to walk into this place and start asking a lot of questions. After all, he wasn't Sam Spade.

He stood still in the stairwell for a moment, collecting his thoughts. If somebody knew where Molly was hiding, they wouldn't come right out and say it. They'd be cagey; they would lie. They would also assess him, check him out, see if he might be trustworthy. Of course, these people might not know anything about this mess. So how to begin? How to approach this? *Do I come at this head-on and just say exactly what I'm up to?* Jack thought. *Or do I pretend to be something else?*

As he was standing there in the stairwell, a woman, mid to late fifties, came down. She was dressed in oversized khaki pants with a waist that came up very high, just below her breasts, and her fancy ruffled white blouse had a high-necked collar. Her hair was dyed very black, and it was very short—a pixyish look, but hip and smart. When she saw Jack, she stopped short.

"Can I help you with something?"

"Yes . . . I'm looking for Ideas on Ice."

"It's on the next floor up, so you've found it. I'm Harriet Potts—I'm with Ideas—so what can I do for you?"

"I've come to apply for a job." He had no idea why he said that; it just popped out.

"Really? We don't get many walk-in applications—we're pretty specialized, so not many folks know about us. How did *you* hear about us?"

Harriet had piercing blue eyes. Jack was going to find it difficult to lie to her. "A woman named Linda Hutzel."

"Ah, I know Linda. I met her at a local chapter meeting of QRCA—oh, that's the Qualitative Research Consultants Association. She gave a talk on trend spotting. Look, I have to run downstairs and get the mail. Why don't you just go on up and sit down. Get some coffee or tea if you like. I'll be right up."

"Okay, thanks," said Jack, not believing his good luck. He'd done just the right thing and gotten in the door without arousing any suspicion.

He found the door and walked into a wide-open office—no waiting room, only a hot pink couch just inside the door. The rest of the space had a few sit-down desks spread out over a large open space— Jack guessed more than two thousand square feet. The walls were covered with white boards; there were flipcharts scattered about the room. There were toys and things everywhere: stuffed animals, balls, squirt guns, balloons, musical instruments, gizmos, and lots of bean bag chairs. An electronic keyboard, a guitar, and a large pair of congas were in a corner area. Oversized antique French posters decorated the walls. It was a bit like walking onto the movie set of *Willy Wonka and the Chocolate Factory*. It was a deliberately fun place.

Jack poured himself a coffee and drank in the surroundings. One of the white boards was covered with sticky notes, clustered in batches. *Molly worked here,* he thought. On a wall just inside the door were some framed black-and-white pictures. He walked over to look more closely. There was Molly in a group picture, sans dreadlocks, looking business-y. She was standing next to Harriet with a couple of other women behind them.

> ONE OF THE WHITE BOARDS WAS COVERED
> WITH STICKY NOTES, CLUSTERED IN BATCHES.
> *MOLLY WORKED HERE,* HE THOUGHT.

Harriet found him there. "We're between projects right now—you dropped in at a good time. It's boom or bust in this business, and to be honest, I'm glad it's bust right now. I need some rest! So tell me, what makes you think you want to work in market research and ideation?"

"I'm new to the area, and I need a job. Linda said you might have use for someone who knew graphics and photography."

"Well, those wouldn't be the first qualifications, although they are interesting ones. Do you know anything about structured ideation?"

"I've been through a couple of . . . brainstorming sessions."

"That's a start. Who did the facilitation?"

"A friend of mine in Chicago."

Harriet paused, her eyes flicking away from Jack for the briefest of moments. The smile left her face. "You're not really here for a job, are you?"

"No, actually I'm not. I'm looking for a friend of mine—Molly Dunne."

"Who are you?"

"My name is Jack Huber."

"Okay, well listen, Jack Huber. Tell Brian Dunne I've had enough of his harassment. Tell him I don't know where Molly is, and if I did know, I wouldn't tell him—or you."

"No, no. I'm not associated with Brian Dunne. I have nothing to do with him. I'm a friend of Molly's from Chicago."

Harriet looked at Jack up and down. "I half believe you, but since you started this conversation lying, it's hard to get my other half believing. Brian Dunne would send a real goon or a lawyer, and you don't fit either part. But like I said, I don't know where she is."

"She did work here?" Jack asked, pointing to the photo.

"Yes, in better days, Molly was my assistant. She's a talented young woman—and a friend. I miss her."

"Look, I got a message from her yesterday. She said Bridgette was in some sort of trouble, and she needed to hide. Do you have any idea where she might be?"

"I don't care to speculate with a complete stranger."

"Okay, I understand you can't trust me. But let me tell you something—I love Molly Dunne, and I mean her no harm, far from it. I was beaten to a pulp two nights ago," Jack added, turning his head around to show Harriet the bandage on the back of his head. "And I was threatened—with my life. I'm here in Milwaukee for one reason, to find her and make sure she's safe. And I'm not leaving this town until I do."

Jack's tone crept into the anger zone as he made this last statement. He turned to leave. He hadn't realized just how angry he was until Harriet had pushed his button.

Harriet put the mail down on a desk near them. "Wait a minute. Like I said, I half believe you. I just don't know you. Before you walk out of here all wound up, you should know a couple things. The first thing is that I'm Molly's friend. If Molly's in trouble, I want to help her, but that won't be easy. That's because you don't know who you're messing around with in Brian Dunne. He's a smart man—and a paranoid man with a lot of resources—but he's lost touch with reality. Anybody who takes him on had better be prepared." Harriet trailed off and sat down on a chair by the desk. She was clearly upset.

"I'm sorry. I didn't come here to bother you. I'm just trying to find Molly, to help her." Jack stood across the desk from Harriet. "I wish I could somehow convince you I'm Molly's friend. It just seems like she's done her Jeannie routine and gone back into the bottle."

Harriet looked up. "What do you mean, 'gone back into the bottle'?"

Jack smiled as he realized what he'd said. "She really liked that old TV show, *I Dream of Jeannie*," he explained. "You should see her apartment in Chicago—she decorated it like the inside of the bottle . . . all paisley and *Arabian Nights*."

Harriet smiled faintly, "She would do that. She was crazy about paisley. When she lived here, her father wouldn't let her wear anything creative. Can you believe that? That he tried to tell her what to wear? A grown woman and a college graduate? Yeah, she was crazy about that old show."

"You are her friend, aren't you?"

"Yes. More than her friend, actually, but yes, her friend." Harriet's eyes misted up. "This is so crazy you would walk in here." She paused to wipe her eyes. Then her expression turned serious. "Be careful with Brian Dunne."

"Why? What's with him anyway?"

"Are you familiar with the Howard Hughes story? Brian Dunne is something like that, a hermit with a bunch of people around him who enable it. Nobody to tell him the emperor has no clothes."

"What do you mean?"

"The rumors were that he had a dirty tricks squad, his own little mob of informants, and that he raised the art of industrial spying to a new level. He was an *information freak* before that term was popular. Whenever he was competing for a contract or whenever he was pushing for a big loan, it always seemed to swing his way. Somebody would get discredited, somebody would sustain a big loss, or a bank official who was dead set against extending credit would suddenly swing the other way. Brian Dunne called it 'the luck of the Irish.' Or it might have been just incredible business skill—I'm sure a lot of it was. But others suspect differently. There was a reporter here who followed Brian Dunne's career—knew where some of the bodies were buried, and I say that only half-jokingly. About a year ago, the reporter moved to Florida, retired at the age of forty-eight."

> THE RUMORS WERE THAT HE HAD A DIRTY TRICKS SQUAD, HIS OWN LITTLE MOB OF INFORMANTS, AND THAT HE RAISED THE ART OF INDUSTRIAL SPYING TO A NEW LEVEL.

"What I don't get is why his own daughters would be hiding from him?"

"I can answer that."

"Why?"

"He wants to control their lives. If he could wave a magic wand, he would have frozen them both at the age of ten."

"You said he wants to control their lives. But I mean, what is he afraid of?"

"I can only guess. We're talking about a warped individual here, someone who's sick. What he's afraid of is losing his daughters, but not just in the sense that they grow up and move away, although I'm sure he would do anything he could to prevent that as well. More like he's afraid they'll lose their innocence."

"Innocence? Are we talking sex?"

"Yes. There were some other rumors from the past, you know . . .

I heard it said that he'd become obsessed with this idea of purity. After Mary died, I learned from one of his former employees that Dunne had lost it, that he'd been . . . *punishing* himself for many years." Harriet paused but then quickly added, "Mary Dunne may not have actually gone crazy at all, at least not in the mentally deranged sense."

"What do you mean by that?"

Harriet paused again but seemed determined to continue. "I knew Mary Dunne—we were friends. Mary had an affair just before she was committed. The affair she had was a desperate sort of thing, but it was hardly insane. When Brian found out about it, he went nuts. There was a brutal beating, and the guy was almost killed. It took a lot of money to clean up that mess. I heard that the guy was paid off, the cops were paid off, a lot of hush money was spread around, and he was sent away. Shortly after that, Mary told me she was going to leave Brian. Then all of a sudden, she was gone—in an insane asylum, committed to St. Leonard's."

"So you think it was all some sort of arrangement? To keep him from looking bad? To prevent her from leaving? From following the guy?" asked Jack.

"That's what I think, all those things."

"Harriet, have you heard from Molly recently?"

"No," she said, looking at him directly.

"Do you think if she was here in town, in hiding with Bridgette, that you would hear from her?" asked Jack.

"I'm not sure. She might call me, but she might be afraid to."

"When her father made life tough on her, when she was working for you, did she talk to you about it?"

"Yes."

"Harriet—will you help me find Molly?"

"I'm afraid—for her, for me . . ." Harriet seemed on the verge of tears.

"She needs your help," said Jack.

"Just let me think about it," said Harriet.

15: SORTING OUT THE OPTIONS

Where a plan begins to take shape
and yet more questions are raised

Manny, Jack, and Linda discuss what they've learned, dig a bit deeper for more data to answer the questions raised, and brainstorm some possible options. In other words, they move into Idea Generation, step four. They don't waste time debating ideas; instead, they list them and then converge on a plan. But they are not finished. It's a temporary plan based on what they know right now, and so, as new facts emerge, they return to Problem Exploration. They use CPS when they separate divergence from convergence—that is, they separate list making from choice making to allow for more options, which leads to better decisions.

Manny had to walk a few blocks before finding a pay phone. "Come pick me up," he said to Jack, giving him the address.

He sat down on a bus-stop bench to wait. Manny had been afraid that Molly was hiding something more than just her sister. The problem had everything to do with Brian Dunne, and now he had confirmation.

He'd found the Dunne place easily enough—a large blue and gray "painted lady" Victorian mansion set in a large corner lot in an old neighborhood, taking up the entire end of the block. He'd noticed a nondescript black car parked at the curb with two men inside. On the other side of the block was another car with two men. Other than the guards, though, there appeared to be no one on the grounds.

Manny had almost made it up the front steps when he was grabbed by the arms, one guy on each side. They'd hemmed him in a practiced maneuver. Probably ex-cops. Especially since there was a shoulder holster on one of them—a gun.

Feigning a Mexican accent, Manny claimed he'd been hired to do some landscaping. The men turned Manny around and led him away from the house and toward a carriage house. Once inside they frisked him and told him this was just a routine check and he was lucky they didn't take him in for trespassing. They looked unsuccessfully for his wallet. Manny had, fortunately, left it in the glove box in his car. One of the guards turned to make a phone call while the one beside Manny told him they'd let him go in a few minutes.

Manny took the opportunity to scan the room. It appeared to be an office for the security staff. He was surprised at how elaborate it was for a residence—a time clock for punching in and out, lockers for hanging coats and jackets, a lounge area, magazines. Next to where Manny had been asked to sit down was a table set up for coffee. That's where he saw the black-and-white notebook. It looked out of place.

"While I'm waiting, could I get a cuppa coffee?" asked Manny.

The guard on the phone looked up and nodded yes to the guard next to Manny.

Manny got up and slowly poured himself a cup of coffee while taking a good look at the notebook. In the lower right hand corner in block lettering were the letters MD. He sat down and drank his coffee until the guard on the phone finished his call.

"So Enrique says there was no order for landscaping, right? . . . Right. Hey, does Mr. D need anything while he is out there? . . . Okay.

Tomorrow afternoon we'll send a replacement out to the farm to cover cottage duty, okay? . . . Okay. Bye." He hung up and looked at Manny.

"Nobody has ordered any landscaping. What are you doing here?" the guard said, staring hard at Manny.

"Okay, lissen, I'm not here to make any trouble. Nobody ordered nothing. I'm just out trying to hustle some work."

"You're probably illegal, I could turn you in right now."

He stopped talking and continued to look at Manny. Then he looked at the guard next to him and simply said, "Get him out of here."

They walked him off the property, the guard giving him a push out the front gate.

Manny walked away.

What had he learned? For one, he was working with a personality who felt like he had a need for a lot of protection. As a retired businessperson, why would Dunne need this level of security guarding an empty house? One guard was reasonable given his wealth, but four guards? And there may have been others he didn't see. These were guards with no uniforms, no security company badges, and no markings on the cars they were sitting in. It was overkill. He'd also learned that Molly may have been in the carriage house for at least a brief period, or the guards had simply taken her notebook. Mr. Dunne was at *the farm,* and there was a rotation of guards there too.

Jack pulled up in the red Cherokee, and Manny jumped in. "Let's compare notes."

Jack filled Manny in on his talk with Harriet. Manny told Jack about his encounter with the Dunne security team.

"It seems like the house is empty," Manny continued. "Although without watching that house for a few days, we can't know for sure. It just isn't a sure thing. The guards did give away Dunne's location. So my bet is they are at this farm."

"So what's next?"

"Let's go back to Linda's and see if we can find this farm. It's been a long day. We'll pick up some eats, rest a bit, and then get back after it later," Manny suggested, settling back into the car seat.

They found a supermarket and selected a sampling of items from the deli counter. And Manny picked up some fresh flowers as a gift for Linda. Jack noted the thoughtfulness, the simple good manners. *I have so much to learn,* he thought.

Linda was home when they arrived back at her place. They recounted their activities of the day for her, Manny hoping she might be able to supply some additional insights.

"Mary Dunne never seemed crazy in the least to me, but I didn't really know her. I'd heard rumors about the affair, long after it all went down," she said.

"Well, what do you know about St. Leonard's?" asked Manny.

"Only what I read in the papers. It was an old-fashioned institution run by Carmelite nuns. It was really more of a home and less of a treatment facility. Very private—maybe that was the attraction—you could send someone there quietly. The nuns who ran the place dwindled in numbers to the point where they had to close it a few years ago. The state took the last few patients to other institutions."

"And what about this farm?" Manny asked.

"I've never been out to Dunne's country place, but in the old days every socialite in town got asked out there for parties and such. It's near Lake Mills. Calling it a farm is kind of a stretch. It's a huge estate, and it's maintained like a park. I've been told it's very pretty. Now that I'm thinking about it, the house was once featured in *Architectural Digest*. And let's see—what else?" She paused for only a second or two. "The horses—the Dunnes were horse people. Mary rode—she loved horses. They kept a couple of Arabians. I know that because there were newspaper stories about how much they paid for that pair. And what else about the farm?" Another moment of thought. "There were pictures of a beautiful French-style garden. Apparently Mary Dunne was a nut for impressionist paintings, and she did a Monet-style garden behind the house. They must have had a pretty big staff out there to deal with the horses and the kitchen, the grounds and such. I have no idea if that's still the case."

"How far away is it?" Manny now asked.

"It's about an hour's drive west."

Manny took a sheet of paper from Jack's notebook and started drawing something. Linda set out the deli food for them, and Jack searched the Web for more information. They ate a light dinner together and discussed alternatives.

"So what are the options here?" asked Manny.

"You could call the police and report missing persons," suggested Linda.

"We could hire a private detective," offered Jack.

"We could go out to the farm, look around, see what we can, and then call the police if we need them," said Manny.

Jack again: "We could spend more time here in Milwaukee first. I'd like to try to find the nuns who worked at St. Leonard's."

"Yes, *and* we could try to find friends of Bridgette's who might have some idea about where she is," said Linda, "or where they might go . . ."

"We could watch the house," said Manny.

"We could watch the farm," said Jack.

"Yes, and we could find that *Architectural Digest* article," put in Linda.

Manny frowned down at the short list of the options and then said, "I think we spend another day here in Milwaukee. We need to know more before we run out to the countryside. I mean, we think that Dunne is there, but he may just be there to enjoy his horses."

"I have a feeling they're out there," said Jack. "I think they got nabbed somewhere along the way."

"I know what you mean," said Manny. "I mean, if Molly was here in Milwaukee, in hiding with her sister, we might have heard from her. When was her last message to you, Jack?"

"She left it on my phone sometime between the time we went over to Geek's and when we were driving up here yesterday afternoon. So that would be between, say, ten and two yesterday. She hasn't left another message—I checked." Jack paused. "I mean, this is the part I don't understand. Even if things are really rough for her, she would call."

"She wants to keep you out of her mess," said Linda, "and she's afraid you'll be hurt."

"Could be," admitted Jack.

"I think she would call you if she could," said Manny. "She knows you'll be worried about her. Let's assume, for a moment, that she would call if she could. If she hasn't called, that means she's being denied access to a phone. Unless you have no resources, you can get to a phone. Does she have credit cards?"

"I don't know," said Jack. "I don't think so."

"Did she have money?"

"I don't know. I doubt she had very much—just what she made at Geek's. Then again, she has some nice things at her place, so she may have a stash of cash. Anyway, we've never had that discussion."

"I think she and her sister are being held by Dunne," said Manny. "And in my mind, the farm is the logical place. Given how paranoid this guy is, he'll have security all over the place. He might even go as far as electric fences, video cameras, armed guards."

"Okay, then how do we get on the grounds?" asked Jack. "Part of me says go out there right now, but I'm beginning to think that a night raid might be ill-advised."

"The best way onto the grounds is to walk right through the front gate," said Manny.

"And how does that happen?" Jack asked.

"A big place like that has all kinds of supply needs. It's regulated, you can bet on that, but still, a Trojan horse of some kind is what I'm thinking," said Manny.

"Okay, let's say we do get on the grounds. We don't know where we're going—where we might look. We'll need time to do that, and it's hard to imagine getting that kind of access," said Jack.

"You're right. Tomorrow, let's make a list of things we need to investigate first. Then we'll make a decision about any drastic course of action," said Manny.

Linda showed Manny and Jack to the guest room. There were a bed and a pull out couch. Manny took the couch and fell asleep immediately. But Jack was wired by a low voltage fear. He tried to sleep, but whenever he closed his eyes, what welled up in him was that familiar sense of mild panic.

He looked over at Manny and wondered how a person could fall asleep so easily in the middle of a crisis. *Of course, it's not a crisis to him like it is to me,* he thought. *Still, he's here trying to solve it.* The question he had asked himself many times in the last few weeks popped up again. Who is this guy? Manny, so vibrant a presence when awake, looked more like an average guy when sleeping—thin, almost under-nourished looking. Jack thought back to their first meeting and real-ized that Manny had always carried a glow.

> *HE'S A THINKING MAN WITH A HEART,*
> *NOTHING MORE—AND NOTHING LESS.*

Manny is what the world needs more of, thought Jack. *No, he's not a saint. He's a thinking man with a heart, nothing more—and noth-ing less.*

His wish now was simply to find Molly. He hoped she was safe.

16: NEW DAY IN MILWAUKEE

Where Harriet comes clean and helps out

Jack acts on intuition and researches the death of Molly's mother. Harriet Potts joins the resource group, and because she and Manny know the language of CPS, they can discuss the situation more efficiently and effectively. Manny shows that he is aware of "where he is" in the problem-solving process. When new information arises, new ideas pop into his head. Being conscious of where he is leaves him open to shifting the problem frame and prevents him from shutting down an idea or deciding on a solution prematurely.

Linda was already up. She'd put out some bagels and lox with tomatoes and capers, and a full pot of coffee was already brewed. Jack poured himself a cup and sat down at the kitchen table.

"How'd you sleep?" Linda asked.

"Okay. I had a little trouble at first."

"That's not surprising," she said. "You must be worried sick about her."

"I am," Jack said grimly.

"How did you meet Molly?" asked Linda.

"At the coffee shop where she works. Just a couple of months ago."

"It's easy to see you're mad about her," said Linda.

"It shows?" said Jack with a half-smile. "By the way, thanks—so much—for letting us crash here."

"Nothing to it. I'm a big fan of Manny's. I've wanted to get to know him better . . ."

Jack got the distinct impression that Linda's interest wasn't merely professional. He'd noticed a picture of Linda with a man on one of her book shelves, but she wasn't wearing a wedding ring. "He's a great guy . . ." he said, leaving an opening.

"And an interesting guy," she added. But that was all.

"So, you're single?"

"I am," she said. "My husband passed away three years ago. But I've just now started thinking about dating again. Actually I'd like to do more than just think about it, but men are so hard to meet."

"I've heard women say that," said Jack. "It must be true."

"It's so true. I've taken to hanging out in bookstores. I get all dolled up and sip tea. I read for hours on end. It's really stupid, but I'm kind of at a loss."

"I've heard the Web is good for matching up," offered Jack.

"I've heard that too, but I just can't go there—yet!"

"Well, maybe you won't have to," said Jack.

Linda gave herself a refill. "Listen, if you need anything, just knock on my office door. I've got a couple of things I've got to take care of," she said. "Feel free to use my kitchen PC."

"Okay . . . and thanks again."

Jack turned Linda's monitor toward himself and Googled St. Leonard's. Not much there. It was on a list of institutions that had closed but nothing about the institution itself.

Jack drank his coffee and ate some salmon. *Brain food*, he thought.

So let me take another tack. He Googled the Carmelites, the order that had run St. Leonard's.

Manny, looking fresh from his shower, walked into the kitchen, fixed himself a plate of food, and sat down.

Jack nodded at him, but he returned to the screen. There was a connection between the Carmelites and St. Therese of Lisieux. She was a Carmelite that had helped "reform" the order. He also found out that the order went all the way back to a sect formed in Palestine at the time of the Crusades.

This was all interesting, but so far none of this was getting him anywhere.

He went to another site and discovered there were several cells of Carmelites in Wisconsin. The "cells" of nuns were kept to twenty-one or smaller, and it seemed the goal of a cell was solitude and silence. One of these cells had run St. Leonard's. There was no Web site for this particular group, since the institution was no longer in operation. However, Jack read that when St. Leonard's had closed, the remaining nuns had relocated to Wauwatosa.

"I wonder where Wauwatosa is," Jack said, looking over at Manny.

"Look it up on MapQuest," Manny suggested. "What's in Wauwatosa, Jack?"

"The nuns that ran St. Leonard's relocated there after they shut down the asylum."

Linda emerged from her office. "Good morning, Manny. Did you sleep well? I see you found the shower."

"Yes, thanks. And another thanks for the breakfast here. I was thinking we'd be making a stop at Dunkin' Donuts."

"Somehow I don't see you as a doughnut kind of guy."

"No, I'm really not, but a nice old-fashioned one—on a road trip, you understand—might be permissible."

"Been traveling a lot?" Linda asked.

"Yes, a good deal, but I'm back in Chicago for a few months now, I think."

"I've been meaning to get down there to see *The Lion King*," she said.

"Well, come on down. Maybe we could go together?" Manny asked.

"That would be great." Linda beamed.

Jack interrupted. "Okay, so Wauwatosa? It's not far from here, about ten miles. It's just out of the city on the northwest side."

"That's right," Linda confirmed. "It's on the way to the farm, more or less. You'd just keep going west to get to Lake Mills."

"What sort of area is Lake Mills?" Manny asked.

"It's nice. Make that *posh*. It's a very pretty area—a spring-fed lake and a lot of recreation around it. Very quiet, the town has a small Main Street area. Some beautiful homes and estates out there."

The phone rang, and it turned out to be Harriet. Linda and Harriet chatted for a few minutes, and then Linda handed the phone to Jack.

"Jack, I've thought this over," Harriet said. "And I want to help. What can I do?"

Jack recounted what they had learned.

"What are you going to do?" Harriet asked.

"We haven't decided yet," said Jack.

"I'm coming over then—if you don't mind."

"Sure, please do." Jack handed the phone to Linda, who gave Harriet directions to the house.

"So what are we going to do?" he asked Manny and Linda.

"Let's wait for Harriet, and then we'll explore this a bit more before making some decisions," said Manny.

They had more coffee and food, and Jack phoned his message machine again. Nothing new there.

When Harriet arrived, Linda introduced her to Manny. Harriet and Manny hit it off immediately—they started talking about creative problem solving.

"This isn't exactly the kind of challenge I'm used to," said Harriet.

"I'm not a card-carrying private eye myself," said Manny. "But as you know, all challenges can be addressed with a deliberate process."

"So where are we in the process?" asked Harriet.

"I think we're still in Problem Exploration, but we've got a foot in Ideas as well. I wish I understood more about what we're up against. We don't have time to explore this the way I'd like to, and time is telling us to get moving." Manny listed the facts they knew so far.

"Let me build on that, Manny," said Harriet.

Jack noted the phrase "let me build on that"—it was a phrase that Molly had used, serving as a painful reminder of her absence. But he liked that it kept the flow of the discussion moving. He listened closely to Harriet.

"Molly Dunne is a clever young woman, but she doesn't have many friends here. Actually, I'm one of the few. After Molly left, her father's people, his lawyer Dave O'Donnell specifically, tried to get me to tell where she went. I told him I didn't know where she was. About a month ago, he asked again, and I said the same thing. Then two weeks ago, my office was broken into. I wondered at the time if it were a threat or conneced in some way to Dunne and his company."

"How did Molly ever end up working in your business if Brian Dunne is so overprotective?" Manny asked.

"Actually, it was Brian's idea."

Linda, Manny, and Jack exchanged glances.

"Molly lived at home when she was going to college. She went about half nuts with all the restrictions and verbal abuse. She got out now and then, she said, so she had some sort of 'life' while she was in school. Brian knew that when she graduated, she'd need to do something, and of course, he wanted to control what it was—at least keep her in Milwaukee and under his thumb. I go back a long way with her mother, and Brian and I . . . knew each other back then. When Molly was about to graduate from school, Brian arranged through O'Donnell to have me meet her and interview her at a career day on campus at Marquette. I offered her a job. She never realized until later that I had known her mother and that her father had arranged for her to get a job at Ideas on Ice. And when she learned it, she was very upset with me. In fact, I think that's what prompted her to leave town. She left not long after that."

"Why did he trust his daughter with you?" asked Manny.

"For a couple of reasons. It's complex. First of all, I think he respected me as a businessperson and a thinker. We used to talk business, and he was always surprised that I kept right up with him and could give him useful ideas. The other reason had to do with my relationship with

Mary—we were very close." Harriet paused and looked down. She seemed to be gathering her strength. "Mary was a social butterfly," she continued, "but Brian isolated her from having close friends. She only had one good friend—and that was me. She told me everything. I was the one she came to when she needed a shoulder to cry on."

"I'd think that would have messed you up with Brian," said Jack.

"Well, it did. At first he just discouraged Mary from seeing me, and then later he outright forbid it. Mary persisted, though, insisting she be allowed to see me. Brian came to me privately and made a deal with me—he'd back off on one condition: that I become his informant and tell him what Mary was up to."

"And you agreed to that?" asked Jack.

"It's pretty simple really. He bribed me," she stated flatly.

Jack was astounded. Harriet seemed like such a straight-ahead person.

"I'm sure you're judging me pretty tough right now," she said quietly.

"Nothing is ever as simple as it seems," said Manny. "Tell us what happened."

"Brian came to see me one day. At the time, I was struggling to get started with my career. I had a low-paying job at an advertising agency—those were the days when glass ceilings were even lower than they are now. I couldn't get anywhere. I had great ideas, and I worked like mad, but I was still just spinning my wheels." She sighed. "I was living hand-to-mouth and really couldn't support any kind of lifestyle on my salary. I really felt like I had no options."

Jack was relating to this part—that hopeless feeling when it seems you've hit the wall. It occurred to him that being able to generate options—ideas on how to break through these walls—was a way to maintain hope. With hope, you are less likely to make poor decisions based on desperation.

Harriet continued, "I had the idea to start my business in qualitative research, but I needed some training, and I needed some money to get it. But there was just no way. My parents had no resources to help me. The only people I knew who had money were Mary and Brian. I talked to Mary about my idea, and she talked to Brian about it. So, he came to see me one day. He'd done his homework. He knew exactly what I wanted. He offered to put me in business—give me everything I needed: money for training, customer contacts, introductions. It was unbelievable. In exchange for this, I was to do two things for him. First, let him know any juicy inside information on things I might learn doing research for companies. And second, keep an eye on his wife. I was afraid of him. And to be honest, I was ambitious and wanted to get my business started. He offered me a shortcut, and I took it. My rationalization was that it wouldn't hurt anybody. And I really thought it wouldn't."

WITH HOPE, YOU ARE LESS LIKELY TO MAKE
POOR DECISIONS BASED ON DESPERATION.

"It's understandable," said Manny.

"Well, I still regret it. I sold my soul that day," said Harriet.

"And the reason he put you in business was to have you beholden to him so you'd tell him what Mary was up to?" asked Jack.

"That's right. He was so paranoid. He was always afraid of Mary cheating, even before she ever considered it. He figured his wife was safe with me—if I was beholden to him. He was right. I was on the phone with her or meeting her for lunch almost every day. She told me everything going on in her life, and I fed tidbits back to Brian. It was a terrible thing to do."

"Did Mary ever find out about this?" asked Jack.

"Yes. And as you might well imagine, she didn't think much of me after that," Harriet said, looking down into her lap again. "And I don't blame her. What I didn't count on was just how unhappy Mary was with him, with her bottled-up life. I knew her, and I didn't know her. She was young and desperate—more desperate than I understood her to be back then." Harriet stalled. "She was a very lonely person. She ended up having an affair with some young guy, a tennis pro, and of course Brian found out and went off the deep end. He confined her to their farm in Lake Mills for a while, and then the story is that she went crazy. She was committed to a mental hospital, and I never saw her again."

"Her being committed must have been very hard on you," said Manny.

"It was terrifying. I knew it was malarkey—just an excuse to take her out of circulation. I tried to connect with her at St. Leonard's, but the nuns had her under lock and key, literally. It was criminal what everyone did to her, and yet it was all perfectly legal. O'Donnell and this psychiatrist, Donald Brennan, arranged everything to get her committed."

"Once she was committed, you had no contact with her?"

"No. It wasn't permitted. It was part of the 'treatment,' I was told. I went out to visit a couple of times, but they only allowed me to drop off gifts. I saw the same nun both times, the one who met with the public, a Sister Marie Teresa. I was concerned, but I thought I'd see Mary when she got a little better. Then I got the call from one of Brian's guys that Mary . . . that she had died out there," said Harriet, pausing. "Everyone was shocked. They buried her on the grounds, and there was no wake or funeral to speak of, only a ceremony at graveside after she was buried, and only a few people made the trip. Brian didn't—he hadn't forgiven her for the affair. Molly wasn't old enough to really feel its full impact. But it was very sad. It still is, after all these years." Harriet began misting up. "And you know, the nun pulled me aside afterward and said something strange. She said if Brian Dunne ever 'turns'—that I should talk to her. I assumed she meant if his grief over Mary got out of control."

"How did he react to her death?" asked Jack.

"He became more reclusive after that."

"So why are you here today?" asked Manny.

"I've been miserable about my decisions, about lying. I don't want to lie anymore. I owe that to Mary—and Molly."

"Thank you, Harriet," said Manny. "All this helps immensely. Now let's talk about what we're going to do."

17: A CLOISTERED CONVENT IN WAUWATOSA

Where Jack and Harriet listen to a Sister

As he enters the Dunne compound, Manny uses his well-trained powers of observation. Observation is a skill that needs to be practiced. Paying very close attention allows you to notice what others miss. In creative problem solving, noticing what others miss, or what you might have missed when you weren't looking at things carefully, is an essential skill. In business, noticing what others don't can lead to a new opportunity for a product, a service, a company, or even a whole new industry. When we truly listen and observe, we learn more.

Manny made the drive to Lake Mills alone in Harriet's car. He'd decided he'd have to park it somewhere and walk onto the farm. On the way out of Milwaukee, he'd taken the time to stop at an

165

Army/Navy store for some clothes and other supplies. He'd bought some work clothes, boots, gloves, and a bandanna that he tied around his head. It had been a long time since he'd done work as a day laborer. *It'll be good for me,* he thought.

He'd also stopped by a library and had found the issue of *Architectural Digest* with the article on the Dunne estate. He copied it and studied the layout of the property.

Manny thought he'd simply inquire about getting some temporary work on Dunne's farm—gardening or other odd work. His father had gardened at home—flowers and vegetables—and Manny had worked beside him. Manny also had done a lot of farm work in Texas for his uncle.

They surely had a gardener, but Manny knew there was day-to-day gardening work, and then there was heavier gardening work, the kind often put off till end of season—or until someone with a strong back and a low price tag came along. And if they didn't need any gardening done, he'd offer to paint, or do low-level carpentry. And he'd keep asking until he got some work. He knew there was a chance he wouldn't get anywhere, but it was worth a try. He was hoping his asking price would be so low they wouldn't be able to resist.

———

Jack and Harriet found the convent in Wauwatosa easily. It was larger than Jack would have thought, given the rule about twenty-one or fewer in a cell. Talking with the receptionist, they learned that this site was a training center, sort of an entry point for young women who wanted to join the order. So that would explain the larger size and number—these women weren't actually Carmelites yet.

The receptionist, a very old woman, seemed happy for a little company to talk to, which helped a lot, since Harriet was very nervous. Her conversations with the sisters had been difficult when she'd tried to visit Mary Dunne at St. Leonard's years before, and on the drive over, she had confessed to Jack that nuns gave her the creeps.

When Jack and Harriet asked for Sister Marie Teresa, the receptionist apologized. "I'm sorry, but Sister Marie is not able to see people at this time."

"Is she cloistered, or is she ill?" asked Harriet.

"She's cloistered."

"I knew Sister Marie when she was at St. Leonard's," said Harriet. "I haven't seen her for a number of years. Are you sure there isn't any chance we can see her, even for a few minutes?"

"Oh, I'm sorry, it's not permitted."

"Sister . . . ?" Jack asked, hoping to learn the nun's name.

"I'm Sister Ruth."

"Sister Ruth, if I told you this was a matter of life and death, a matter that could determine the fates of two souls, would that make a difference?"

"Oh, my . . . of course, but I'd have to know the circumstances."

"We're searching for two missing persons, and we think Sister Marie might be able to help us find them," said Jack bluntly, thinking the truth might just work here.

"Recently missing?" asked the old woman.

"Yes," answered Harriet.

"Well, but how would Sister Marie know anything about it? She's cloistered, after all. Are you with the police?"

"No, Sister, we're here privately—we're friends of the missing," said Harriet.

"I'm sorry, but this just doesn't seem like anything Sister Marie could help you with. She's been cloistered for almost five years— how could she possibly know anything about two missing persons?"

Harriet felt they were about to fail in their efforts to see Sister Marie. "Well, can you take a message to her?" she asked.

Sister Ruth paused, but finally said, "I suppose so."

Harriet scribbled quickly on a piece of paper.

> *Sister Marie Teresa,*
>   *We met years ago when I tried to visit my friend,*
> *Mary Dunne. As you know, she passed away at St.*

*Leonard's. Her daughters, just young children then,
are now missing. I suspect foul play. I'm afraid for
them. I really need to talk—you may be able to help.
Please see me.*

Harriet Potts

She folded the note and handed it to the nun. Once again, Sister Ruth hesitated for a moment, but then she walked away with the note.

"I wonder if this visit is a waste of time," said Jack.

"It's a long shot," admitted Harriet, "but, you know, I've always wanted to look that nun in the eye one more time anyway. She knew something about Dunne, I think. I was so emotional about losing Mary, and so afraid of Brian Dunne, that I chose not to push it at the time."

"Well, we'll learn what we can, and then we'll drive out toward the farm and find someplace to kill the afternoon."

Sister Ruth reappeared. "Come this way, please."

They followed Sister Ruth down one hall and then another and then another. She led them into a small and very spare sitting room with a crucifix on one wall, a painting of Madonna and Child on another. "Please sit down," she said.

Sister Ruth left them, and a few minutes later, Sister Marie entered the room. She was a small elderly woman. She walked slowly, appearing to be in some pain. But there was dignity in her presence. She sat down in a chair facing Harriet and Jack.

"So, Harriet Potts, I remember you. You came to visit Mary Dunne years ago."

"Yes," said Harriet. As an experienced interviewer, she did not want to put up any barriers, and since she sensed that Sister Marie was prepared to be defensive, she thought it best simply to let her talk.

"Your note said that Mary's daughters are missing. What's happened?"

Harriet noted that the old nun had already taken charge.

"Molly and Bridgette Dunne have been missing for about a week, and Brian Dunne may be restraining their freedom. As friends, we're quite concerned about their safety."

"Brian Dunne has been reclusive since Mary's death, and people used to gossip about him and his tragedy. I met his daughters years ago and haven't seen them in quite some time. I'm not sure how I can help you. I'm sorry."

"Brian is a recluse, Sister. That's true. But let me bring you up to date. Molly, that's Mary's older daughter, left Milwaukee six months ago because her father wouldn't stop interfering in her life. She kept her whereabouts secret from him until just recently. Her sister, Bridgette, has also dropped out of sight—she was living in a dorm room at Marquette. We have reason to believe they are together."

"Couldn't this just be a case of these two girls running off somewhere?"

"Yes, it could be, but we don't think so."

"Why?"

Jack spoke up. "Sister, may I please say something? I've spent the last few months working with Molly—we are good friends. Actually, we're more than friends. And I don't believe she would go somewhere without telling me."

"Are you in love?" the nun asked.

Jack tried to hide his surprise, but he didn't hesitate with his answer. "Yes, Sister, I am in love with her."

"Is she in love with you?"

"I think so, yes, she is," said Jack.

"Do you plan to marry her?" the nun asked quietly.

"Well, yes, if I ever get the chance."

"What kind of girl is Molly Dunne? Is she at all like her mother?"

"If you mean, 'Is she crazy?' then no, she's not crazy. But I don't think her mother was either," said Harriet.

"I never said her mother was crazy," said Sister Marie. "What her mother was—was a fine actress."

"I'm not sure what you mean," Harriet said, puzzled by the comment.

"It doesn't matter. What matters are those two girls."

"I NEVER SAID HER MOTHER WAS CRAZY,"
SAID SISTER MARIE. "WHAT HER
MOTHER WAS — WAS A FINE ACTRESS."

"Yes, Sister—exactly," said Jack.

"I'm still not sure how I can help you."

Harriet spoke up. "Sister, I should have said this years ago, but I'm going to say it now. I've always suspected that Mary Dunne was killed by her husband. I don't know all the details, and maybe not by his hand directly, but I do know that the Carmelites helped him by holding her prisoner at Old St. Leonard's."

The old nun's face went red at this remark. "That's preposterous. Mary Dunne was never a prisoner at St. Leonard's, and she was not killed by Brian Dunne. I'll tell you what she was if you want to know the truth. She was a prisoner in her own home. And you know that's true, but you don't know the half of it."

Sister Marie was still quite upset. She pulled a handkerchief from inside her robes. After she blew her nose, she continued in a softer tone, "The Carmelites were not party to any imprisonment. We took Mary Dunne in when she was almost crazy from acting crazy, and so weak she could barely walk. We brought her back to health. Actually, I brought her back to health."

"Brian Dunne was very controlling," commented Harriet, hoping to encourage Sister Marie to continue talking.

"It went beyond that. Just before she came to St. Leonard's, Brian was keeping her under lock and key. She was kept in a small cottage on the grounds of their farm in Lake Mills. He even had bars built into the windows. I said Mary was a great actress because the only way she could get out of that cottage and off that farm was to act crazy. Brian didn't believe it at first, but she sold her performance with a suicide attempt. She almost bled to death."

"You say you brought her back to health, but she died at St. Leonard's."

"Yes, that's true. Mary Dunne died at St. Leonard's." She paused, hesitating. "It was a tragedy. She'd recovered from her faked suicide attempt, but then something unexpected happened . . ."

"What was the cause of death?"

"A broken heart, I think. She missed her children. She missed you—her best friend—in spite of your betrayal of her confidences." Harriet's eyes grew wide. "Oh, yes, I knew about that."

Harriet was getting angry, but she worked very hard to control herself. "I never understood why she was buried before anyone could get out to St. Leonard's."

"Mr. Dunne was too distraught to see her, and he left it up to us."

"Sister, is there anything else you could tell us that might help us find these young women?"

"I don't think so, except to say Brian Dunne is a dark and troubled soul, and you'd be well-advised to steer clear of him."

Harriet stood and said, "Thank you, Sister."

"Where are you going now?"

"We're on our way out to Lake Mills," said Harriet.

"Before you go—is there some way I could reach you?"

Harriet gave Sister Marie her business card after writing down her cell phone number on the back.

The little nun looked at the card and then looked up at Harriet. "Harriet, I have to ask you something."

"What is it?"

The nun moved closer to Harriet, then reached out and held her hand. "Have you suffered a great deal?"

"Yes," said Harriet quietly.

"You should know that Mary forgave you."

Harriet felt her eyes well up with tears.

Sister Marie said, "I'll pray for you, this young man, and those girls. I'm sure things will work out. God bless you."

Sister Marie bowed with her hands folded in front of her and then walked away from them down the hall.

As Jack and Harriet left the convent, Jack said, "This is like a soap opera."

"Worse," said Harriet, who was clearly shaken up by the meeting.

"But what did we really learn in there?" asked Jack.

"That Brian is worse than I ever thought he was, even in the days when I thought he wasn't. I'm surprised by how much Sister Marie knew."

"Are you okay?" asked Jack.

"Yeah, I'm okay. I'm angry. We've got to get those girls. I owe this to their mother, and I owe this to Molly."

"I'm wondering if history is repeating itself. Molly and Bridgette might be in that same cottage Brian held their mother in," said Jack, "the one with the bars."

Jack borrowed Harriet's cell phone and made calls to Manny and Linda.

18: LAKE MILLS

Where Manny plays Trojan horse

The team moves into the last phase of CPS, Getting into Action. They did as much Idea Generation as time allowed, and now they are taking action on what they know to be true with the best plan they have. By moving into action, they increase their odds of success by placing themselves in a place to take advantage of opportunities that arise and accidents that occur.

Effective, creative people get into action on their ideas even when they are not sure, not fully informed, or are afraid. If better ideas occur to them, they can adjust their plans. If the original ideas don't work, they can back up and generate new ones and take advantage of what they've learned. They can even use step three, Problem Framing and Reframing, as Manny and Linda do in this chapter.

173

Manny walked up to the front gate of the Dunne farm, which was locked tight. Then he noticed the intercom and walked over to press the button.

"Yes?"

"Lo, I'm Manny—lookin' for day job gardening," he said, using the accent he'd heard every day growing up.

"We don't need any help, thank you."

"Lissen, I just want a day's work—I'll do any work you have. Can I speak to the head groundskeeper?"

There was a delay, then, "He'll come out to the gate to see you. Just wait there."

Manny looked down at his clothes, not that convincing because they were too new, too clean. His hands were also a bit too manicured-looking for a day laborer. He'd keep his hands in his pockets for now and put some gloves on later—if he got in.

Ten minutes went by, and then Manny heard a vehicle coming down the long driveway from the main house. It pulled into view, a small red pickup truck, then slowed down, stopping in front of the gate. An older man got out—short, solid, with dark, gray-streaked, well-groomed hair. As the man got closer, Manny felt a surge of hope since he was obviously Hispanic. He looked like an old-fashioned Mexican gentleman, complete with a guayabera shirt. The man came through the gate, then carefully locked it behind him.

Manny addressed him first in broken English, but then he asked if he spoke Spanish. The man nodded, so Manny began speaking in Spanish, careful to keep his language simple and not betray his education. The man came closer. Manny explained that he had just moved to the area with his family and that he'd had trouble getting work. He said that he needed a couple of days of work—and cash—desperately. That he would do any kind of work he was asked to do—dig ditches, anything. That he had experience with landscaping, painting, carpentry, and even simple electrical work. He dropped the names of two large families in Mexico City that he and his father had done work for years ago.

The man responded courteously. He said he was sorry to see a man down on his luck and would do what he could to help him. But, he added, the owner of this farm is a very peculiar man, very private, and were he to bring him in, he would insist that Manny do whatever was asked of him with no questions asked. There were areas on the property that were off-limits to all employees, and under no circumstances should he go near those areas.

When Manny agreed, the man said there was a project that he could use some help with. They were rebuilding some of the stalls inside the horse barn. The man had hired someone last week who had not worked out, but if Manny could take over the project, it would be very helpful. Then the man told Manny what he would pay him. The fee was ridiculously low.

Manny was careful here. He was portraying a desperate man, and yet the culture demanded a negotiation, a bargaining. Manny fell into the drill, not working it too aggressively, and after a couple of rounds, he agreed to a fee that was a bit closer to what Manny would have considered reasonable. They shook hands.

The man's name was Enrique. As it turned out, Enrique explained, most of the staff were Latinos, except for the security group. Enrique warned Manny not to speak to any of them unless they asked him something. He led Manny through the gate and motioned for him to get in the truck.

Manny was elated to be on the grounds, but he coached himself to stay in character and observe. Enrique said it was a long drive back to the house from the road, and Manny made sure to look at the mileage on the car odometer. The grounds were beautiful. Manny said so, and Enrique smiled, pointing out his residence, a cottage, which was up the road about a quarter of a mile. It was set in a cluster of trees just off the road and to the west of the main house. They passed another cottage on the other side, Manny noting several cars parked there. This cottage was larger and had been modified—the large picture windows looked like an architectural mistake. Inside, three men were visible through the windows, one on a phone, the other two smoking cigarettes. Enrique said, with barely disguised contempt, that this was the security team.

Manny asked why they needed so much security for a family estate. Enrique hesitated and then said they had some very valuable art in the main house and Arabian horses also. According to Enrique, Mr. Dunne was very concerned about his privacy. Enrique also said he wouldn't be surprised if Mr. Dunne had created some enemies in his business dealings before he retired. When Manny asked if Mr. Dunne had any family, Enrique ignored the question, suddenly noticing a flower bed alongside the drive that didn't look the way it should and muttering comments to himself.

> THIS COTTAGE WAS LARGER AND HAD BEEN MODIFIED—THE LARGE PICTURE WINDOWS LOOKED LIKE AN ARCHITECTURAL MISTAKE.

When they pulled up to the main house, Manny scanned the site carefully. The residence was an immense English Tudor. It was stately and complemented on each side by clusters of mature pin oaks and silver maples, with an informal garden that was just coming to life. It could have been a postcard for a mansion in the English countryside. There were several outbuildings: a long and low barn about one hundred yards northwest of the mansion, painted white, and another smaller building of a circular shape that Manny imagined was for horse training.

Enrique parked the truck. As they walked in the direction of the barn, he pointed out some of the landscaping features on the grounds, Manny making appreciative comments. As they neared the barn and crested a rise, a large pond became visible on the other side, just northeast of the barns. Directly opposite the barns, to the east and across the expansive pond, Manny noticed a Tudor-style cottage built into the side of a ridge. The ridge ran north-south, and at the top were dense woods. Enrique noticed Manny looking in that direction. He warned Manny again not to roam around the grounds but to stay in the barn. Manny noted that the cottage was clearly visible from the back of the main house. Taking one last glance, he also noticed a man in an Irish walking cap sitting on a stool under a tree about twenty yards further up the hill from the cottage.

Inside the barn, the construction job was well underway. It would be a lot of work, but nothing too difficult. Enrique showed him where the tools were, and then he sat and watched for a half hour to see if Manny could do the work, speaking in Spanish occasionally about the weather and asking him a few questions about his background. Manny kept his answers short, being careful again about his language. Enrique was soon satisfied that he'd struck a good bargain, and he left Manny on his own. But before he left, he showed Manny an intercom, telling him that if he needed him, he was to call security and have him paged. And for a third time, Enrique told him not to wander around the grounds.

Manny continued at his work for some time after Enrique left, making sure that if Enrique checked back, he would find progress made. At one point, he heard a vehicle outside, and when he looked out the window, he saw Enrique's pickup going by, heading back toward the front gate. As Manny walked through the barn, a horse nickered and pranced in his stall. Manny looked in and saw a beautiful white horse, an Arabian by the looks of it. A man walked by the window on the other side of the horse's stall and stopped when he heard the horse. He talked in low tones—in Spanish—to the horse. Manny could see that it was a young guy in work clothes, probably a groom.

"Hola," Manny said.

"Who's there?" asked the worker, in English.

"My name is Manny—I'm working on the new horse stalls, but I was just looking for a place to go to the bathroom."

The groom laughed. "Enrique told me he found somebody to bang on that stuff. Yeah, just keep walking to the end of the barn. It's on the right side."

"Hey thanks, bro," said Manny.

Inside the bathroom, he locked the door and looked out a small window. He could see the cottage from this vantage point. He reached deep into one of his pockets and brought out a small pair of binoculars. Getting a closer look, Manny could see that the cottage had well-disguised iron bars built into the window design. The glass on the windows facing the lake was an old-fashioned style of frosted glass that distorted shapes on the inside. He noticed movement in the cottage.

Then he shifted his view toward the watchman on the hill. The guy was middle-aged, but he looked fit. He was wearing a leather coat, and as he shifted his position on the stool, a leather shoulder strap came briefly into Manny's view. He was armed.

Manny tried to use his cell phone, but he was in a weak coverage area and couldn't connect to the outside. When he got back to his work area, he picked up the intercom phone. A female voice answered.

"I'm working in the barn. Can I call home?"

"Who is this?"

"My name is Manny. Enrique has me fixing the horse stalls. Just need to call home and talk to my wife a minute."

There was a pause. "Okay, here's a line."

Manny dialed Harriet's cell phone. Speaking in his Spanish accent, he said, "Rosa, got day work on the Dunne farm repairing a horse's stall in the barn. Very beautiful home and garden; they have a pretty pond behind the house with a little cottage on the hillside; it looks like a postcard. There's even a shepherd on the hillside, like back home. I'll call later so you can come pick me up."

"Okay, adios," said Harriet.

Manny hung up the phone.

———

Linda wasn't cut out for work that required patience. She'd driven over to the Dunne mansion, essentially to keep an eye on it and note the comings and goings of the security guards and house servants. She watched for a half hour. No sign of Brian Dunne or the girls. Worse yet, she'd not planned things very well because the coffee she drank earlier was pressing on her bladder.

After a while, Harriet and Jack called, explaining that it was likely that Molly and Bridgette were being held at the farm. It was her job to help them locate the whereabouts of Brian Dunne and to get a sense of how much security he could muster in an emergency. She watched for another half hour. Nobody went in or out of the mansion or the carriage house.

————

Harriet and Jack were halfway to Lake Mills. When she glanced over at Jack, she noticed his troubled expression. "This is all going to work out," she said.

"Uh-huh—what makes you so sure? We're dealing with a complete nutcase, and he's got armed guards. We're driving to rescue my girl and her sister—me, an underemployed photographer, with who? An idea generator, backed up by a trend analyst, and led by a pacifist problem-solving consultant. Yeah, we're in good shape."

"That's one way to look at it," said Harriet.

"And just how are you looking at it?" Jack said peevishly. He was getting annoyed with this "other perspective" thing that Harriet—and Manny—constantly seemed to be doing.

"We have a lot of skill on our . . . team for one thing," she said.

"And they have guns," Jack said emphatically.

"We'll never get those two out of there with direct confrontation," stated Harriet. "We'll either avoid the guns, or we won't do it."

She was right—they had a choice, and after all, this wasn't a movie.

"What we also have is the element of surprise. Dunne has no idea we are on to him."

"As far as we know. He knows I'm out there somewhere," said Jack.

"Well, he's paranoid, that's for sure. So we'll have to expect this won't be easy on those grounds alone. You called him after the beating you took, didn't you?" she asked.

"Yeah, yeah, I did. That was stupid."

"Well, it's easy to see why you made that call when you did. Now that we know more about him and what's going on, it's easy to look back and see what else you might have done. So, no, you're not stupid." Harriet looked over at Jack and said almost as an afterthought, "I'd call you a person with more courage than I ever had."

Jack took this in and thought about it for a moment. Perhaps he was brave *and* stupid. Looking at Harriet again, he was struck with the intense reality of his situation. He didn't want to see anyone hurt.

"I'm sorry to have gotten you involved in this, Harriet."

She didn't say anything at first, but then she answered in a slow, measured tone. "I've been involved in this for a long time, Jack. And I'm scared for Molly and Bridgette. In my own way, I feel very responsible for them. I played games with their father, and it may have contributed to their mother's losing her life. You know, I still don't buy that heart attack story. Mary seemed like such a healthy woman. Anyway, I may sound like I'm in a mafia movie here, but part of it is about settling an old score."

"I know. And I'm glad you're part of the team." Jack smiled briefly at her, but then his thoughts returned to Molly. He stared out of the window at the Wisconsin landscape. "How are we going to get them out of there?"

"I don't know yet, but I have some ideas."

"Ideas on Ice," said Jack.

"More like ideas on fire, but, well, this will put my skills to the test in a way they've never been tested before."

"What are you thinking? I need to hear some kind of possibilities here or else I'll go crazy."

"Well, the challenge of all this could be viewed as a rescue mission. But that would be the traditional view."

"And so . . . ?" asked Jack.

"It could also be viewed as liberation."

"Isn't that the same thing though?"

"Just go with the flow, okay?" Harriet asked.

"Okay—sorry."

"Or it could be viewed as a rekidnapping . . . or a performance . . . or as persuasion . . . or as a con job . . . or as a diversion . . . or a preemptive strike . . . or a Hollywood movie . . . or some combination . . . or all of the above. The task really is to get Brian and his security team to look the other way while we find the girls. And to not have him catch on until it's way too late. We also have to plan for what happens after we get them out. He won't give up easily," said Harriet.

"It really is a performance," said Jack, "a con-job performance piece."

"I think that's how we should look at it," said Harriet.

Her cell phone rang, and they both jumped.

Harriet answered and heard a woman's voice. "Harriet, did you ever quit smoking?"

"I quit about five years ago. Who's asking?"

"It's taken a bit of a toll on your voice."

"Who is this?" Harriet repeated.

"You don't recognize my voice, do you, old friend?"

But suddenly, Harriet did. "Mary? It can't be . . ."

"Mary's dead. My name is Gina Mooney. I'm a pottery artist and a horse trainer. It's way too long a story to be telling you right now. I want you to pick me up. I understand you're on your way to Lake Mills? You might find me helpful in your efforts."

Harriet burst into tears. She pulled the car over.

Jack took the phone from her. "Who is this?"

"I was just telling Harriet, my name is Gina Mooney. What might be interesting for you to know is that I'm Molly and Bridgette's mother."

Jack was speechless.

"Listen to me," the voice went on. "This is no joke. Sister Marie called me from the convent. I've been living under a new identity for years—you might call it the Carmelite Victims Protection Program. My death was faked. I live near Lake Mills in Johnson Creek. Pick me up at the Johnson Creek Outlet Mall. There's an Eddie Bauer store there, and I'll be standing in front of it. I'm wearing jeans and a light brown suede jacket. I'll have glasses on. Anyway, I think I can help. Please, let me help. It's time."

"This is so weird," Jack said. Taking a deep breath, he continued. "Okay, I believe you. We'll pick you up in about a half hour."

"See you."

Jack clicked the cell phone shut, handed it back to Harriet, and relayed what they were supposed to do next. "Can you believe this?"

"No. No, I can't believe it. Mary Dunne was dead. I've lived without her for years, and now, she just pops up like some Lady Lazarus."

"You're sure it was really her?"

"It was her. Nobody could fake that voice. I know her voice," said Harriet. She straightened herself up in the seat, wiping mascara from under her eyes with a Kleenex from her purse. "I'm in absolute shock. It's like somebody just threw a bomb at me."

"Or at least an M-80," said Jack without thinking.

"M-80—that's like a cherry bomb, right?" asked Harriet.

"Yeah, much like a cherry bomb," said Jack, looking at her inquisitively.

"Those things are really loud, aren't they?"

"They really are," he said. "Surprisingly loud."

"Can you buy those this time of year?"

"In Wisconsin, I think you can buy them year-round," said Jack, remembering that Rob occasionally made a trip up here to buy them. "Why do you ask?"

"Just thinking out loud. Let's swing by Eddie Bauer and pick up my old friend," said Harriet. "I still can't believe it."

"Gina Mooney," said Jack. "A pottery artist, a horse trainer—and a ghost."

———

Manny had been sawing and hammering for over an hour and decided he could take a break. He wandered outside the front side of the barn, the cottage in his view across the pond. Positioning himself by a flower bed, he knelt down and pretended to examine the ground, pulling out a blade of errant grass as if it were a weed. He snuck as long a peek as he could at the cottage. The guard was still up on the hill.

He saw a tall black woman in a maid's uniform start up the path toward the cottage from the back of the house. She had not seen him, but Manny walked back into the shadow of the barn entrance and watched as the maid walked up the hill. She had a tray of food, complete with a portable coffee holder. The guard got up from his stool and walked over to meet her at the door, pulling a key from his belt. The maid stepped in, and he locked the door behind her. Just then, Manny heard the whine of the engine from Enrique's truck, so he stepped further into the shadows then went back to work on the stall.

Enrique checked Manny's work and was pleased with his progress. "Good job, Manny. Think you can finish this up in a couple of hours?"

"I can finish."

"When you are done, have me paged. I'll pay you and drop you back at the front gate."

"Okay."

———

Linda was still monitoring the Dunne mansion when Harriet called.

"I have an idea about how to thin out the security at the farm," Harriet said. "We'll need you to help us on that end in a couple of hours."

"How so?" Linda asked.

"I want you to stop and visit a fireworks store and pick up a large bag of M-80s and a couple of smoke bombs if they have them."

"I haven't set off an M-80 since I was twelve years old," said Linda, "but my brother was an expert."

"And pick up a good cigar as well. Do you smoke? Do you know how to get one lit so it won't go out?"

"My father smoked cigars—I know the drill," said Linda.

"So get one. I'll speak to you again in about an hour," Harriet said. "Oh, and we've picked up another player on this end."

"Who?"

"Mary Dunne . . . or I should say Gina Mooney."

"What?" asked Linda, confused.

"Long story, but we just picked up the real article at Eddie Bauer," said Harriet.

"Is this some kind of code?"

"No. Mary Dunne, in the flesh, is in the car with us right now. She's going to show us the keys to the kingdom in Lake Mills."

———

Jack was still getting used to the idea that he was in the car with Molly's mother. If you looked very carefully you could see some of

Molly's features, but she was very deliberately plain-looking. She wore no makeup, and her face was weathered and taut—she'd spent a lot of time outdoors. Her hair was completely gray—and she made no attempt to cover it. She wore oversized round black glasses. Her appearance was so changed that Harriet didn't recognize her when they'd first pulled up—she had been a pretty and very polished woman back in the day, and now she was hiding herself in plain sight by dressing like a ranch hand with very poor eyesight.

The meeting at Eddie Bauer's had been a cool one. Harriet had stepped forward to hug Gina, but Gina had stepped back, clearly not wanting to be touched. She shook Jack's hand and then got in the front passenger seat. Harriet and Jack filled her in on the situation, and a period of silence followed.

Harriet was the one who started things up again. "Mary, I can't believe you are sitting here with me."

"Call me Gina. I don't feel much like Mary anymore."

"Gina—why did you pick that name?"

"My grandmother was named Regina, and her nickname was Gina. She was sweet and funny, so I took up her name. And I had some cousins named Mooney."

"How did you fake your death? I mean, somebody has to be buried at St. Leonard's."

"Somebody is buried behind St. Leonard's. A woman showed up at the doorstep about a month after I got there. She was homeless—no family—and she had a terminal case of TB. The nuns did what they could for her, but she was too weakened for any treatment to work. When she died of a heart attack, Sister Marie and I cooked up the scheme. The county coroner came out and declared me dead, only it wasn't me. The doctor took the nun's word for the identity. Then she somehow convinced Brian that the respectful thing to do with a suspected suicide—they told him I killed myself—was have a closed casket. They said they would report the death as a coronary if he agreed to that. He agreed. Mary Dunne was buried and in the ground, and Brian never knew it wasn't really me.

"So, why did you decide to come out of hiding?" asked Harriet.

This gave Gina pause for thought. "Well, my girls are in trouble. I've not done much for them; I've been too afraid. I'm older now, and I guess I just think I have less to lose. In a way, I don't care about just myself anymore. I want to, finally, take their side. So, Harriet, whose side are you on now?"

"I'm sorry Mar . . . Gina. I'd do anything to change what I did," said Harriet.

Gina looked at Harriet for a moment before she spoke. "Ambition got the better of you, didn't it?" She stopped and sighed. "It's not so surprising what you did, really, and I'm sorry—I know the kind of pressure he must have put you under."

"I have no excuses, I was a gutless wonder. Right now, whatever our differences were, I just want to get the girls to a safe place," said Harriet.

"Yes," said Gina, "their safety is the thing. And I must say, I was a gutless wonder myself."

"Maybe being scared isn't so gutless—maybe just human," put in Jack.

"Well, maybe you're right. But it cost me. I didn't raise my daughters; I wasn't with them. But I won't let him mess up their chances for freedom. I'll die first—I mean really die—before I let that happen to them. I've spent years trying to justify what I did. I thought it was my only option, my only chance—and their only chance. I should have found a way to go back and get them, but I was scared and I had no resources. And I was damaged goods—I've spent years in therapy trying to make sense of my life and reduce my own paranoia. As the years went by, while I was trying to stabilize myself, I saw them going to school, and it looked like they had something close to a normal life. I suspected worse, but I wasn't able to do anything about it. I heard that Molly got into college and graduated, and I thought maybe she had gotten away. But when Sister Marie called I realized that I had to do something. Brian does love them, but he's sick. He can't stand the idea of either one of them being grown women, of being anything but a perfect little girl. The idea of them out in the world experiencing things he can't control . . . that's why he's done this. I feel sorry for him, but he's not going to take Molly and Bridgette down with him."

———

Manny was nearly finished with the stall. It was almost six o'clock, and he'd been after it all afternoon. He tried his cell phone again—still no signal. Then he picked up the intercom. A different voice answered this time.

"Could I get an outside line?" Manny asked.

"You guys aren't supposed to use this phone."

"Listen, I just need to call my wife to get a ride home. I won't be back tomorrow."

"Okay . . . this is it, though."

"Gracias."

Manny called Harriet. "I'm done in here," he said, maintaining his accent. "Pick me up by front gate of Dunne's farm at 6:30."

Enrique came by soon after that and examined Manny's finished work. "You can get spot work here a lot if you want it. Do you have a phone number?"

"No, not yet," said Manny.

"Any way I can get in touch with you?" asked Enrique.

"How about if I call and see?"

Enrique looked a bit disappointed. "Please do," he said. Then he switched over to Spanish. "Are you working tomorrow?"

Manny carefully led Enrique to believe that he was interested but remained noncommittal. He was as polite as he could be.

Enrique paid him in cash then gave him ten more. In Spanish again, he said, "You seem like a good man. I wish you luck."

"You were very kind to hire me today. I needed help, and you gave me work," said Manny.

"I wish I could hire you full time, but this place is run by that mob that surrounds Mr. Dunne. They are not good men. And he's a strange man."

"What's wrong with him?" asked Manny.

"He's wounded . . . ," the man said, pausing before continuing in a wistful way. "I remember when there were good times at this place. Maybe they will happen again." But he didn't look too hopeful. "Mr.

Dunne, I think he will probably die soon—he's given up on living. Then I don't know what will happen here. The girls will probably sell the place. It would hold bad memories for them."

"What's so bad in a beautiful place like this? Horses, gardens, swimming pools?"

"You don't want to know," said Enrique.

"I guess not," said Manny.

"Let me drive you down to the front gate."

Manny and Enrique got into the truck. As they were driving down the road, they passed a large black limo.

"Is that Mr. Dunne?"

"Yeah, everyone will be thrilled to see him," he said sarcastically.

"The guards?"

"No, I mean . . . yes, the guards. His daughter—she wouldn't even know him in her condition."

"What's wrong with her?"

"She's sick. It might be drugs."

"That has to be tough," said Manny.

"It is. You should be glad you're not around at night to hear her crying and screaming."

"Who's taking care of her?" asked Manny.

"Her older sister," said Enrique. "She's a good girl."

"I see."

"Listen, remember what I said about this place. Don't talk about it to anyone, okay?"

They pulled up to the gate, and they both got out. Manny watched Enrique carefully as he punched the code into the keypad, and he memorized the four-digit code: 5-8-5-4.

"Thanks again. Be in touch—I can give you a lot of part-time work here," said Enrique.

"I will," said Manny. "Gracias."

The gate shut behind him. Manny watched as Enrique drove off. Then he walked down the road about a quarter of a mile to the car and called Harriet and Jack from his cell phone. He asked them to rendezvous at a pub in Lake Mills.

Linda hadn't been to a fireworks store in years. Her father had always made a yearly visit around the Fourth of July. Fireworks stores dotted the landscape in Wisconsin. She got a shopping cart and wound her way through the store. She avoided the Roman candles and other exotics and instead focused on the large firecrackers. She picked up several smoke bombs as well.

At the checkout counter, the man behind it looked at her curiously. "Stocking up for the Fourth of July?"

"Exactly."

"Pretty early."

"I always plan ahead. By the way, do you sell cigars?"

"We sure do."

"Great. Pick out a couple for my husband, would you? Some good ones that don't stink too much . . ."

The clerk laughed, and then he put a couple of medium-priced cigars on the counter. "These are pretty mild," he said.

"Good. Thanks. Oh, one more thing—a pack of Camel filters, please."

Linda walked out of the store with a shopping bag filled to the brim. She felt giddy.

Harriet, Jack, and Gina met Manny at the brew pub. Harriet did the introductions.

"Manny, I'd like you to meet the woman formerly known as Mary Dunne."

Manny looked at Mary and back at Harriet and Jack. He smiled, and Jack noticed the glow that seemed to radiate toward Molly's mother. "I'm pleased, and surprised, to meet you, Mary."

"You can call me Gina. I'm pleased to meet you as well—it's a shame it had to be under these circumstances."

They sat down at a table and ordered sandwiches and coffee. Manny described the layout of the farm in as much detail as he could remember. Gina confirmed and elaborated. Manny ate with vigor, pausing every once in a while to add more information.

"According to Enrique, Molly is taking care of Bridgette. I wonder if the drug habit is a story Dunne tells his employees, or if it's true. We really don't know what's wrong with her."

"Does it matter?" asked Gina.

"It may matter once we get to her. We don't know if she's fit to travel."

"I don't think this can wait," said Harriet. "I think we've got a good distraction set up with Linda at the Dunne residence in Milwaukee. It should be enough to have him go back home," said Harriet. "Hopefully he'll take most of his boys with him."

"Breaking in won't be easy even if they are out of the way—and he'll leave behind a couple of guys, at least. That cottage is a prison cell. The doors are reinforced, and the locks are strong. You won't kick that door down, I know," said Gina.

"So we need to distract the guys who are left. Then we'll need to get the keys off the hillside guard," said Manny.

"There are other problems too," said Jack. "If we break into the property, they'll call the police."

"It's about a fifteen-minute drive from Lake Mills out to the farm," said Gina, "ten if you're speeding. The local cops used to work with the security guys pretty closely, I remember. They all know each other. But I think I know a way to get onto the property without setting off an alarm."

"Good, but just in case, how many local cruisers are there—were there?" asked Manny.

"Just two," said Gina.

"Well, the other problem is the getaway," said Jack. "And then, how do we prevent ourselves from being taken to court after all this?"

Manny said, "I think we can balance the scales of justice with some evidence. You make a good point—Brian Dunne is a dirty-tricks expert, so he'll have ideas on how to dodge this, how to explain it. We don't want to give him a chance. We need to be able to prove what's been going on, if we have to. Jack, you'll want to fire up your camera and flash unit. I'm calling my legal team in Chicago."

19: Smokin'

Where passion and diversions rule

The culmination of Problem Exploration, Idea Generation, and creative action takes place in this chapter. The team has done its best preparing but now must rely on passion for the rescue plans. They all care deeply about the outcome and are fully committed.

Passion is infectious. It's one reason some ideas—and some organizations—succeed in spite of mistakes, miscalculations, and Murphy's Law. Sometimes, but rarely, our success is like a slow swan dive—graceful and flawless; more often we stumble into success only because we keep trying. When implementing a plan, move forward with passion in your heart and with as many creative ideas as you can muster. Be ready to change the plan if an opportunity arises. If you don't have passion for an idea, you need to find some—or refocus on a challenge you care about.

On the backseat of her car, Linda found the baseball cap that she used for bad hair days. She tucked her hair under the hat and put on a pair of sunglasses. She'd made it back into Milwaukee and had resumed her spot watching the Dunne house. The mansion's lot was ringed by a wrought iron fence, interrupted in the back by the carriage house, which was set into the corner of the lot, its front entrance facing the forest preserve on the other side of the street.

Linda pulled her car around the house and turned onto the street behind it. She parked behind the next house up, her car now obscured from view of anyone who might look out of the windows of the Dunne mansion. She opened the pack of cigarettes and went to work.

Her older brother, Bill, was infamous as a child for pranks and general mischievousness. One of his favorite tricks was putting firecrackers on a "cigarette fuse" and blowing up people's mailboxes in the dead of night. An M-80 could blow the top completely off, leaving only the post and the floor of the box. And the sound! It was like an invasion. Of course, once this was discovered, he'd had hell to pay—he'd had to get a paper route just to pay everyone back.

Linda opened the cigarette pack and shook the cigarettes out on the passenger seat next to her. She took an M-80 out of the shopping bag and jammed the fuse through a cigarette filter and into the back end of the tobacco. How long would it take for the fire to reach the fuse? She tried to guess, but as a nonsmoker she was at a disadvantage. She guessed the fuse would take about ten minutes, maybe less. She loaded up all the fireworks she could with the one pack of Camels, regretting she hadn't bought more. Then she put all the M-80–loaded cigarettes into a Starbucks bag.

The sun was setting, and only a faint glow of the day remained in the sky. She unwrapped one of the cigars and got out of the car with her bag. She sauntered down the street and peered around the carriage house toward the back side of the house. There were lights on in the kitchen, and she could see a cook working behind a counter. There were at least two guards inside the house and two parked out front. The guards were joking around with the cook, who was trying to shoo them away. They were obviously not on "high alert" with Mr. Dunne out of the house.

Linda walked down the back alley and lined the little strip of grass at the back of the carriage house with the fireworks, setting them so that the cigarettes faced the alley. Then she looked at her watch.

After walking back to the car, she got out her cell phone, dialed the number, and then said simply, "I'm ready in Milwaukee."

———————

Manny was sitting in the car, parked behind some trees about one hundred yards from the entrance to the Dunne farm. He reached into the backseat and pulled out a cowboy hat. He put on the colorful western-style red shirt taken from his Cherokee—the one he wore to his square dancing class—and he tied a purple handkerchief around his neck.

"You ready to ride, cowboy?" asked Harriet.

"Oh, yeah."

———————

Jack and Gina were in the other car, driving down a country road bordering the back side of the Dunne farm. Gina was riding shotgun and was looking carefully at the white fencing. They reached a stretch of trees and the wooden fencing stopped, replaced by three strands of barbed wire.

"It's there," said Gina.

"What's there?" asked Jack.

"Park the Cherokee."

They both got out, and Gina led Jack to a spot in the white split-rail fencing where there had once been a gate. The weathered posts on either side of the missing old gate remained; barbed wire was now stretched across the opening. Inside the fence, Jack could make out the faint outlines of what had once been a service road, now grown over with weeds and tall grass. Bushes had been planted at the fence line to obscure the opening, but looking over the bushes, the road outline was clear on the other side.

"I see the road, but how are we going to get through this fence and these bushes?" Jack asked.

"Watch this. Step aside."

Gina put on a pair of gloves and pulled a pair of wire cutters from her back pocket. She cut the wires, carefully pulled the strands back, and twisted them around the old fence post.

"Okay, Jack, get in the Cherokee and get a running start. Plow right over these bushes. Put it in four-wheel drive."

"Will it go through?"

"I think so. Wear your seat belt."

Jack had no sense of how well a Cherokee would do running over those large shrubs. They're bushes, not trees. But still, that's a lot of bush to go through. He was afraid of the impact. He looked back and saw Gina standing near the entrance, and he was reminded of Molly. *Molly's on the other side of this obstacle,* he thought, *locked up and thinking what?* He felt a bead of cold sweat running down his side. *I've got to do this,* he thought as he got into the Cherokee and strapped himself firmly in.

He backed it down the road about fifty yards from the opening. It would be tricky because he had to turn toward the bushes. He couldn't drive too fast, or he'd flip the vehicle. As he was struggling to get the vehicle into four-wheel drive, he had an idea.

He drove slowly up to the turn and noticed Gina looking at him quizzically. He edged up to the bushes and stepped on the gas. At first, nothing much happened. The wheels spun around, and he could hear gravel spitting backward, but then the back wheels gripped and the bushes started to give. He gave it a little more gas, and the bushes gave some more.

Then the Cherokee stalled, but he started it up again, backed up a few feet, and rammed the bushes. This time he heard the branches break under the impact. He backed it up again and rammed away. More snapping branches. He eased back one more time and then pushed forward. He gave it some gas, and more bush gave way; then he felt a hard thump on the front underside of the Cherokee and another hard bump as the back wheels were over the bushes. What was left of the bushes sprang back up behind the vehicle. Gina came through a small opening and got in.

"Okay. Now, call Manny," she said.

Jack called, "We're in the back door."

Manny got out of the car—looking like a Hispanic Roy Rogers—and walked up to the Dunne front gate.

He took his cell phone out from inside his underwear and called Linda. "Let her rip," he said.

Then he called Jack and Gina. "Move in as close as you can, and be ready to work fast."

He stood behind a large tree and waited. Ten minutes later, he was talking to himself. "Come on, Linda, come on."

Linda put the cigar in her mouth and realized immediately she had forgotten something. Matches. She went back to the car and looked in her glove box—nothing. She groaned. Then she checked the trash bag in her backseat, hoping somebody had put an old pack in there. Nothing. She looked in every nook and cranny of her car. Still nothing. She was going to screw the whole thing up.

She closed her eyes and rubbed her temples. How to light a cigar without matches or a lighter? I need heat. The engine? How could you get a flame off the engine? There were spark plugs, but that wouldn't do it.

She opened her eyes and stared at the dashboard. The cigarette lighter. Why hadn't she thought of that? Because I don't smoke, she thought. She pushed the button. A few moments later, the lighter popped out, and she pulled it out, its tip glowing red.

She got out the cigar, licked the sides, and snipped a little piece off the mouth end with her Swiss army knife. Then, using the lighter, she puffed away. Her father said it was important to get a cigar going well or it would burn unevenly and require relighting. She puffed aggressively until the fire at the end of the cigar was three inches high. Satisfied the cigar was burning strongly, she proceeded quickly down the alley, lighting the tips of the cigarettes on the M-80s. In about ten minutes, hopefully, all hell would break loose behind the Dunne mansion. She got back in the car and arranged more M-80s and the smoke bombs on the seat next to her. Then she opened the car's skylight and puffed on the cigar. Nothing to do now except wait.

Fifteen long minutes later, the first one went off. She knew it was coming, but she still wasn't prepared. The explosive sound made by the firecrackers made her jump. She put her hands to her ears. *Whew! Those suckers are loud,* she thought. *Perfect.* She got out of the car and lit the smoke bombs, throwing them as close to the back porch as she could. The first one made it only halfway. She tried harder, and the second came within about ten yards of the back steps. Smoke filled the backyard.

Back in the car, she drove down the alley past the house as the guards cautiously stepped out of the back door. She lit another M-80, threw it out her skylight, and then sped around the corner. Her bomb went off, then another of the timed ones, and another, then another, then several at once. The guards were on their bellies in the backyard now, trying to see though the smoke.

Linda continued away from the house, hearing more bombs go off every so often. She drove to a nearby McDonald's, got out of her car, and made a 9-1-1 call from the pay phone outside.

"I'd like to report gunfire. It's still going on! . . . No, I can't wait, this is an emergency. The Dunne mansion is under some kind of attack . . . I can't stay on the phone—I might be in danger. I hear gunfire! It's terrible—his servants are under fire. You need to get people over there now!"

Taking another puff on the cigar, she sniffed the smoke and decided she could get to like these. But she put it out and threw the stub away before going into McDonald's and ordering a cherry Coke. She was walking out with her drink when she heard the sirens. The M-80s were still going off. Time to drive back toward the Dunne house. As she passed it, she noticed there were already six squad cars. She grinned. Her brother must have felt a bit like this.

Hiding behind some bushes, Manny watched the front entrance to the Dunne farm from across the road. He heard cars coming fast down the drive, then the gate opened and the limo shot out, followed closely by another sedan holding four more men. Manny calculated. *That leaves three,* he thought—*two in the house and my Irish walking-cap friend guarding the cottage.*

Manny stole across the road and punched in the security code. The gate swung open. He entered the property and ran along the edge of the woods, staying out of sight. In about ten minutes he reached the back of the barn. He found the stall with the Arabian and whistled to the horse who came over to the stall window. Manny spent a few minutes befriending the animal in soothing tones. Then he opened the stall's half door and grabbed the bridle. He led the horse to the front entrance of the stable. He mounted the horse bareback and urged it toward the house. As they approached the house, Manny began to yell and whoop at the top of his lungs.

Jack and Gina parked the Cherokee at the edge of the woods and walked to the top of the hill overlooking the cottage and the main house. After about twenty minutes, Brian Dunne and his men ran out of the house and left in a hurry. The cottage guard had walked down from his post but then turned back. He was out of sight now, behind a tree. They waited.

Five minutes later, Manny appeared, as if in a western, on a white horse. The two guards came out of the house on the run. As they approached Manny, Manny turned the Arabian around and rode away from the house. The guards hopped into an open-air Jeep and gave chase.

"So far so good," said Jack. "We just have to contend with the guard at the cottage."

"What can we do to get him away from the cottage?" whispered Gina.

"We could jump him."

"Too dangerous," said Gina. "And he'd probably hear us coming, so we wouldn't get the chance."

"Wait a sec . . . He's going into the cottage . . . Let's get down there."

They rushed down the hillside then walked carefully toward the opening of the cottage door. Jack tried to peer in the bottom corner of the doorframe, but Molly spotted him. She tried to mask her surprise, but the guard caught the look. He turned around and started toward the door. Molly tripped him, and he fell, sprawling on the floor. Jack pounced inside, pinning the guard to the floor. The guard was shaken but began to struggle and cry out for help.

"Give me something to tie him up—fast!" Jack said.

Gina took the belt off her jeans, and Jack tied the man's hands behind his back with it.

When Jack stood, he turned toward Molly. They quickly moved toward each other and embraced, Jack wrapping her tightly in his arms. Bridgette sat up slowly in her bed. Both of them were dressed in flannel nightgowns. As Jack took in his surroundings, he couldn't believe what he was seeing. The cottage interior was like something out of Hansel and Gretel. It was all done as if it were an overly decorated room for a seven-year-old girl, with two matching brass beds, lace curtains, and porcelain dolls. Children's toys everywhere. Then, he saw the chain around Molly's ankle. His blood went cold instantly.

> THE COTTAGE INTERIOR WAS LIKE SOMETHING
>
> OUT OF HANSEL AND GRETEL.

"Are you okay? Is she okay?" asked Jack.

"I'm okay—mostly. They've got Bridgette on tranquilizers," said Molly.

Bridgette was awake but only dimly aware that something was happening. She waved a wan hand at the guard on the floor and seemed to be on the verge of saying something but couldn't quite manage it.

Molly tried to make Bridgette more alert by lightly slapping her cheeks. It didn't have much effect.

Jack snapped back from his shock over the chain. He saw a key chain on the guard's belt, grabbed it, and started trying keys. Then, remembering, he took his camera out of his pocket. He gave the keys to Gina who kept trying while he snapped several pictures of the bizarre scene as fast as the flash would recycle.

"Are you fit to travel? We need to get out of here as quick as we can," Jack said as he clicked.

"This is it," said Gina as she unlocked the leg bracelet.

"Thanks," said Molly. She looked at the woman. "Who are you?"

"Gina Mooney."

Molly looked more closely at Gina, and then suddenly realized who she was. She stood still in utter shock for a long moment, then she slowly shook her head, speechless.

"Listen, we need to hurry right now," said Jack. "Where are your shoes?"

"They've taken all our clothes. All we have is what we have on."

"No way. Okay. Take his shoes, Molly. And, Bridgette, hop on, you're going for a ride."

———·———

Manny had taken the guards on a loop around the far west side of the ranch. He took the Arabian over rough ground, and he was able to stay in front of them. He changed directions frequently. He suspected that as long as he stayed on the horse they wouldn't shoot—the Arabian was too valuable.

During the chase, one of them took a call on a two-way radio. The ruse in Milwaukee had been discovered.

———·———

Jack had started up the hill with Bridgette on his back in a rush, but after about twenty yards he was huffing and puffing. Bridgette wasn't helping much, and he struggled to keep her on his back. As he neared the top of the hill, he wondered if his heart would explode. His injured ribs screamed with every step. He fell to his knees; Gina and Molly came back and helped him up. Then suddenly gunshots sounded from downhill and across the pond. While he doubted they were shooting directly at him, it gave him a rush of energy. He scurried the last few yards to the Cherokee.

Molly and Gina helped him get Bridgette into the backseat, and they piled in after her.

"Put your seat belts on," Jack said. There wasn't time or room to turn around quickly, so he floored the car in reverse, heading them wildly back down the old service road and all the way out to the fence at the rear of the property.

"Hold on, everybody," Jack warned, shooting the Cherokee into the broken mass of bushes without slowing down. The impact was jolting, but after a lurch they thumped out onto the road. Jack braked, changed gears, and they were soon speeding down the road.

Molly whooped. Bridgette raised her head from Gina's lap and asked, "What's going on?"

"Nice to meet you, Bridgette," said Jack. "We're going to Chicago."

"That's nice," she said quietly.

————

Enrique had seen the limo and the escort car leave the property in a big hurry. He'd looked out his window and wondered what the emergency was. He thought of calling the main house, but truthfully he didn't care. He knew what was going on in the cottage, and it disgusted him. Those two beautiful girls—he'd never understand how a man could do that to his own daughters. In his heart he knew it was just a matter of time before all this blew up in Dunne's face. Then again, maybe not. This was a guy who had made a life-long habit of avoiding consequences.

He heard the shouting near the house. He looked out the window and saw a cowboy riding toward him on Rooster, their Arabian. As the horse and rider passed his window, he realized it was the man who'd done the work for him that afternoon. He thought about this. Manny's being here couldn't be an accident. This wasn't Manny acting loco or trying to steal a horse; it was Manny pretending to act loco and steal a horse. Enrique remembered the language slips. He'd known Manny was more educated than he'd let on. He might be an undercover cop. Or just a scam artist. He didn't know quite what to make of all this, but the horse was his responsibility, so he'd better get out there and see what he could do to make sure it wasn't harmed.

Manny looked over his shoulder and saw that the guards had abandoned the chase and were driving back toward the main house. He hoped he'd bought Jack and Gina enough time. He pulled the horse up and gave him a pat on the neck. "Well done, well done," he said. He headed the horse back toward the barn at a trot, not sure how he'd manage to return the horse and stay out of harm's way, but he rode on anyway.

The guards drove the Jeep around the pond to the cottage. They found and untied the guard, and the three of them got into the Jeep and started up the ridge.

Enrique watched the activity on the far side of the pond and smiled to himself. *Somebody sprung the girls*, he thought, *good for them*. He heard the sound of a horse at his back and saw Manny riding Rooster toward the barn. He walked over and met him there.

"Out for a recreational ride, or are you trying to steal our horse? Are you a cop or Roy Rogers?" asked Enrique.

"No. I'm a friend of Molly's. Really, a friend of a friend. I know what's going on in the cottage. I'm not a cop, but I'm on the right side of the law here," said Manny, "and the right side of what's right."

"The guards—they're going up the ridge, but they'll be back here in a few minutes."

Manny dismounted and tied the horse to a post. "I don't have time to do much explaining here. I'm just going to ask for your help; I need to get out of here in a big hurry."

Enrique made a quick decision. "Come with me," he said.

The two ran toward Enrique's cottage and hopped into the pickup. They sped toward the front gate, and in minutes they were off the property. Enrique dropped Manny at his car.

"I can't thank you enough for this," said Manny.

"Hey, who can refuse Roy Rogers?"

"I'm thinking more like the Lone Ranger."

Enrique grinned.

"Thanks, my friend. This is not the end of this, as you might well imagine. I think we've got Dunne boxed in. I'll call you and tell you the whole story. If anything happens to you—you call me," Manny said, scribbling down a number on a piece of scrap paper from the car. "Right now, you want to get back in there and pretend like you just woke up from a nap. We'll let my escape be thought of as aided by my trusted Indian scout."

"Just call me Tonto. And yes, call me. I have to know how you pulled this off."

"With your help, that's how," said Manny, shaking Enrique's hand.

Manny got into the car, and Harriet sped off.

20: REUNION

Where love and forgiveness win the day

Safely away from their father, Molly and Bridgette are confronted by their emotions. Manny advises them to forgive. From the standpoint of preserving personal energy, sometimes it makes more sense to forgive and let love and kindness win the day. Creative people do not deny their feelings, but they also do not let their emotions rule. Creative thinkers also choose their battles wisely.

The ride back into Milwaukee was uneventful. Manny had seen Brian Dunne's limo speeding in the other direction on I-94. Jack, in the other car, hadn't seen it because Gina took them east on back roads. Bridgette was asleep, her head on Gina's lap; Molly was on the other side of her mother. They didn't talk, but Molly rested her shoulder on Gina's shoulder and cried softly. After a while, she fell asleep from exhaustion.

She woke up when they got to Linda's home in Milwaukee. She followed Jack, who was carrying Bridgette into the house. He took Bridgette to the bed that he had used the night before.

Manny was already there, having taken the more direct route. Linda had gotten home first and was waiting with him on the front steps.

"Welcome," said Linda, "nice dreads."

"It's nice to be back," said Molly. "Thanks."

"*De nada*. Molly, this is Manny Gibran," said Linda.

"Heard a lot about you, but I wish we were meeting under different circumstances," said Molly.

"Are there better circumstances than lovers reunited?" asked Manny.

Molly blushed. "I guess not," she said.

"Get some rest," said Manny after giving her a hug.

Linda drew a bath for Molly. Molly shut the door to the bathroom and took off her clothes. Her hands were shaking, so she hugged herself to stop them. As she stepped into the hot tub, it hit her that the events of the past few days were finally over. She burst into tears and then just as suddenly laughed. The heat of the water was wonderful, and she stopped crying and relaxed for the first time since she'd been abducted in Chicago.

Linda had ordered pizza. As they ate, Manny made phone calls back to Chicago. He talked at length with his lawyer, who advised him to get out of Wisconsin and back to Chicago as soon as possible. Manny and Jack decided to let the girls rest for a few hours before they would leave.

Gina and Harriet promised to follow them down a day later. Gina had asked Harriet if she would travel to Chicago with her—she wanted to get to know her daughters. Harriet agreed.

At five in the morning, Manny got up and roused Jack from a dead sleep. "Jack, come on. Let's get the girls up and blow this town."

While Linda made coffee and packed a bag with some sandwiches and fruit, Molly and Bridgette were proving difficult to rouse. Molly finally got up and wordlessly got dressed into some clothes Linda provided. She then helped her sister.

Linda walked them all to the Cherokee, which now had dents,

scratches, and mud all over it. "I think I'm going to come down to Chicago with Harriet and Gina, if you don't mind," said Linda to Manny meaningfully.

Manny was at a loss for words. Finally he said, "I'd see that as a great opportunity." Then he grinned and leaned down to kiss Linda good-bye.

As they were leaving Milwaukee, Manny was already planning. "My lawyer will call Dunne later today to begin negotiations," he said. "And, Molly and Bridgette, if you—and your mother—agree, here's what I think we ought to do. Your father is a powerful man, but kidnapping is a very big deal. He's boxed in. We have evidence. What we're going to insist on is that, if he wants to avoid prosecution, he needs to promise not to interfere, to provide financial support for you girls and your mother, and then get psychological help. If he agrees, we won't go to the police."

Bridgette spoke up. "I want to press charges." Her eyes, while still tired looking, were now clear.

"You have that right. The question is, do you want to spend the next two or three years of your life tangled in the courts? You are entirely right to seek justice, but what I want you to think about is the impact that the legal battle is likely to have on you. It will consume your life, and it will be all over the media. The anger you have in your heart right now—how does that feel?"

"I . . . I think he should be punished," she said.

"Okay. You don't need to make a decision right now. We have some time. All I'm saying is, for the sake of your own life, I'd try to get this incident behind you," said Manny.

"It's not an incident. It has been my life for years." Bridgette looked to her sister for support.

Molly spoke. "Bridgette, come live with me for a while. You can transfer to DePaul or one of the other schools in Chicago. Let's take some time and get you healthy. I think we both should probably see a counselor, get some help," she added. "Personally, I'd just like to kill him. And I don't want his money—I'm sorry . . ."

"It's understandable," said Jack. "You were imprisoned."

"I want to thank you guys for riding in on your white horses," said Molly. "Now my life can start again."

"What happened on your end?" said Jack.

"The short version is they found me walking to work. I was on my way down to Geek's, and they pulled up in a van, surrounding me before I could even think about running. They talked to me at first. One was the guard at the cottage that you tied up—and two other guys. They told me that my father needed me to come home to help him take care of Bridgette. They said that she was addicted to heroin, and he needed my help taking care of her. When I said I wouldn't come without speaking to Bridgette first, they just snatched me. They forced me to leave messages—they knew about you—and said you'd be killed if I didn't say what they told me to. I had no choice but to cooperate."

"Unbelievable," said Jack.

"We were at the house in Milwaukee at first. I managed to sneak out of there with Bridgette in the middle of the night, and we crashed at a friend's house. But they found us there early the next afternoon. Then they took us to the farm and locked us in the cottage."

Bridgette put in, "I'm sorry about all this."

"Why are you sorry?" asked Molly.

"I knew Dad was taking a turn for the worse a few months ago. He'd promised to let me go to school without interference, but I caught one of his goons tailing me around campus—he was so obvious. I thought I could keep my life a secret, but it wasn't possible. I'd been seeing a guy. We had a wild party one night, and I got a little stupid and started throwing bottles and screaming at the guard Dad put on me. They snatched me up the next morning, and I woke up at home in a straightjacket. They put me on so much dope that all I did was sleep. I barely knew where I was."

"Your father is a sick man," said Jack.

"You don't know how sick. He came over to the cottage every day and read to us from the Bible. Made us kneel and pray with him. He lectured us on sex and told us he was going to keep us pure for the rest of our lives." Bridgette looked at her sister.

"I'm still in shock at mother showing up after all these years," said

Molly. "I can't wait to talk to her . . . although I hope I can stay calm. To be honest, I'm pretty angry at her. Why didn't she do something before? Why did she leave us to deal with him alone all those years?"

Manny took a deep breath before speaking. "You know, I lost my mother when I was young. I can barely remember her face. Really, I can't remember it in my own memory, but I've looked at her picture so many times, I kind of blend the memory and the picture. I'd give anything to see my mother again."

"Oh, I'm glad to see her—I just don't know how to deal with it," said Molly.

"If you love each other, it'll work out," said Manny. "Keep in mind that your mother had to fight just to survive. She found a way to escape the cottage—by acting insane. When she faked her own death, she probably felt like she'd gone beyond a point where she could ever return. She must have hung on to her new identity for dear life. She had no resources. She was alone in the world. She was afraid. When you talk to your mother tomorrow, I ask . . . I ask you to listen with a forgiving heart. She loves both of you, and she risked her life to come get you last night."

> I ASK YOU TO LISTEN WITH A FORGIVING HEART.

"I have no anger for Mom. I'm very sorry for her. We're all Dad's victims," said Bridgette.

"You are victims no longer," said Manny. "You are making your own choices now."

They drove south as the sun rose. Jack updated Molly on events in Chicago—the studio space behind Geek's, business ideas, and the upcoming photo shoots for Tony Cooper. They got out a pen and started making notes of ideas she had to build on Jack's. Manny chimed in now and then too. Bridgette fell back asleep.

As they approached Chicago, Manny got a phone call. It was his contact at the building downtown. They had two more days to find a solution before the software company would be forced to pay for an expensive multi-floor easement—or find a more convenient space in another building.

Manny brought Molly, Bridgette, and Jack to his condo—which had a doorman and tight security. Until things were settled down in Milwaukee, he thought it best to keep them somewhere Brian Dunne didn't know about. Jack and Molly put Bridgette to bed in a guest room. Then Manny showed Jack the other guest room, saying he was going upstairs to bed. They all hugged and off he went.

It was the first private moment Jack and Molly had shared since she'd left Chicago. Jack pulled her close and held her head in his hands, feeling those sweet dreadlocks. Molly moved her hands to touch his face as well. They looked into each other's eyes for a long moment, then gently kissed.

"No more of these sudden vacations, okay?" said Jack, grinning.

"Absolutely not, unless you're going with me."

"I was so scared for you," he said.

"I was scared for myself. It was a nightmare."

"I still can't quite believe any of this," said Jack, shaking his head.

"Believe it. And thank you. I haven't said thank you. I prayed to God you'd come find me. I didn't know how long it would take—or even if you would."

"At first I didn't know what to do. I wasn't sure what the best thing to do was, but I had an instinct, deep down, that things were not okay. Of course, the beating was a clue! I'm still sore."

"Tell me about that—what happened exactly?" she asked.

Jack filled her in on the beating, the night in jail, the hospital visit, and the morning meeting with Tony. At a certain point, Molly drew into herself. Hearing about the violence done to Jack and the danger he'd been in reminded her of the danger she herself had been in. Her mother had to fake her own death to escape her father, and if Jack and Manny hadn't come for her, what would she have done? The horror of the last few days hit her again. She started crying. She tried to hold it back, but it was a useless effort.

Jack stood there for a moment, not sure what to do. He put his hand on her shoulder and slowly moved closer to her, and then he wrapped his arms around her.

"Hey, it's going to be all right now. You're back. You're home now," he said softly, feeling his own tears on his face.

"I never felt like Chicago was really home—until now. Maybe it's not Chicago, though. It's really just you. Wherever you are, I'll feel at home," she said.

"And someday we'll have our own home, a real home. Manny's will do for tonight. All of this was a team effort, you know. Manny's the miracle man. I'm still amazed that he just dropped everything and took me up to Milwaukee."

"I love that guy. And Harriet sure came through," said Molly.

"She did. And so did your mother, and Linda too."

"My mother—my mother! I'm going to get to know my mother!"

Jack couldn't help but notice the little girl sound in her voice. "Yeah, you are. I'm happy she's back in your life."

Molly looked at Jack again and said, "And I'll have you. You, you, you." She said the word *you* differently each time.

Jack echoed the phrase, "You. You. You."

CONCLUSION: UP ON THE ROOF

The value of persistence
and musicals

Manny and Jack make one last visit to the building in downtown Chicago. They are persistent—a trait of creative problem solvers—and continue to seek a solution to Manny's wiring challenge. To cheer Manny up, Jack starts having some fun. They play with ideas—and take time out for play to refresh their minds. They get ready to tackle another tough, serious challenge.

Breakthroughs sometimes occur when we relax, have a bit of fun, or simply try again with a lighter heart. Fun is an underrated principle of effective creative problem solving. Play and fun are necessary, not optional.

The next afternoon, Manny decided to pay one last visit to the building downtown. He asked Jack to come with him.

"Let's try this one last time," said Manny. "Maybe something will show up for us."

"So you're still looking for a place to put a vertical shaft, right?"

"Right. I still think that's the best bet. Let's walk through the basement again. Then let's look at the floor the software company wants to move into. Then we'll take a last look at the roof."

Manny had the pictures laid out on the coffee table in his living room. Jack picked up a picture of the roof.

"Not much to see up there—it's just a flat roof. I don't see any indentations or marks," said Jack.

"On a building like that they tend to relayer the roof with tar every few years. Like a stack of pancakes. They do it five or six times like that, and it all tends to even out. Without taking the whole roof off—and that's not going to happen—it's pretty hard to see anything. So how else could we get a sense of where the shafts might be? If there are any . . ." Manny wondered out loud. "We might take a look through the crawl space just under the roof—if we can get in there."

Manny gave Molly his cell phone number, and then he and Jack drove downtown to the now-familiar site. When they got into the building, they poked into every nook and cranny they could find. On the empty floor, Manny compared the blueprints to what he was seeing. The area that had held the AC and heating unit for the floor seemed bigger than it needed to be. It was empty now, so there was no way of telling why it had been that large. He looked up at the ceiling, which was sealed.

Then they went up to the roof. Manny found the entrance to the crawl space, and he went in with a flashlight. Jack followed. Insulation had been put in everywhere, and it was clear after looking around for a short time that they did not have access to all of the crawl space. Sections of it had been walled off. They backed out and went up to the roof where they searched every inch but didn't notice anything new.

"I know there is a solution to this," sighed Manny. "I think I've just run out of time. There may be a better answer here, but I can't find it."

Jack noted to himself that this was the only time he had ever seen Manny in a truly down spirit. "So if it's over, how about a song?" suggested Jack.

Manny laughed wearily. "Sure, that'll do it."

They had walked the length of the roof, and now as they crossed it again, Jack noticed a small puddle of standing water. He started goofing around, doing a bit from *Singing in the Rain* to cheer up Manny. He stomped on the puddle and then stomped again on another puddle a few feet away. He started playing the roof like a drum. He did a very poor Gene Kelly impression, but it was fun, and Manny seemed to be enjoying it. Then in the back of his mind—almost unconsciously—Jack noticed something. One part of the roof had more thump, more echo. He stopped singing and walked back to the spot where he'd started. He tested it, stomping his foot hard. Manny watched with growing curiosity as Jack stomped around the roof. There was, indeed, a bit of hollowness to the area just to the right of the puddle. Jack defined it by stomping all around, eventually putting himself in the center of the "drum" area.

> ONE PART OF THE ROOF HAD
>
> MORE THUMP, MORE ECHO.

Manny backed away to the edge of the roof and got on his hands and knees. From that angle it was just possible to discern the slightest rise in the area where Jack had found the hollowness. Jack was standing on it.

"Jack, there was something in this area. Let's take a closer look."

Manny and Jack went back downstairs to the open floor. The corresponding area to the hollowness was a wall—a weight-bearing, brick-supporting wall. It was on one side of the old AC/heating area. Manny called some engineers to drill holes. The drills went through two thicknesses of brick slowly, and then they punched through into a hollow area. They took out enough bricks to get a mirror and a lamp into the space—it was about three feet wide. They looked up and down, and it was clear that the shaft went all the way down to the first floor and up to the roof. They took out more bricks, and when they were able to see better, they noticed that at every floor there was an old window, all sealed with bricks. When they opened up the corresponding space on the roof later in the afternoon, they could see a narrow ventilation shaft that had been completely sealed off in the renovations of years past. It dropped down the entire length of the building. The engineers had it marked on the redone blueprints as a very thick brick support column.

Manny introduced Jack to the building owner and an executive with the software company. They'd come over when they learned about the discovery. This was a good day for both of them. The software executive was going to be able to get into his new space economically and in fairly short order now that the wiring issue had been resolved. The building owner was delighted because the new data shaft could also be used by other tenants in the building who wanted to upgrade their data and telecom lines. He thought his two empty floors might lease faster now that the building would have improved data service.

The two businessmen shook Jack's hand, and they chatted with him briefly about how they'd discovered the shaft. The feeling Jack had when they looked at him was—well, new. He felt they respected him. He was comfortable talking with these men because it was clear they appreciated what he had helped them get done. They asked him questions about what he did, so Jack took the opportunity to talk about his new business. As they were about to leave, the software company executive gave him a business card and asked him to call and set up a meeting. They needed a set of portraits of their management team for their Web site and annual report.

Driving away from the building, Manny said, "Jack, since you were so instrumental in saving that deal for me, I'm going to give you some of the fee."

"No, no, no—I can't take it. You've done so much for me already."

"Listen, I bought an old car from you—that's nothing," said Manny.

"Hello? You saved Molly's life!"

"Hey, we did that together. We went to Wisconsin, we zipped in, we zipped out," said Manny.

"*Stripes*," said Jack, "where would we be without *Stripes*?"

"If you won't take the money, I have another idea," said Manny.

"What?"

"Let me invest in your business. Take half the fee and give me 15 percent of your company."

"How much was the fee?" asked Jack.

"Thirty grand," said Manny.

"Really?" Jack was incredulous.

"Yeah, really."

"So for fifteen thousand dollars you get 15 percent of the company?"

"Right," said Manny.

"Ten percent."

"You dog! I value your nonexistent—okay, barely started—company at $100,000 and give you the cash you need to get started, and you'll look that gift horse in the mouth?" Now Manny was incredulous.

"Someday my company will be worth millions." Jack had no idea where this was coming from. But having said it out loud, somehow he felt it was true.

Manny looked over at Jack. "You know, you just might do that. Do you really want to grow something? Something bigger than a two-person commercial art shop?"

"I do. I have . . . a wish . . . a vision . . . that we'll start there and grow into other things. Like corporate training, publishing, and Web services." Jack realized he'd been thinking these things over since the day he'd walked into the back of Geek's, looking at the space. Until now he hadn't dared to express these ideas.

"Sounds interesting. Okay, let me revise my offer, Mr. CEO guy. How about 10 percent and chairman of the board?"

"Deal—as long as Molly buys in. She's half of this you know."

"Okay, so let's get started." Manny cleared his throat. "As the new chairman of the board of JackNewCo company . . ."

"Call it High Definition, Inc.—it's a working name."

"Okay, as chairman of the board of High Def, Inc., I would like to review your action plan. Get out your sketchbook. Let's hear it."

"You don't rest for a minute, do you?" asked Jack.

"No, not really. Let's say I've reframed rest as 'doing something interesting.' No, check that. 'Doing something creative.'"

CPS Quick Reference Guide

Guidelines—Review before you begin

When List Making

- **Defer judgment**—Don't criticize as you go.
- **Strive for quantity**—The longer the list, the better. Take your time and push yourself beyond the obvious.
- **Seek wild ideas**—They expand your thinking and sometimes lead to breakthroughs.
- **Combine and build on other ideas**—A small change can make a big difference.

When Choice Making

- **Be deliberate**—Consider every idea or item.
- **Check your objectives**—How does it meet the challenge? Your chosen wishes?
- **Improve your ideas**—What would make the idea work? Or work better?
- **Be affirmative**—Look for the positive in every idea and item.

Where to Begin? Challenge Triage!

You can start at any step, depending on what kind of thinking you need, how well you understand your challenge, and if you already have ideas in hand.

Challenge Triage

- If you believe you really understand your challenge but need ideas, start in Idea Generation.
- If you are unclear about what the challenge is, or what challenge to work on, start in Identifying the Challenge.
- If you have a good idea about what you want to implement, begin with Solution Development.

CPS Process

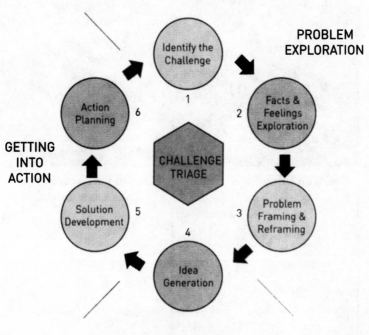

PROBLEM EXPLORATION

GETTING INTO ACTION

BRAINSTORMING

CPS Steps At A Glance
Read across each row for guidance on each CPS step

STEP ➡	PURPOSE ➡
Identify the Challenge	To identify a goal, wish, or challenge that you are motivated to work on with CPS.
Facts and Feelings Exploration	To list all the facts, feelings, or questions about the challenge.
Problem Framing and Reframing	To state or frame the problem/challenge as a question then to reframe the question as many different ways as time allows. Then choose the one that most clearly identifies the challenge you wish to work on.

CPS Steps At A Glance

HOW TO MAKE LISTS ➡	HOW TO MAKE CHOICES
List your goals, wishes, or challenges—even if they seem obvious. The list items should begin with "I wish . . ." or "It would be great if . . ."	Choose one goal, wish, or challenge. This becomes the starting point for Facts and Feelings Exploration. Check the chosen objective for ownership, motivation, and imagination.
Make a long list of facts about the situation. Use Who, What, When, Where, Why, and How to stimulate your thinking.	Highlight all the facts that seem important or interesting. Use the highlighted facts as a starting point for Problem Framing and Reframing.
Write as many "frames" as you can. This is another list! Use key facts from the previous list. Begin the framing question with these words: "In what ways might I/we . . ." or "How to . . ."	Select a single "challenge frame" question that, if answered, would address the challenge.

CPS Steps At A Glance
Read across each row for guidance on each CPS step

STEP ➡	PURPOSE ➡
Idea Generation	To generate as many ideas that answer the frame question as possible.
Solution Development	To find strengths and weaknesses of promising ideas and decide which ones to use. When a weakness is found, generate ideas on how to fix it. Look for any possible way to enhance a good idea to make it a great idea!
Action Planning	To develop an action plan for your improved idea or ideas. Before creating the plan, list assistors, resistors, resources, and ways to generate excitement.

CPS Steps At A Glance

HOW TO MAKE LISTS ➡	HOW TO MAKE CHOICES
Brainstorm a list of ideas that answer the "In what ways might I . . ." question selected. **Key:** This is the heart of the CPS process—make as LONG a list of ideas as you possibly can. Take the time! Go nuts! Get help!	Narrow the list down to a few or even one idea that is "intriguing" or "might work."
List criteria for judging ideas. What factors will determine whether or not an idea works for you? Typical criteria have to do with Time, Money, Resources, and Acceptability. **Be specific:** "Money" is not a criterion, but "Does it cost less than $350?" is. "Time" is not a criterion, but "Can I get it done by June 1?" is.	1. Narrow the list of criteria down to the most important criteria. 2. Judge the ideas selected from Idea Generation by using the final criteria. A matrix is a convenient way to keep track. Solutions that work for you go into Action Planning. **Option:** Use the PPCO tool to develop and improve ideas.
List all the things you need to do to get the idea implemented. **Questions:** Who will be involved? Whose approval do you need? What has to happen? When are the deadlines?	1. Narrow the list to the action steps necessary to get the idea or ideas implemented. 2. Commit to the dates and resources for completing the action steps.

ASKING BETTER QUESTIONS
MEANS MAKING BETTER LISTS

CPS is about making lists and making choices. In every step, you make some kind of list, and later you make choices from that list. Below are some questions to ask yourself. These will help you make longer lists.

IDENTIFY THE CHALLENGE
Where your list is about what challenge or wish you want to work on
To make a long list, ask:
- What would you really like to improve?
- What sorts of situations have you been thinking about?
- What are some goals that you would like to meet?
- What's on the horizon?
- In your life, what opportunity might you like to maximize?
- Imagine yourself a year from now. What would you like to accomplish or begin in the next year?
- You have Aladdin's lamp in your hand and can have any wish you want—in any part of your life: What do you wish for?

FACTS & FEELINGS EXPLORATION
Where your list is about the data that surrounds your challenge
To make a long list, ask the five "W" and the "H" questions ... Who, What, When, Where, Why, and How:
- Who is involved?
- Who else?
- Who makes decisions?
- Who gains if this situation is improved? Who doesn't?
- What is the background story here?
- What is the obvious solution?
- What does your intuition tell you about this situation?
- What is an ideal outcome?
- What successes have you achieved so far with this situation?
- What are the obstacles?
- When did this come to your attention?

- When is the situation occurring?
- When would you like to take action?
- Why is this important to you or your organization?
- Why has this situation come to your attention?
- Where does the challenge happen?
- Where does the situation show up?
- How has this been addressed in the past?
- How do you feel about this challenge?

ACTION PLANNING
Where your list is about assistors, resistors, resources, and things you get to do
To make a long list, ask:
- Who might assist you?
- Who do you need to convince?
- What steps might you take to get into action?
- What additional resources might help you?
- How do you gain broader acceptance?
- How do you inspire enthusiasm for your solution?
- What's your plan B?
- What special times might you use?
- What are some times to avoid?
- When do you start?
- Where might you start?
- How might you pilot-test your solution?

Jack's Notebook with Author Tips

Jack's Notebook contains some of the lists that Jack created during the story. Also, at the beginning of each chapter, I've provided for you a few of my own notes—additional CPS information.

As Jack did, I recommend keeping a notebook with you at all times because ideas will occur to you when you least expect it. Write them down immediately, or you'll forget them. If it's not practical to carry around a standard-sized notebook, get a small one that can fit in a jacket pocket. If you're truly desperate, carry a pack of sticky notes! If you resort to a cocktail napkin, that's okay, but transfer it or tape it into a notebook at your earliest convenience.

Following are more lists from Jack's notebook and more tips from me.

1: The Ride

Jack's wish list

I wish I was a photographer
I wish I had a car
I wish I had a girlfriend
I wish I had my raincoat with me
I wish I could find a way to have more fun in my life
I wish I had more ideas
I wish I had better ideas

I wish I had finished college
I wish I could confront my demons
I wish I knew more about computers, e-mail, and the Web
It would be nice if I never hurt anybody
I wish I had a family, kids

3: AS THE STONE TURNS

Author's Note: In this chapter, Jack is exploring the problem. He and Molly use observational research and a form of qualitative research, but they also could use experiential research and quantitative research. You, too, can consider using these methods for deep challenge understanding:

OBSERVATIONAL RESEARCH: This is about *watching*—with an open mind! Imagine you are trying to come up with new products for washing cars. Instead of sitting in your office thinking, go to a car wash and watch for a few hours. Take notes! If you observe with an open mind and with thoughtfulness, you will learn useful things and get ideas.

EXPERIENTIAL RESEARCH: This is about *doing*. One way to get a better understanding of something is to simply do it. For instance, you might wash a car if you're looking for ideas for new car-care products. Or if you are trying to understand a brand experience, make yourself a consumer and go through the experience of buying a product or service. Is it easy to find? Does the packaging have the information you need? Have you ever called your own company? Would you like to be your customer? You get the point—find a way to experience aspects of your challenge.

QUALITATIVE RESEARCH: This is about *listening*. Talk to your customer or someone who has information relevant to your challenge. Ask questions, sit back, listen carefully, and take notes! Don't be defensive if you are on a learning mission only—in other words, defer judgment. Remember, it's not what you think that counts; it's what they think.

QUANTITATIVE RESEARCH: This involves *asking questions— and asking as many people as you can*. For instance, you might issue a survey to know how many of your current customers are likely to buy a new product from your company. This type of research can provide scientifically based results if done properly and with a large enough sample. You can learn a great deal from a good survey or question-naire, even from a small sample. Just remember to keep it simple and to the point. Also make sure that you don't ask leading questions. Before you send out a survey, test it with a friend; in fact, try it out several times with several friends in order to perfect your questions.

Summary of Facts & Feelings Exploration

Web searches at Geek's (bookmarks of all kinds of things related to photography)

Visit to Columbia College

Visits to local commercial photo studios

Feeling: Not sure what kind of photography to do (journalistic, fine art, etc.)

Observation: Interested in studio photography

Studio photography requires space*

Studio photography requires expensive equipment

How to get customers for studio work?*

Ideas for Coffee-Table Books

Chicago at night

Illinois landscapes

Neon lights of Chicago

Best local rock bands

Funky old Wicker Park

Street scenes in Wicker Park

People drinking coffee

Outside cafés, Chicago-style

Famous Chicago hot-dog stands

Chicago tourist traps

Chicago-style patriotism

Deep-dish patriotism—Chicago war heroes

Chicago murals and graffiti

Ashland Avenue book

4: A FRESH PERSPECTIVE

Author's Note: In this chapter, Manny assigns Jack the task of reframing his original wish of being a photographer. Manny, too, is trying to reframe his wiring challenge as he clues Jack into the language of reframing, using the phrase "In what ways might I . . ."

Another way to see a challenge differently is to become someone else. Think of someone you believe is wise, perhaps a minister, teacher, or business leader. It could be a historical person like Winston Churchill or Abraham Lincoln. How would he see your challenge? How would he state it? You could also call a wise friend and ask him or her directly— use your friend as a resource to gain a fresh perspective on your challenge.

Manny's Reframes of the Building-Wiring Challenge

In what ways might we widen the stack?

In what ways can we create an alternative stack outside the building?

In what ways might we create an alternative stack within the building?

In what ways might we drill a new shaft economically?

In what ways might we drill a new shaft without disruption?

In what ways might we locate unused space within the building?

Jack's Problem Frames and Reframes

In what ways might I become a photographer?

In what ways might I become a successful photographer?

In what ways might I become a successful art photographer?

In what ways might I become a successful fine-art photographer?

In what ways might I become a successful artist?

In what ways might I become a successful commercial photographer?

In what ways might I become a successful commercial artist, specializing in photography now, learning about other related media?

In what ways might I become a successful commercial artist, specializing in photographic fine-art books, learning about other related media?

In what ways might I become a commercial artist, specializing in photographic fine-art books, learning about other related media?

5: A Smashing Night for Ideas

Author's Note: In this chapter, Jack and Molly brainstorm after SMASH closes. Listed below are the "first blast" ideas that Molly and Jack created. Molly introduces the tool of forced association (she calls it *force fit* in the story). Another tool to stimulate your thinking further is called SCAMPER, which is an acronym that stands for these words:

> **Substitute**
> **Combine**
> **Amplify**
> **Maximize or Minimize**
> **Put to other uses**
> **Eliminate**
> **Reverse**

Ask yourself what your challenge has to do with any or all of the above words. How might substituting something help? What ideas might you combine to make a new one? Even one more good idea can make all the difference.

Force Fit Attributes (of the Southern Comfort bottle)
See-through
Full
Tall
Brown
Southern
Comfortable
Sweet
Potent
Tea-colored
Old-fashioned

First Blast of Ideas
Do fine art photographic books
Do fine art coffee-table books

Go back to school
Apprentice to someone doing art books
Take a class in Flash Animation
Start taking pictures of a certain topic area
Make a list of possible books
Add on to my existing list of possible books
Do a book about me (Molly)
Do two books about you (still Molly)
Study art books at the library
Create the largest coffee-table book ever
Create a book that is a coffee table
Go to work for a big commercial studio and learn
Work for a big studio then open your own studio
Rent the back room at Geek's

Digital Photography Ideas

Learn digital photography
Learn digital photography at Columbia College
Buy a cheap digital camera and teach myself
Get a book on digital photography
Get an Idiot's Guide to digital photography
Learn Adobe Photoshop inside and out
Learn FrontPage
Take a drawing class

More Ideas on Fine Art Books

Do a series of shots on barns
Do a series of shots on cows
Do a book on barns and cows
Do a book on Milwaukee Avenue
Do a book on Ashland Avenue
Do a book on shots from Wicker Park
Do a book on bands that live in Wicker Park
Do a book on the local rock scene
Do a book on one particular band in the local rock scene

Do a video documentary of a band
Do a book of flowers
Do a book on prairie flowers
Do a book on endangered species in Illinois
Do a book on endangered species in the Midwest

6: 100 IDEAS INSIDE JEANNIE'S BOTTLE

Existing Ideas
Chicago at night
Illinois landscapes
Neon lights of Chicago
Best local rock bands
Funky old Wicker Park
Street scenes in Wicker Park
People drinking coffee
Outside café Chicago style
Famous Chicago hot dog stands
Chicago tourist traps

Marketing Ideas
Take a marketing course
Read books on marketing
Read book on starting a new business

More Studio Ideas
Talk to someone who has started a small business
Research what the government can do for starting a small business
Research what kinds of services are in high demand in commercial art

More New Business Ideas
Research loans for new businesses
Research grants for new businesses
Join the American Marketing Association
Join the Chicago Chamber of Commerce

Brochure Ideas

Do a brochure for photographic services

Do a brochure specific to documentation photographic services

Documentation Services Ideas

Do a brochure offering photographic documentation services for
businesses

Do a brochure offering photographic documentation services for
homes

When brochures are finished, hand deliver them to several property
managers to get reactions

Do a Web search on photographic documentation

Convention Business Ideas and Other Events

Develop events photography brochure

Find out how they hire photographers at McCormick Convention
Center

Find out who makes all the arrangements for out-of-towners for all
of those meetings

Get a good instant camera and take pictures at the Blues Fest

Get a booth at the Blues Fest

Roam around at the Blues Fest and sell pictures to couples

Take pictures at the Jazz Fest

Take pictures at Taste of Chicago

Take pictures outside Wrigley Field

Permits, Bears, and More

Check with the city of Chicago about permits for soliciting at
public events

Find out who hires photographers for the city

Take pictures outside Soldier Field at Bears games

Take pictures at the big running races like the Chicago Marathon or
the Shamrock Shuffle

Do a Web search on city of Chicago events

Do a Web search on cultural events

Check the newspaper every Sunday for upcoming events where I
    might take pictures

Charity and Fashion Ideas
Show up at charity events and offer to take snapshots
Call charity event planners and offer your services
Offer your services at fashion shows
Call Cheryl and ask about who does fashion shows
Ask Cheryl if hairdressers want pictures of their best do's

The Five Best Ideas that Suggest Starting a Business
Do a brochure offering photographic documentation services for
    businesses*
Partner with Molly and open up a commercial art studio*
Promote yourself as an events photographer*
Exchange work for use of space behind Geek's*
Read a book on starting a new business*

Ideas to Do Right Away or Revisit Soon—"The Short List"
Get a yellow pages listing as a photographer
Check with the city of Chicago on permits for soliciting at
    public events
Find out who hires photographers for the city
Check the newspaper every Sunday for upcoming events
Call Cheryl and ask about who does fashion shows
Ask Cheryl if hairdressers want pictures of their best do's
Get a book on digital photography
Read books on marketing

7: Razor's Edge

Jack's Criteria for Evaluating His Business Ideas
Generate cash in three months
Is it in Jack's (or Molly's) skill set
Can find the work

PPCO Tool Used to Evaluate JackNewCo and Develop a Solution from Jack's Ideas

Positives List
Focus my efforts
There are always events happening
Molly will be a great partner
The studio is big enough for almost anything
We could do photography and all kinds of commercial art
There's space for a lot of people
Documentation is something businesses need for insurance
There must be a ton of books out there on how to start a business

Potentials List
Molly and I might make a decent living
Build up the business into something really big
It would be fun work, fulfilling work
I'd learn a lot
It might enable us to have a more interesting lifestyle
We might do something very valuable for our customers

Concerns List re: JackNewCo
In what ways might we avoid the most common mistakes of new
  businesses?
In what ways might we avoid an embarrassing failure?
In what ways might we speed up the cleanup of the studio?
In what ways might we get some cash to fund equipment and
  general start-up costs of this JackNewCo?
In what ways might we generate cash?
In what ways might we find customers?
In what ways might we get Molly back to Chicago?

Overcoming Concerns List
Get advice from a SCORE counselor (www.score.org)
Don't incur debt unless there is income to cover it

*Take the attitude to try as hard as possible to succeed and not to worry
    about failure or be embarrassed as it is a learning experience*
Work with local Chicago area recyclers to sell whatever possible
Generate cash by selling services and by selling my broken-down car

Author's Note: CPS has two tools for very careful and deliberate choice making: PPCO and the Idea Evaluation Matrix. The latter involves making a table. You list the ideas down the left side, and you list criteria across the top of the columns. Below is an example of an Evaluation Matrix using three of Jack's ideas. He has rated each idea against one criterion using a simple scale of 1 to 3, with 3 being very good, 2 being fair, and 1 being poor. What the Evaluation Matrix does is point out weak spots in an idea. If you address the weak spots, you enhance the idea and raise the odds for successful implementation.

Ideas to Improve the Ideas Based on the Evaluation Matrix

1. Do a brochure offering photographic documentation services for businesses and distribute it to the security departments of the top 100 Chicago businesses.
How the idea changed: By making the idea more specific and getting it into the hands of potential buyers, it becomes a much more powerful idea.

2. Partner with Molly and open up a commercial art studio and solicit subcontracting work with large ad agencies.
How the idea changed: To address the weakness of selling, they make the idea more specific by going after "piece work" from large agencies. They've focused their business.

3. Promote myself as an events photographer through the Chicago Convention Bureau.
How the idea changed: It was made more specific to include a way to get business. It doesn't address the fact that Molly does not know photography and can't contribute directly to this kind of idea. Further development could be done to address this, such as photography training for Molly, or ideas could be added in to get her involved in events in some other money-making and value-oriented way.

IDEA EVALUATION MATRIX

Ideas listed down the side, evaluation criteria across the top	Generates cash in 3 months	Is in Jack or Molly's Skill Set	Can sell the work	Total Score	Evaluation Analysis
1. Do a brochure offering photographic documentation services	3	2	1	6	The weak spot here is that the idea doesn't directly connect to finding or selling work. It's strong potentially as a tool for selling.
2. Partner with Molly and open up a commercial art studio	2	3	1	6	This idea is also weak in connecting to customers but strong in skill sets.
3. Promote yourself as an events photographer	2	1	1	4	Weakest idea overall, so you might choose to rule it out. Still, if you can address the weak areas, you can save it.

8: TONY, TONY, TONY
Jack's Assistors, Resistors, and Resources List

Assistors
Manny Gibran
Molly Dunne
Layne—Geek's owner
Tony Cooper (first customer?)

Resistors
Jack's family (highly critical people)
The market? (may not accept a new photographic service provider)

Resources
Rob's photo equipment
The new studio space behind Geek's
Molly's computer and ideation skills
Jack's photographic skills

SCORE
Columbia College

Author's Note: Following is Jack's Action Plan. When creating one, follow these tips:

1. Make yourself accountable to somebody for doing things.
2. Include in your plan ways in which to make the idea exciting to anyone involved. Don't be boring! If you can work a party into a plan, I'd advise it.
3. Take the first step of execution as soon as you possibly can. The longer you wait, the less likely you will do it. Projects that are underway often gain momentum.

JackNewCo Action Plan

WHAT	WHEN/ STARTING	COMPLETED	WHO'S RESPONSIBLE
Sell the car to Manny for $500	Pick up Tuesday morning	Tuesday at noon	Jack
Get all the stuff out of the car and find the title and such to sign	Monday	Monday 6:00 p.m.	Jack
Generate new-term business First try: Tony Cooper	Now	Monday mid-day	Jack
Visit the SCORE office downtown on Madison; learn as much as possible about government help for small businesses	Wednesday p.m.		Jack and Molly
Entrepreneur education		Ongoing	Jack and Molly

WHAT	WHEN/ STARTING	COMPLETED	WHO'S RESPONSIBLE
Marketing education		Ongoing	Jack & Molly
Write up new JackNewCo statement of purpose with core values, including: • Name the company! • Create logo • Rules about debt • How to handle failure • Making honest efforts • Partnership agreement with Molly	Next Tuesday	By May 1	Jack & Molly
Studio cleanup	When Molly returns	By June 1	Jack & Molly Sandy as resource for ideas on clearing up rehab sites
Research recyclers	Now	April 15	Molly

WHAT	WHEN/ STARTING	COMPLETED	WHO'S RESPONSIBLE
Arrange for pick up or drop-off of recyclable materials		May 1	Molly
Rent an empty Dumpster for the non-recyclable trash	This week	By Saturday	Molly
Do a brochure offering photographic documentation services for businesses*			Jack writes Molly edits and computerizes
Do research on likely upcoming events			
Solicit Web development business	May 1		Molly
Find somebody to help with accounting, books	June 1	June 15	Jack

ACKNOWLEDGMENTS

I've had a good deal of help in writing this book, so some acknowledgments are in order.

First, I want to acknowledge the CEF (Creative Education Foundation) for furthering the work of Alex Osborn and Sidney Parnes over the last fifty-three years. Their annual CPSI (Creative Problem Solving Institute) is where I learned CPS. Beyond CPS, I found myself in a community at CPSI, and I learned how empowering a belief in the power of creative thinking can be. There are numerous people in that wondrous creative community to whom I owe a lot and without whom this book may never have happened. In particular, I thank Sid Parnes for the inspirational example he's set and for his lifelong commitment to CPS, CPSI, and the CEF.

At CPSI I met a number of people who are now life-journey friends. First and foremost among them are the first three readers of this book. They provided me with crucial early feedback. I'm referring to Jean Bystedt, Siri Lynn, and Deborah Potts. Their feedback on the book itself was valuable and insightful, but their friendship and support, both personally and professionally, these last few years are even more meaningful to me. Good friends with creative hearts and heads are the kind that sustain a creative soul.

A number of people read this book in its various versions. These readers all provided insights that made this a better book. Thank you to my daughter, Meghan Fraley; my sister, Marijo O'Connell; Mark Maguire, Paula Rosch, Danica Novgordoff, Beverly Bond, Caroline

Pakel-Dunlop, and Alex Aixala. I thank you all most sincerely for marking up my book and taking the time out of your busy lives to help me. Please allow me to return the favor someday.

Thank you, Anne Pici, for your advice on my writing. Your help on the first version of the manuscript took my work to another level.

Diane Fraley signed me up, somewhat reluctantly, for my first CPSI conference. Without her influence and interest in creativity, I might never have become aware of CPS, and this book would never have happened. Thank you.

Doug Stevenson, my good friend and partner in The Innovise Guys podcast, hooked me up with Pat Friendlander who gave me good advice on how I might find an agent. Doug, you are one of those people who simply live and breathe creative thinking; thank you for your generous assistance and friendship. Pat, I thank you for ideas on how to navigate the publishing world and for pointing me toward Jack Covert.

Jack Covert (founder and president of 800-CEO-READ) was the first publishing professional to read this book. His immediate enthusiasm for it was a real shot in the arm. Jack, I thank you for helping me get this book published and for connecting me with Tom Ehrenfeld and Daniel Greenberg of Greenberg-Levine. I hope your track record of spotting great new books holds true here! Tom was kind enough to help me with query letters and marketing plans; thank you so much, Tom.

Daniel Greenberg is quite simply a terrific and effective literary agent. I appreciate all the hard work and time he put into getting me a book deal, my first, and his continuing support and interest. Thank you, Daniel.

Finally, I thank Thomas Nelson Publishers and my editors at Nelson Business. Kristen Parrish's good advice has made this a more powerful book. I thank Kristen for sharing her wisdom and insight. I thank Paula Major for her fine work readying this book for publication. Lastly, I thank Jenny Baumgartner, who helped me streamline the story and perfect the final version of this book; her help was invaluable, and it was a pleasure working with her.

ABOUT THE AUTHOR

Gregg Fraley works as an innovation consultant to Fortune 500 companies and does keynote speeches and workshops on creative thinking, innovation, problem solving, and new-product development. An idea generation expert, Fraley leads on-site and virtual brainstorming sessions for his clients. He has credentials as a classic artistic "creative"—doing illustration and improvisational comedy—and as a creative entrepreneurial business professional.

With Warner Cable's QUBE interactive television project in the early 80s, Fraley worked on production teams that won Emmys and cable's ACE award for innovation. His entrepreneurial career includes senior management and/or ownership positions in software companies and a qualitative research firm. He was also a founder of Med-E-Systems, a software firm that developed the first wireless prescription system for physicians, "Smart Scripts." And he led the PR and marketing effort that took Advanced Health Corporation public in 1996.

Fraley is currently a partner in The Innovise Guys, a leading innovation podcast that combines humor with innovation content. *Innovisation* is a term Fraley and his partner, Doug Stevenson, have coined to describe the use of improvisation techniques to spur spontaneous thinking in structured creative problem solving. To hear the podcasts, visit http://dainnoviseguys.libsyn.com.

Fraley did his Improv training at Player's Workshop of Second City and Improv Olympics, both in Chicago. He is a board member of the Creative Education Foundation (CEF) and teaches creative problem solving at CEF's annual Creative Problem Solving Institute (CPSI) and other creativity and innovation conferences worldwide. He is also a professional member of the National Speakers Association (USA). Fraley resides in Chicago.

CPSIA information can be obtained
at www.ICGtesting.com
Printed in the USA
LVOW07s1806221117
557232LV00003BA/19/P